Toronto Sketches
"The Way We Were"

Toronto Sketches
"The Way We Were"

MIKE FILEY

Dundurn Press
Toronto & Oxford
1992

Editing: Nadine Stoikoff
Design and Production: Green Graphics
Cover design: Andy Tong
Printing and Binding: Gagné Printing Ltd., Louiseville, Quebec, Canada

The publisher wishes to acknowledge the generous assistance and ongoing support of **The Canada Council, The Book Publishing Industry Development Program** of the **Department of Communications, The Ontario Arts Council,** and **The Ontario Publishing Centre of the Ministry of Culture and Communications.**

Care has been taken to trace the ownership of copyright material used in the text (including the illustrations). Credit for each quotation is given at the end of the selection. The author and publisher welcome any information enabling them to rectify any reference or credit in subsequent editions.

J. Kirk Howard, Publisher

First Printing: December 1992
Second Printing: January 1993
Third Printing: February 1995

Canadian Cataloguing in Publication Data

Filey, Mike, 1941 –
      Toronto sketches

ISBN 1-55002-176-1

1. Toronto (Ont.) – History. 2. Toronto (Ont.) – Pictorial works.
I. Title.

FC3097.4.F55 1992   971.3'541   C92-095288-7
F1059.5.T6857F55   1992

Dundurn Press Limited
2181 Queen Street East
Suite 301
Toronto, Canada
M4E 1E5

Dundurn Distribution
73 Lime Walk
Headington, Oxford
England
OX3 7AD

Dundurn Press Limited
1823 Maryland Avenue
P.O. Box 1000
Niagara Falls, NY
U.S.A.

TABLE OF CONTENTS

FOREWORD

Toronto has changed dramatically in the last half-century from a reserved provincial city that was more concerned with Sunday activities and liquor laws than about its position in the world community. The 1970s and '80s have changed all that and vaulted Toronto into the major league.

We have managed to maintain our solid image of being a livable community while at the same time providing our citizens the excitement, pizzazz and flair that is so necessary to attract tourism, industry and commerce. Toronto is an exciting world centre with big league sports (including home to the World Series champions, the Toronto Blue Jays), first-rate entertainment and sophisticated cultural activities that compete with the best anywhere.

Toronto will never forget its yesterday because it is important to build one's future on the solid foundation of our past. Positive traditions and wonderful memories will always be an important keepsake.

Mike Filey, our great historian, reminds us every week in the *Sunday Sun* of the "way we were." He brings the positive past back to us and reminds us of how deep our roots really are. This book is not only a tribute to Toronto, but a reminder that where we come from can only help us with where we are going. Mike Filey is very much the human chain that links the dreams of the future with the memories of the past.

Paul V. Godfrey
Chief Executive Officer, *Toronto Sun*

PREFACE

Several months prior to the October 30, 1971, demise of the *Toronto Telegram* newspaper, I was approached by the editor of the paper's real estate section and asked whether I might be able to provide copy and photos for a Toronto history column that would run if and when space was available.

I said I could and over the next few weeks, my material ran on a few occasions before all columns, and the paper itself, came to an untimely end.

While the termination of the 95-year-old "*Tely*" was unquestionably a sad event in our city's history, there was one positive side-effect. Just two days after the last *Telegram* was published, the city witnessed the birth of a new city paper, the *Toronto Sun*.

Many of the former *Telegram* people threw their lot in with the *Sun*, and before long I was again asked to provide historical photos and cutlines that would run on an irregular basis. This time, however, the uncertainty as to whether my material would appear wasn't predicated just on the availability of space, but on the uncertainty as to whether the paper would be around long enough to run the column. The so-called experts didn't give the *Sun* much hope of survival.

But survive it did and in 1973 a Sunday edition appeared. Two years after the arrival of the *Sunday Sun* I was asked if I'd like to be a regular contributor to this edition of the paper. I accepted, and since then I have contributed more then 800 columns on subjects as diverse as the origins of Toronto street names to the history of the city's streetcars, prominent sports personalities to little-known morsels of Toronto trivia.

Unless otherwise stated, photographs are from my private collection. The dates under each storey's headline is the date the article first appeared in the *Toronto Sun*.

What follows is a selection of columns each of which has received some sort of special feedback from my readers. I hope you enjoy them the second time around.

Mike Filey

IN APPRECIATION

In preparing a newspaper column such as "The Way We Were," it's always helpful to have nice people on whom I can call in my search for hard-to-find historical data and/or photographs. With some trepidation that I've forgotten the names of a few such individuals, listed below are those who I can remember:

Julie Kirsh, Catherine Webb Nelson, Glenna Tapscott, Joyce Wagler, Sue Dugas and Robert Smith (Toronto Sun Library), Marilyn Linton, Vena Eaton and Linda Fox (Sunday Sun's Life section), Eric Leverton and Don MacPhail (out back in the Sun composing room), Paul Godfrey (we all know who he is), Victor Russel and his staff (City of Toronto Archives), Michael Moir (Toronto Harbour Commission Archives), Ted Wickson (Toronto Transit Commission Archives), Catherine Webb (Toronto Historical Board), Linda Coban (Canadian National Exhibition Archives), Linda Heath (House of Providence), Margaret Bowser, Bruce Croft, Paul Culliton, Andy Donato, Warren Evans, Douglas Seuvage, Rand Sparling, and Jack Webster. To those I've forgotten, sorry, but thanks anyway.

To my wife Yarmila, thanks also, especially for putting me onto WordPerfect.

This book is dedicated to all the *Toronto Sun* readers who make putting together a column such as "The Way We Were" a lot of fun.

A Street by Any Other Name . . .

June 9, 1985

While the origins of a great number of Metro Toronto's street names are relatively easy to deduce (pretty words, catchy words, simple words), there are a few names that we'll probably never discover the reasons for since the story behind the selection years ago was never documented. I can think of several that seem so obvious yet, so far, the reasons remain obscure; Pharmacy, Martin Grove, McNicoll and Robina, to name just a few.

Scattered around Metro are many streets whose names have come about as a result of an association with a historic event in the city's past. Take Temperance Street, for instance. Running between Yonge and Sheppard streets in downtown Toronto, this little thoroughfare was cut through the property of Jesse Ketchum who, as a young man of 17, moved to the fledgling Town of York from New York State, eventually settling on the farm of his brother near the busy little community of York Mills, several miles north of the little town.

At the age of 30, Jesse moved into town and bought a tannery on the west side of Yonge Street just south of Queen. In 1845, he laid out a street through his property and, because of his aversion to the consumption of liquor (his father had been an alcoholic) named the new thoroughfare Temperance Street. Land deeds drawn up for property on the new street decreed that liquor would not be sold in any building fronting on the street. It was only natural that the street took the name Temperance.

In the Queen Street/Broadview Avenue part of town there's a small thoroughfare called Sunlight Park Road. Back in 1886, the city's first professional baseball team began playing at a base-ball field that was located just east of the mouth of the Don River and south of Queen Street. Because of the field's proximity to the Sunlight Soap factory (now Lever Brothers) and with the ever-present smell of Sunlight soap in the air, the name Sunlight Park was a natural.

For a time, we also had Baseball Place in the same part of town. However, with the expansion of a Japanese car dealership on Queen Street just west of Broadview Avenue, that name disappeared in the name of progress.

One of Etobicoke's major north-south streets is Kipling Avenue. The assumption has always been that it was named for the famous English author,

Jesse Ketchum (1782–1867).

Toronto's first extensive industry was Ketchum's tannery that occupied the Yonge/Queen/Bay/Adelaide block.

Rudyard Kipling, but why and when remains a mystery. Some investigative work has produced the following details that may (or may not) shed some light on the events leading up to the street's name.

In 1907, Kipling visited Toronto as part of a North American tour. On his itinerary was a visit to the Woodbridge Fair where he was to officially open the event. At the last minute he was forced to cancel his visit to the fairgrounds, but it's not difficult to imagine that the trip to Woodbridge from the city might have included using some portion of what was called in those days, simply, the Second Line. Perhaps someone dubbed it Kipling's road (to Woodbridge) and the name stuck even though Kipling never made it to Woodbridge.

If you have any interesting stories about how some of the streets in and around Metro Toronto got their names, I'd be glad to hear about them. Perhaps they'll even find a place in a new book I plan to write listing the origins of as many Toronto street names as I can find.

Yuletide in Little York

December 24, 1989

Well, the big day is almost here. Soon family and friends will gather to exchange gifts, enjoy fabulous taste delights and share all the good feelings that this special time of year brings, feelings that we wish could prevail all year long.

It goes without saying that our Toronto, the Toronto of 1989, is very much different than the city our parents or their parents knew. Better? Perhaps. Different? Without question!!

Back in the 1930s and 1940s, a gentleman I'd like to know more about, Mr. Percy Ghent, contributed a multitude of stories to the old *Telegram* newspaper, stories that focused on the changing face of his Toronto.

One of those stories is particularly interesting, especially when read at this time of year. Ghent's Christmas offering first appeared on December 23, 1933, the year before Toronto celebrated its 100th anniversary as a city, and in it Percy took his readers on an imaginary trip around his hometown as he believed it might have looked 100 years earlier.

His story brought to life the hustle and bustle throughout York, as Toronto was then known, on Christmas Eve in the community's last full year as a town. On March 6, 1834, the Town of York became the City of Toronto. Now, 56 years after his story was first published, Percy Ghent's story is even more entertaining.

I'd like to share with my readers Mr. Ghent's entertaining story, "Yuletide in Little York."

Yuletide in little York – what was it like here during the festive season a century and more ago? What was it like, say, on December 24, 1833, when the town boasted less than 10,000 souls, but was sticking out its chest with pride at the prospect of becoming a real grown-up city in the New Year? Henry Scadding and other historians of Toronto's infancy have left such detailed records of the scene that it is easy to make a tour in fancy, a sleigh ride if you like, around the little town; and the sights are well worth seeing.

That giant sign above the Steamboat Hotel on the bay shore, for instance, is one of the star attractions. Over the upper veranda of the hotel, it extends for the entire length of the building and on it is a steamboat of almost the same length. Smoke belches from the stacks and the bow wave breaks in spray, and there's a foamy wake from sidewheel to stern.

At Front and John streets stands the Greenland Fishery Inn. Its famous sign depicts whaling vessels capturing one of those sea monsters. All on Yonge Street, and all with their quaint old signs, you'll find the Bird In Hand, the Sun Tavern, the Golden Bull and the Red Lion.

On Front Street there's the White Swan tavern, but if you prefer the Black Swan, it stands on King. They are all busy and boisterous. So are the Black Horse and Antelope Inns on Church Street, and a long list of others elsewhere in town.

But we are quiet, sober folk who would like to know what the merchants in York are offering for sale this Yuletide season, 1833. John Betteridge has a shop on King Street with a window of small square panes. He's busy, too. Turkeys, we learn, are a dollar apiece, but you can get a plump goose for 50 cents or 2 chickens for the same price. Beef? Four to eight cents a pound, according to cut. Mutton is a dime a pound, and for the same modest sum you can buy a dozen eggs or a pound of cheese. Butter is 15 cents a pound and people are beginning

York's second market and Town Hall located on the south-west corner of King and Jarvis streets. It was on the second floor of this building that the Council of the Town of York met in 1833, the date of Percy Ghent's Christmas tour. Following incorporation of the new City of Toronto in 1834, this building became the City Hall until a new structure, a block to the south, was opened in 1845.

Sketch from Toronto's 100 Years.

to ask when this outrageous price will come down. Tea and sugar are luxuries out of the reach of ordinary folk. Good tea costs $4 a pound. Folk in York will never stop drinking cheap beer and whiskey unless the price of tea goes down, a citizen tells us, and if they want sugar in their tea, he adds, it costs 50 cents a pound.

Mrs. Lumsden has a little shop on King Street too. There's an array of long clay pipes in the window, and papers of pins just as long are hanging behind the square panes. Children are Mrs. Lumsden's steady customers. They're not keen about the clay pipes, of course, nor the pins. But look at the gingerbread cookies! Scores of them, Gingerbread men, prancing ponies, fishes, parrots, dogs and gingerbread hearts with a sprinkling of fine pink sugar on them. One price for every delightful design – a half-penny. Or a cent. Both are in circulation. For a dollar you could buy a whole sackful of juvenile joy.

Any music in York to brighten

Christmas? Of course there is. Here comes the band now. It belongs to the Volunteer Artillery Company, and the man carrying the gorgeous standard struts ahead of the trumpets and drums. That standard was presented to the band by the ladies of York last June. They wanted to encourage the bandsmen. You see, the citizens of York, like those of the bigger Toronto, had a special affection for a good band. They used to go out in crowds to hear the band of the 66th Regiment. During the exile of Napoleon the 66th was stationed at St. Helena, but whether the martial airs of Britain blared forth by the trumpets had any charm for the Emperor is not on record. But they thrilled the citizens of York and there was gloom in town when the regiment left for home and England at the end of 1833.

There are Christmas travelers in York, too. At the coach office citizens are booking seats for journeys afar. Stage coaches on runners await passengers and a chilly and arduous trip over bumpy roads awaits them. What says the notice posted on the wall? "A stage leaves York every day at 12 o'clock noon and arrives at Hamilton at 9 o'clock the same evening. A stage leaves Hamilton at 12 o'clock at night and arrives at York the next day at 10 o'clock in the morning. Fare, 12 shillings and sixpence."

As well, a stage leaves every day at 5 pm for the Carrying Place which is reached at an indefinite time the next day. For Holland Landing, the coach departs every day at noon and arrives at 7 in the evening. What would the good citizens of York think could they but speed in some magic coach through the years dividing their day and ours and see the bustling we Torontonians of 1933 know? Perhaps in some realm beyond our ken they do live on and see the transformation. Who knows?

Who knows, indeed, Mr. Ghent. Merry Christmas!

Waterfront's Steamy Past

September 17, 1987

Recently, I was given the honour of officially opening the 16th annual Uxbridge Threshing Show on behalf of the Ontario Heritage Foundation, of which I am a director.

To signal the opening, I was asked to blow the whistle on a huge 1922 steam tractor that had spent its life, before being proudly restored by the steam show chairman, chugging away at a lumber mill near Lindsay, Ontario.

I found it fascinating to think that the sounds and smells made by the steam equipment on display at the Uxbridge Museum that hot Saturday afternoon in the middle of the summer of 1989 were the same sights, sounds and smells one would have found all over the Toronto of the last century. In particular, the hundreds of steam railway engines that criss-crossed Toronto's waterfront added a sight, sound and smell that has virtually disappeared from the big-city scene.

Interestingly, the very first steam locomotive to be built anywhere in Canada was manufactured in the factory of James Good, located on the east side of Yonge Street right across from today's glitzy Eaton Centre.

Mr. Good had set up a metal fabricating shop in 1852 and, a year later, received an order for a 25-ton, 4-4-0 wood-burning steam locomotive from the officials of the new Ontario, Simcoe and Huron (OH&S) Railway who were in the process of constructing the province's first railway line to connect the capital city with Georgian Bay.

In April of 1853, the citizens of Toronto were both impressed and awestruck when the balloon-stacked steam engine, christened naturally enough, *Toronto,* was hauled south down Yonge Street and put on the OH&S tracks, newly laid across the city's bustling and smoke-drenched waterfront.

A month later on May 16, 1853 (to be precise), the *Toronto* hauled the first passenger train in the province northward to it's destination, Matchell's Corners, a community we now call Aurora.

One last bit of trivia. Uxbridge gets its name from Uxbridge in Middlesex, England.

6

Engine #2, **Toronto,** *manufactured by James Good in his Yonge and Queen Street factory in early 1853.*

One of the early waterfront stations was that of the Great Western Railway. Erected on the east side of Yonge, just south of Front in 1866, the structure burned to the ground in 1952.

Toronto's Island Airport

February 26, 1989

It was exactly 50 years ago this month, February, in 1939 that Toronto's new Island Airport opened with the arrival of one Harry Falconer McLean in his Stearman airplane.

Born in Bismark, North Dakota, in 1883, McLean had worked his way up the ladder from a water boy with a Minneapolis railway construction company, then a timekeeper with a Helena, Montana, construction company, through various other positions with numerous other construction enterprises until he was appointed superintendent of the Toronto Construction Company in 1905.

That same year, he became president of the Grenville Crushed Rock Company and the Dominion Construction Corporation. McLean moved to Canada and took up residence in Merrickville, Ontario, and with his aviation skills was able to visit his construction and quarry sites all over the country. In fact, listed under the heading "Recreations" in his entry

in *Who's Who in Canada, 1938–39* are golf, hunting, fishing and aeronautics.

Apparently McLean's arrival at Toronto's new airport on the waterfront didn't amount to a "hill of beans" to the representatives of the city's media 50 years ago. A thorough search of the February papers didn't even hint that the airport had opened.

In retrospect, that's probably because there were plenty of other airports around town and the one on the "western sandbar," as the Island Airport was originally described, just added to a list that included Barker Field on Dufferin Street, the Toronto Flying Club Field a little further north at Wilson Avenue, and the old De Lesseps Field on Trethewey Drive near Jane Street.

What was different with the Island facility was that it, along with the "auxiliary" airfield at Malton (for use in the event of thick fog), were to be municipally owned while the others had been developed over the years as business ventures. The significance of these two

The main building at the Island Airport was erected in 1938–39 using the same blueprints developed for Malton Airport's first new passenger and operations facility.

Courtesy of Toronto Harbour Commission

government-owned and -operated airports was not yet apparent to Torontonians of a half-century ago.

In late May of 1939, just a few short months after the little "airport on the sandbar" opened, King George VI and Queen Elizabeth arrived in Canada. In and its fleet of Dash 7 and 8 aircraft became major tenants of the Island Airport.

In an attempt to meet the ever-increasing traffic demands, there have been numerous improvements to airport facilities, although the original adminis-

Courtesy of Toronto Harbour Commission.

Access to the Island Airport was via a "rope" ferry from the foot of Bathurst Street. The now-demolished Maple Leaf Stadium is evident in the background of this 1955 photo.

tribute to the royal couple's first-ever appearance in the provincial capital, the Toronto City Council decreed that, from henceforth, the airport would be known as Port George VI, Toronto Island Airfield, a term that was slightly altered to the present Port George VI, Toronto Island Airport, still its official title.

The airport was little more than a year old when, in November of 1940, it became the home base to almost a thousand members of the Norwegian Air Force who, having established living accommodations across the Gap in behind the ball stadium (a place that was soon to become affectionately known as Little Norway), trained long hours at the Island Airport in anticipation of seeking out and destroying the Nazis, who had so callously and swiftly overrun their homeland. Today, a Norwegian flag flies alongside Canadian and Toronto city flags on the site of Little Norway Park at the foot of Bathurst Street.

As the years rolled by, traffic into and out of the Island Airport grew steadily. Starting in 1984, City Express

tration building (constructed from the same set of blueprints as those used to construct Malton's first administration building) is still used by Island Airport passengers. A new $7.3 million passenger terminal building is on the horizon with its opening scheduled for 1990. The old building will be retained.

In an effort to define the future roll of the Island Airport, former Toronto Mayor and Federal MP David Crombie has recently completed extensive public hearings and will soon release a Discussion Paper prior to his final recommendations that will set the course for the next 50 years of our Port George VI, Toronto Island Airport.

[Since this column first appeared in February 1989, City Express has gone out of business. Today, only Air Ontario operates commuter flights to and from the Island Airport using Dash 8 aircraft.]

Filling Up on Waterfront History

January 31, 1988

Looking north up Yonge Street from the Yonge Street slip. Note trucks dumping fill into the slip. The curved-roof Great Western Railway station, the skyscrapers at the Yonge and King corner and the 1920 addition to the King Edward Hotel are evident in this 1923 view.

Courtesy of Toronto Harbour Commission

What a difference 60 years can make! The accompanying photograph was taken in March 1923 and captures the view looking northward from a vantage point on the frozen surface of the old Yonge Street slip. Note the trucks dumping fill just outside the curved-roof former Great Western Railway station, now the site of the O'Keefe Centre.

Over the years, our city's waterfront has undergone continual change, thanks primarily to major landfilling operations along the edge of Toronto Bay. In fact, during construction of projects all along the city's waterfront, projects such as the CN Tower, SkyDome, the Harbour Castle Hotel and Harbour Square condominium tower, to name just a few, remnants of a much earlier and different shoreline, have been uncovered.

Even now, the tunnel being excavated under Bay Street between Front Street and Queen's Quay for the new Harbourfront streetcar line, is progressing through landfill, as are the numerous pilings being placed for the foundations of the No. 1 York Quay condominium tower and phase 2 of Water Park Place at the foot of Bay Street. The concept of creating "new" land along the water's edge actually started, in a minor way, shortly after our city was established in 1834. Back then owners of the private wharves at the foot of Church, Yonge and Bay streets would simply extend their wharves further and further into the bay, thereby creating for themselves more property from which they could load and unload an ever-greater numbers of ships and, not coincidentally, increase the wharves' profitability.

This all came to an end in 1840 with the creation of the Windmill Line, an imaginary line drawn between the old Gooderham and Worts windmill (in today's terms, just south of the corner of Trinity and Mill Streets) and the site of the old French fort, Fort Rouillé or, as it was more commonly known, Fort Toronto. In modern day delineation, the fort would have stood just west of the

Similar view 1987.

CNE Bandshell. The Windmill Line, which is still on the surveyor's books, prohibited the extension of wharves further south than this boundary.

During the 1800s several landfilling projects were carried out, including the Esplanade Plan of the 1850s that saw the creation of a substantial right of way across the waterfront for the new Grand Trunk Railway. Other railways were created on paper, so too were tracks, and soon the entire width of the shoreline was encumbered with smoky steam engines pulling slow-moving passenger and freight trains.

In 1911, to try and make some sense out of the chaotic conditions along the water's edge, a new harbour commission was established. As part of its mandate, the Toronto Harbour Commission (THC) began the controlled development of what was called the Central Harbour Section of Toronto Harbour. Hundreds of depth soundings and miles of drawings of the bay were undertaken, but any real work was held up until landownership rights (some of which are still undetermined) were settled. Finally, the federal government gave approval to extending the old harbourhead line 1,100 feet into the bay, behind which land could then be reclaimed using landfill from construction sites, street sweepings (in today's terminology – garbage) and dredgings from the harbour bottom, the latter process giving the harbour a 24-foot depth for ocean-going vessels that would use a planned new seaway (that didn't open until 1959).

The first part of the Central Harbour project to be completed was the westerly stretch between Bathurst and Yonge streets where, in the 1920s, new buildings like Maple Leaf Stadium, Tip Top Tailors and the massive new Loblaw's warehouse, as well as several new streets like Queen's Quay, Harbour Street and Fleet Street (now Lake Shore Boulevard) appeared on the 266 acres of reclaimed land. Harbourfront now occupies much of this area.

The easterly section, Yonge to Parliament Street, wasn't extended out into the bay until the cross-waterfront elevated railway viaduct was finally completed in 1929. This added another 52 acres of new land to the waterfront. Marine Terminals 27, 28 and 29 and the large Redpath Sugar refinery were erected on this portion of the Harbour Commission's new Central Harbour.

Let the Games Continue

August 7, 1988

The year was 1883 and Torontonians were looking forward to the following year when they would celebrate the community's semi-centennial, 50 proud years as a city. It was a matter of record that the city had made great strides since its incorporation back in 1834.

With the arrival of 1883 the population finally broke through the 100,000 barrier, with many hundreds more living in suburban communities such as Leslieville out Queen Street East way, Brockton on Dundas Street West and Doncaster a way up the Don Mills Road (now Broadview Avenue).

In fact, one of those suburbs, the former Town of Yorkville at the Second Concession Road and Yonge Street, had just been annexed by the city. And with the city growing so fast, the private company that had been providing minimal public transportation services was compelled by civic officials to start constructing additional horsecar lines to serve the ever-increasing number of commuters. And there was even talk about electrifying the system just like they had done in several big European

The first police-sponsored Miss Toronto was selected at the 1937 edition of the games held at the CNE grandstand. Billy Hallam is seen being congratulated by a dapper Mayor Robbins. The Miss Toronto competition ended in 1991.

Courtesy of City of Toronto Archives

and American cities.

Both Timothy Eaton and Robert Simpson were doing extremely well in their respective stores on Yonge Street, in spite of all those dire predictions that they would soon be bankrupt because they hadn't heeded advice to build on the city's main thoroughfare, King Street.

While on the subject of financially sound enterprises, the young city had a total of 12 federally chartered banks in operation, plus 20 loan and investment companies and a dozen insurance companies, 6 of which had their head offices in the city.

In the wonderful world of politics, Oliver Mowat was in the middle of his 23-year tenure as premier of the province and sat firmly ensconced in his office in the Parliament Buildings on Front Street West.

And just up the street in his residence at the south-west corner of King and Simcoe, the popular John Beverley Robinson was in his third year as lieutenant-governor of the province.

Further east on Front Street over near the St. Lawrence Market, Arthur

Radcliffe Boswell was settling into his new position as Toronto's new mayor, an office he would be elected to for the next two years, municipal elections being an annual occurrence back then.

Two of the mayor's key officials were Police Magistrate Colonel George Denison (remembered in Denison Avenue) who resided at Heydon Villa on the Dover Court Road out in the west end of the city, and the Colonel's senior police officer, Chief of Police Major Frank Draper (of Draper Avenue fame).

Together, this well-respected duo kept close check on the young city's criminal element. It was during the Major's tenure that the idea of holding a get-together for members of the force (there were 115 officers and men in 1883) arose, where the men could demonstrate their prowess at various sporting activities – running, jumping, hammer throwing and the like. As the years passed, the games grew both in numbers of participants and in popularity amongst the public. Venues for the games have included the old lacrosse grounds at the north-west corner of Jarvis and Wellesley streets, Hanlan's Point Stadium on the Island, Sunnyside Amusement Park out near the Humber and, most recently, the CNE Grandstand.

No one will question the fact that our city has changed greatly since 1883, but the Police Games now held under the auspices of the Metro Toronto Police Amateur Athletic Association continue, as ever, to be one of the city's most popular summertime attractions.

Let the games begin!

Members of the 1924 Toronto Police tug-of-war team were Canadian champions.

Metro Toronto Police Museum

13

Everything Old is New Again

June 10, 1990

Assuming there are no last-minute hitches, the first new streetcar line in Toronto in more than 60 years will be officially opened in less than two weeks' time. The public is invited to the ceremonies which are planned for 11 am, June 22, at the Ship Deck at Harbourfront. After all the speeches streetcars of the venerable PCC "Red Rocket" style, that are to see service on the new Harbourfront line, will do a ceremonial first run. Included in the ceremony will be PCC #4500, recently rebuilt to its original 1951 look by the Commission's own experts at its Hillcrest shops on Bathurst Street.

Toronto's first new streetcar line in six decades, 604-Harbourfront, went into service on June 22, 1990.

Running a distance of slightly more than a mile and a quarter (2 kilometres), the new Harbourfront route will have its northern loop underground at Union Station where the streetcars will interface with the Yonge/University subway. The cars will operate in a tunnel under Bay Street south to Queen's Quay, where they will curve westerly and come to the surface, gliding along the middle of Queen's Quay on a private reservation. The terminus of the line will be a loop at the north-east corner of Queen's Quay and Spadina Avenue.

Streetcars on the new line will run in and out of service over the new Spadina bridge. Sometime in the future we may see this route extended either westerly to the Exhibition grounds or northerly up the middle of Spadina Avenue to Bloor Street.

Historically, the last time the TTC laid track on a street where there hadn't

been some form of electric streetcar service was in 1925, when the cars on the St. Clair line began operating on Mt. Pleasant Road.

Some readers may think I've forgotten the Queensway extension of the Queen streetcar line that occurred in 1957. That project was really a realignment of the Queen line that had been operating on Lakeshore Road since 1923 and originally designated the Beach route. The Queen cars moved onto a private right of way on the newly built Queen Street extension called the Queensway on July 21, 1957.

Long before November 3, 1925, the day the Mt. Pleasant extension opened, there had been agitation by the citizens of the Town of North Toronto for another route into the city other than the busy Yonge Street route. One possibility, they

Work progresses on the extension of the St. Clair streetcar line from the Moore Park loop through Mt. Pleasant Cemetery to a loop at Eglinton Avenue, August 1925.

maintained, was to extend Mt. Pleasant Road, that existed north of Merton Avenue, through the cemetery property and connect it with St. Clair to the south.

With the annexation of North Toronto in 1912, this agitation increased and discussions were then held with the trustees of the Mt. Pleasant Cemetery for a right of way through their property. Needless to say, the trustees weren't happy with this plan since they felt its implementation would lower the value of undeveloped cemetery plots at the east end of their 200-acre holding. Nevertheless, three years later the city received permission to expropriate a 76-foot-wide strip through the cemetery, paying the trustees almost $100,000 in compensation. Road construction started almost immediately and the unpaved extension through the cemetery was ready for traffic (except when it rained) in 1918.

Unfortunately for the northenders, the opening of the roadway didn't mean they would get a public transit line on the street right away. In fact, another seven years went by before the newly established TTC felt there was sufficient ridership potential to build a new line on the new (and old) sections of Mt. Pleasant Road.

Prior to 1925, streetcars on the St. Clair route crossed the Vale of Avoca bridge, a few hundred yards east of Yonge Street, as far as the loop at the entrance to Moore park. With the laying of track on the old and new sections of Mt. Pleasant Road, the cars could now curve north onto Mt. Pleasant and trundle along 2 1/2 miles of track to a new loop at Eglinton Avenue.

On June 22, 1990 (almost 65 years after the Mt. Pleasant streetcar-line extension went into service), Toronto's newest streetcar line will be officially opened. On the following Saturday and Sunday, June 23 and 24, the public is invited to take a free ride on the new Harbourfront line.

Only the Sky is the Limit for the Time-Honoured CNE Air Show

August 27, 1989

One of the most popular features of our annual Canadian National Exhibition is the thrilling air show that fills the sky over the waterfront on the last weekend of the fair.

Now officially known as the Canadian International Air Show, the genesis of this extremely popular event goes back to the year 1914, when a small three-seater flying boat called *Sunfish* made daily flights over Exhibition crowds. All eyes stared skyward; the crowds were totally and absolutely thunderstruck.

Over the next few years one of the old Exhibition buildings would be devoted exclusively to the newest wonder of the age, the flying machine, and now not only could the public see and hear these objects as they roared overhead, but here at the good old EX, they could actually touch them.

In 1917, a car and a biplane raced each other around the oval track in the old grandstand and the car driven by American auto pioneer, Gaston Chevrolet (what a perfect name for a brand of automobile, the "Gaston"), won.

In that same year a demonstration of flying in formation was held over the fairgrounds. Again, the crowds were spellbound.

Two years later in 1919, aeroplane races between New York and the little Leaside field northeast of Toronto were held, with many of the participants cracking up somewhere along the 1,150-mile route. These races were followed a decade later by air races between Cleveland and the CNE waterfront. Then in 1930, a triangular course was set out over Lake Ontario, south of the CNE grounds, and seaplanes battled for the prize money.

Static aircraft displays also drew large crowds at the annual CNE. War was raging in Europe as visitors to the 1941 EX marvelled at a Canadian-built Bolingbroke reconnaissance bomber in front of the now demolished Electrical and Engineering Building. This would be the last Exhibition for five long years.

In 1939, once again the winds of war were blowing in Europe and at that year's edition of the CNE Fairy Battle bombers, Oxford light bombers and a Hawker *Hurricane* gave aerial demonstrations. No one could anticipate what carnage the *Hurricane* and its companion, the *Spitfire*, would soon be facing in the skies over Britain.

The war arrived and, in 1941, the fun-seeking crowds were replaced by young men in army, navy and air force uniforms. Our Exhibition had become a military camp. The annual fair wouldn't return until the fall of 1947.

In late August 1946, a real air show was held, not at the Exhibition grounds, but at the de Havilland Airport, a way up Dufferin Street in the Township of North York. When the air force opened a base there years later, the airport was renamed Downsview. The event was rather grandiosely billed as an International Air Show and proved highly entertaining for the thousands who, with all the newspaper and newsreel reports of wartime aerial activity still fresh in their minds, eagerly made their way to the airport to discover the thrill of airplanes first hand.

The eight-day event was sponsored by the National Aeronautical Association of Canada and endorsed by the City of Toronto. Using the airfield and a few of the de Havilland buildings (in some of which more than a thousand of the incredible wooden twin-engined *Mosquito* fighter-bomber aircraft had recently been assembled), the show claimed the distinction of being the first show of its kind ever held in the country.

The star performer of the 1946 International Air Show was just that, a Lockheed P-80 *Shooting Star* jet fighter.

"It had no propeller," wrote one of the Toronto papers and "the wooshing sound amazed every one of the 78,000 who attended the show."

Other highlights of the show were Royal Canadian Navy *Seafires* and Royal Canadian Air Force *Mustangs*, a C-47 *Dakota* transport, several American Air Force *Black Widow* and *Thunderbolt* fighters plus a flock of small private planes.

Things were back to normal at the CNE in 1947, and there was even a special appearance by several Avro *Lincoln* bombers of the famous Dambusters Squadron at that year's fair.

Succeeding editions of the EX continued to include aircraft as part of the entertainment package, but their appearance could hardly be termed an air show.

On September 16, 1950, the Toronto Flying Club sponsored a "flying program" out at Malton Airport (now Pearson International) that included, to quote from the *Telegram* newspaper, "aerobatics, jet fighter displays, static displays and the latest in personal aeroplanes, radar equipment etc., etc."

Some of the aircraft seen at Malton were the RCAF's first jet fighter, the de Havilland *Vampire,* and one of their brand new F-86 *Sabres.*

In 1952 and 1953 what was billed as the National Air Show moved to the Exhibition grounds, though the event was held on the third Saturday of September, almost two full weeks after the fair had closed.

Then in 1954 a one-day show, which was opened by General Jimmy Doolittle who led the air attack on Tokyo during the last war, was rescheduled to run early in the month of June. Prominent in that year's show (admission 50 cents, special reserved waterfront bleacher seating, an extra 50 cents) was the first Canadian-designed and - built jet fighter, the RCAF's CF-100 along with a gigantic B-47 six-engine jet bomber of the United States Air Force.

On June 2, 1955, Minister of Trade and Commerce, the ubiquitous C.D. Howe (who a few years earlier had dealt a death blow to North America's first jet passenger plane, the Canadian-designed and -built *Jetliner*) opened the next year's show, now identified in the advertising as the Canadian International Air Show. This time the stars were the U.S. Navy's *Cougar* jet fighters and the RCAF's CF-100s and T-33s.

"One of the air force's *Sabres* stole the show with a 708 mph flypast," wrote a *Tely* reporter.

One year later in 1956 the Canadian International Air Show, complete with CF-100s, F-86s and T-33s, *Banshees,* the U.S. Navy's Blue Angels aerobatic flying team and the United States Strategic Air Command's huge B-52 *Stratofortress* eight-engine jet bomber, became a permanent feature of the Canadian National Exhibition.

The Fall of an *Arrow*

August 16, 1987

Avro Canada's first Arrow *lands at Malton Airport as a* CF*-100 chase plane keeps close watch following one of many highly successful test flights in April 1958.*

So there I was, walking through Yorkdale Shopping Centre, not really looking for anything in particular, when I decided to peruse the plaza's hobby store. Entering the store I was absolutely flabbergasted to see a huge display of plastic models of a Canadian-designed and -built jet aircraft that has been deader than the proverbial door nail for almost three decades, an airplane that continues to elicit controversy every time its name is mentioned. The Avro *Arrow*.

In April of 1953, the Royal Canadian Air Force issued specifications for a new supersonic all-weather jet interceptor to replace the venerable CF-100. The specifications were so demanding that, if they were all met, the resulting aircraft would exceed any aircraft then in service or under development anywhere in the world.

Nevertheless, in the incredibly short span of just four years, the engineers at

A.V. Roe Canada, whose factory was adjacent to Malton airport (now Pearson International), had succeeded in creating the required aircraft and on March 25, 1958, the first Avro *Arrow* made it's maiden flight.

The new *Arrow* was better than anyone had hoped for and on November 11, 1958, just 7 1/2 months later, the second *Arrow* aircraft, #25202, was flown at Mach 1.96 or almost TWICE the speed of sound. And that flight was nearly 30 years ago!

Over the next few months, a total of five *Arrows* were built and flown and another five were in various stages of completion when, on Friday, February

Soon after the project was canceled on February 20, 1959, Arrows RL *201 through* RL *205 were cut into pieces on the tarmac outside the plant. All that remains of this remarkable Canadian creation are portions of* RL *206 on display at the National Science and Technology Museum in Ottawa.*

20, 1959, the Conservative Government of John Diefenbaker canceled the entire project. Then, in an incredible demonstration of shortsightedness (or was there something to hide?), company welders were ordered to cut the revolutionary craft into small pieces. Not one *Arrow* would be kept, nor would any be turned over to the Americans or British

to continue with the revolutionary aircraft's development.

Now here we are, 28 years later, and Canada's *Arrow* is back, though it took a local plastic model aircraft company to make something out of what, if it were still flying, would probably continue to be one of the world's most advanced fighter aircraft.

Toronto Swimmer Stuns World

April 20, 1986

In an effort to raise money for a much-needed swimming pool for the children at Variety Village, a special celebrity marathon swim was held this past Friday and Saturday during which well-known personalities from the business, entertainment and political worlds swam in relay from the beach at Port Dalhousie near St. Catharines, the 30-some miles to Marilyn Bell Park on the Toronto waterfront just south of the Exhibition grounds.

Marilyn Bell and her coach, Gus Ryder, after the 16-year-old's successful crossing of Lake Ontario, September 8–9, 1954.

All participating celebrity swimmers had received pledges of specified amounts of money for their efforts, all of which will go towards the construction of a new pool at Variety Village.

On hand to welcome the arrivals at her name-park was Marilyn DiLascio who, as a 16-year-old schoolgirl, became the first person in history to complete the treacherous crossing.

The story of the youngster's accomplishment is a fascinating one. For one thing, Marilyn Bell wasn't even supposed to be a starter, but rather simply a back-up (and a female at that) in a four-man relay effort to conquer the lake, a special attraction held during the 1954 Canadian National Exhibition.

And even after Marilyn decided to attempt her own solo crossing, CNE officials refused to recognize that the teenager was even in the water hoping, instead, that American long-distance swimmer, Florence Chadwick, with whom they had a business arrangement to complete the crossing, would become the first person to successfully conquer the treacherous waters of Lake Ontario.

As fate would have it, Florence was beaten by the lake about half way into her attempt. Young Marilyn, however, kept going and, after a total of 20 hours and 57 minutes in the chilly water, completed the 32-mile ordeal, touching the breakwall opposite the Boulevard Club where thousands had gathered to welcome Marilyn home.

Interestingly, this weekend's celebrity swim falls on the anniversary of another famous swim featured at the EX. As part of the 1927 CNE, it was decided that the Wrigley gum people and the CNE would hold the Second Wrigley Marathon Swim on a triangular course south of the CNE breakwall. And there was absolutely no question that Toronto's own George Young would be the winner.

After all, George had been victorious earlier that year when, as an unknown amateur, he completed the First Wrigley Marathon Swim crossing the treacherous 20-mile stretch from Santa Catalina Island to the California mainland ahead of 102 other highly experienced participants, thereby capturing the coveted Wrigley trophy and, more importantly for George, $25,000 in cash.

Welcomed home by cheering crowds, starry-eyed George was worshipped like a hero. From then on, he could do no wrong. Except he did. He lost the Second Wrigley's marathon swim to Ernst Vierkoetter. Actually, lost isn't the word. George didn't even finish the swim.

The instant hero became an instant bum. Until the day he died in 1972, poor George never lived down his humiliating defeat.

Torontonians went wild as Marilyn and Gus made the traditional victory parade up Bay Street.

Toronto Telegram *photo.*

Picture Perfect

December 4, 1988

The Front/ Wellington/ Church intersection showing the original "coffin block," c. 1870.

Anyone who drives or walks along Front Street between Jarvis and Church will, I'm sure, have noticed tour buses stopped on Front Street while their complement of passengers disembark and busily snap pictures of the beautiful old Gooderham Building, posed in a kind of postcard setting with the modern Toronto skyline in the background.

But this setting wasn't always so picturesque. In the accompanying photos we see the same view over a period spanning more than a century. The earliest view, taken sometime in the 1870s when Toronto's main streets were still mud, shows the three-storey structure that occupied the Front/ Church/Wellington corner years before George Gooderham built his new office building on the site in 1891–92. This old building, known locally as the "coffin block" because of its dimensional resemblance to a coffin, was built in the early 1830s and for a period of years served as the western terminus of the Kingston to York stage coach line, a trip that took at least 28 hours to complete (in good weather). In the photo we can also see that the local Dominion Telegraph Company office had an office in the building, along with a coal and wood merchant whose name is obscured by the telegraph pole.

In the early 1890s, business mogul George Gooderham (of Gooderham and Worts, and Bank of Toronto fame) purchased the corner, had the old "coffin block" demolished and erected a new five-storey head office building for his business empire to the design of prominent Toronto architect, David Roberts Jr.

The building's proximity to the busy St. Lawrence Market is evident in the second photo taken sometime in the early 1950s. Delivery trucks and vans crowd Front Street and the TTC streetcar tracks, as produce, meats and other commodities are delivered to or picked up from the market and the surrounding warehouses that use to line Front Street.

Several years ago the Gooderham Building was given a new lease on life, though for a time it looked like it would be demolished to permit a large office tower to be erected on the corner. Today it's one of our city's few remaining landmark buildings.

Same view taken in 1975 showing the 1892 Gooderham Building. Note the CN Tower under construction in the background.

Toronto's Old Gates
Took Their Toll on Us

April 23, 1989

You know, there's an old saying,"what goes around, comes around." Take, for instance, the incredibly naïve plan recently put forward by some of our politicians to erect toll-gates to control the flow of traffic into the city's downtown core. I wonder if any of our city hall wizards realize the collective sigh of relief that was heard around the province when toll-gates were finally abolished in December 1896, nearly a century ago!!!

Actually, the original idea behind the installation of toll-gates on some of our community's major thoroughfares was quite sound. The money collected was used to ensure the necessary upkeep of the rather primitive road system. After all, in those far-off days there were very few other sources of money needed to fill potholes, grade rough thoroughfares and to generally maintain the province's pioneer highway system.

With a toll-road system in place, Yonge Street, being the main route into and out of the principal city in the province, was naturally the first thoroughfare to have gates put in place, with the money collected used to help pay for its ongoing maintenance. One of the first toll-gates, if not the very first in the entire province, was the one erected at the King and Yonge intersection just after the turn of the last century. A few years later, as the town expanded, a new gate was built further north at College Street. However, the gate that seems to have lasted the longest was the Yorkville toll-gate that "opened" (actually closed) for business in 1820.

Situated first at Bloor Street (which for a time was called the Tollgate Road), the booth was soon moved further north to Davenport, then north again to

Toll-gate on Yonge Street north of Davenport Road, c. 1865.

Cottingham Street and finally to the top of what was then called "Gallows Hill" (so named for a tree that had fallen across the road giving the impression from a distance of a hangman's gallows), a few hundred yards south of St. Clair Avenue.

Another Yonge Street gate barred the way at the south brow of the hill into Hogg's Hollow. Other toll-gates were constructed at various points along Yonge Street, well out into the countryside to the north.

Yonge Street, however, was by no means the only Toronto-area street with toll-gates. Dozens were scattered along roads leading to the city with four on Dundas Street in a 10-mile stretch between Brockton and Islington. Progressing westward they were the Brockton gate (on Dundas between Sheridan and Brock), one at the northeast corner of Bloor and Dundas, the Lambton check gate at St. Clair and Dundas and the Mimico gate (Mimico being the original name for what is now the Islington area) on Dundas just west of St. George's Church.

Other gates were located on the Lake Shore Road just west of Ronces-valles with another opposite High Park. There was one on Davenport Road at the Avenue Road intersection and another near Davenport and Bathurst.

To the east there was a gate on the Kingston Road at Norway (near today's Woodbine Avenue) and another further north on the Danforth between Little York (Main Street) and the city limit.

There was even one for a time at College and St. George streets, now a midtown intersection.

Here are some typical toll rates in the mid-1870s: 7 cents for a loaded one-horse wagon, 10 cents if a second horse helped pull, 4 cents for horse and rider and one cent for each and every sheep, pig or goat driven past the gate. There's no indication of what a road hog would have paid.

The "blind" toll-gate at Dundas and Bloor streets, c. 1890. It was called a "blind" toll-gate, as it served to catch those approaching Toronto from the west who tried to evade the Brockton village toll-gate at today's Dundas and Lippincott intersection.

The "Lead Sled" in Plastic

February 7, 1987

Several months ago I wrote about my amazement at discovering in a Yorkdale shopping plaza hobby store a plastic model kit of the late, lamented Avro *Arrow*, without question, the most advanced jet aircraft ever produced in this country. So advanced, in fact, that all traces of the *Arrow* were unceremoniously cut into tiny pieces in hopes that this world-class engineering triumph would vanish from the minds of all Canadians. Even now, when the flying capabilities of new jet fighters are discussed, the extraordinary abilities of our *Arrow*, dead now almost three decades, still enter the conversation.

Well, there I was back at Yorkdale perusing the women's wear shops for a Christmas gift for my wife (and even if I found that certain something, I still had to get up the nerve to go in the store, guess at sizes and actually buy the thing) when I was again drawn to that same hobby store, this time by a sign advertising a new, larger-scale version of the original Avro *Arrow* and a brand new kit, this one replicating the first all-Canadian designed, mass-produced fighter aircraft ... the CF-100.

Again I was surprised, but this time for a different reason. After all, it was one thing to offer a model of the truly unique *Arrow*, but it was an altogether different matter to see offered for sale a model of an aircraft that was virtually unknown outside of this country.

Nevertheless, the "Canuck" (as the CF-100 was dubbed, though it was also known by the less flattering terms "Lead Sled," "Aluminum Crow" and "Clunk") was ours and it too was now in model kit form, thanks to a local company called Hobbycraft.

A quick telephone conversation with a company representative revealed sales were brisk on both the *Arrow* and CF-100 models; and who knows, maybe we'll even see more Canadian technology in kit form.

Now that I've recovered from my amazement at seeing the good old CF-100 again (albeit in kit form), let me recount the story of an airplane that was a landmark in the frequently happy, yet more frequently unhappy, story of Canadian aviation. According to Larry Milberry's fascinating book, *The* Avro CF-100, the "Canuck" really was created as merely something to wrap around a revolutionary jet

Avro Canada's CF-100, the first Canadian-designed and -produced jet fighter. The aircraft shown in this photo, VC FBS, was the prototype Mark 4 and flew October 11, 1952. It crashed near Ajax, Ontario, in the summer of 1954 with the loss of one life.

One of the CF-100s that rolled off the Avro assembly line between 1950 and 1958. Only a few were preserved. This Mark 5 model, #18619, sits on a pedestal in the community of Malton, northwest of Toronto, just a short distance from the factory in which it was built.

engine known as the *Chinook*. The engine had been developed in the closing days of the Second World War in, of all places, the Toronto suburb of Leaside by Turbo Research, a small crown-owned operation that would be acquired by the huge A.V. Roe Company out at Malton after the war.

Realizing that Canada's aircraft defences required modernization, especially in view of what the Russian Air Force was putting into the air, government and military officials decided to phase out the obsolete propeller-driven *Mustangs* and *Sea Furys* and the small single jet engine de Havilland *Vampire*, replacing them with a new Canadian-designed and -built, all-weather, twin-seat, twin-engine jet fighter.

Exactly two years after the first drawings of this new aircraft appeared on Avro sketchpads, Canada's prototype CF-100 Mark 1 (powered by two English jet engines as the *Chinook* was not yet ready) took to the air over the little Town of Malton on January 19, 1950.

One year later, the highly modified version of the *Chinook* engine, called the *Orenda*, was installed in a Mark 2 model CF-100 and in June, the first *Orenda*-powered CF-100 roared into the air.

Over the years, 692 CF-100s were produced at Malton in five variants and there was even a proposal for a four-engine version, the two additional engines to be fitted at the wingtips. In 1958, a short takeoff/vertical landing model, similar in several ways to today's unique *Harrier*, was proposed but no action taken.

By late 1961, Canada's NORAD (North American Air Defence Command) squadrons had been converted to the American-designed *Voodoo* and the "Canuck" was fast becoming just a memory of a time in our aviation history when we did it ourselves, and did it well.

By 1981, only eight CF-100s were still flying; today there are none. However, a few survivors can still be viewed and admired. One is in the National Aeronautical Museum collection in Ottawa,and another is on display near the Belleville Airport. two others are on view at CFB Borden and Trenton and, closer to home, a fifth CF-100 sits proudly on a concrete pedestal in a small park off Derry Road in the community of Malton, just a short distance from where #18619 first took to the air 22 years ago.

The Story of the Osgoode Hall Gates

May 27, 1989

Osgoode Hall and part of its wrought-iron fence.

Flanking the south and west perimeter of Osgoode Hall's beautifully manicured lawn is an ornately carved wrought-iron fence complete with a sextet of so-called "cattle gates" that permit, with some manoeuvering, entry into the grounds.

Osgoode Hall itself was erected in three separate stages with the most easterly wing dating from 1829 to 1832, the west wing from 1844 and the centre block from approximately 1856 to 1861. There have been numerous alterations and additions to the structure over the past 163 years leading to the sprawling complex that occupies much of the original 6 acres of land purchased by the Law Society of Upper Canada for the sum of 1,000 pounds ($5,000) back in 1829. The Hall, named for William Osgoode, the province's first Chief Justice, is the home of both the Law Society and the Supreme Court of Ontario.

Interestingly, when the first part of Osgoode Hall opened in 1832, it was illegal to hear cases in the building as it was outside the boundaries of the Town of York. City status and expanded boundaries that would enclose the hall and grounds wouldn't be granted to the little community for another two years.

Of particular interest today, especially to those attempting to enter the grounds, are the gates which, with their 18-inch wide openings, occasionally pose problems for the corpulent members of the legal profession.

From the earliest days, Osgoode Hall was surrounded by a simple wooden picket fence. Then in the mid-1860s, it was decided to replace this common wooden fence with an expensive fence of wrought iron whose individual component pieces were strung on steel rods like pearls on a necklace. To provide places of access, architect William Storm designed a series of intricate entry gates which people have come to regard as cattle gates, supposedly because they prevented cows from a nearby farm from entering the grounds where they would lunch on the lush vegetation and succulent flowers and shrubs.

A nice, folksy story to be sure. However, by the time the fence was completed in 1868 at a cost of £12,242.10 (about $60,000), there wasn't a cow within a mile of the place. In fact, the 1868 edition of the City of Toronto street directory tells us that the area around the hall had developed into a rather busy neighbourhood, with shops and stores stretching in both directions along both sides of Queen Street.

Just to the west of Osgoode Hall was, and is, University Avenue, though in those far-off days it was called the College Avenue, as it led to King's College. The thoroughfare, though legally private, was frequently traversed by riders on horseback as a rather delightful bridle path. Horses trying to get at the Osgoode flowers? Maybe. But cows? No way!

A more plausible reason for the unique gates has to do with ongoing political unrest. South of the border memories of the recently ended American Civil War were still in the minds of many, as was the fear that the dastardly Irish sympathizing Fenians might try to upset things like they had done two years earlier in and around Fort Erie.

To prevent the possible storming of the law courts by insurgents, the architect was either instructed or decided himself to incorporate entry gates which would require all those seeking admission to slow their pace and enter the grounds one at a time. The unwelcome visitors, possibly with the overthrow of the provincial legal system in mind, could then be easily "picked off" by defenders.

Toronto Telegram *photo.*

A local newspaper cooked up a story about how the unique Osgoode Hall gates could indeed be considered practical "cattle gates."

Waiting for a Bus

July 24, 1988

Several weeks ago it was announced that Toronto's downtown bus terminal at the corner of Bay and Edward streets, a short distance north of City Hall, would be getting a $10 million renovation, an amount that would be paid for in total by the building's owner, Gray Coach Lines, Limited.

This Toronto landmark first opened for business in December of 1931, and since then literally hundreds of thousands of newcomers have been introduced to our city via the building's front doors. Research reveals that from almost the day it opened, there have been plans to replace it with a more modern facility. Now it looks like something's finally going to happen.

The Toronto Coach Terminal which opened 57 years ago was without doubt one of the finest, most up-to-date of its kind on the entire continent. But the world of 57 years ago was a very different place.

In 1931, the Great Depression had the country very much in its grip. Toronto's population had reached 627,231, with Bill Stewart serving as the city's new mayor. Just north of the city the Township of North York was, for the most part, acres and acres of farming country.

Toronto's best hotel, the Royal York, was just two years old, Union Station had been in operation for four years and right across Bay Street from the new bus terminal's main doors stood another new hotel, the Ford.

A few months before the new terminal was to open its doors, John David Eaton opened his new uptown College Street store, the TTC had increased the price of a car ticket from 7 to 10 cents, and the Maple Leaf hockey team had just moved into their new home at the corner of Carlton and Church streets.

Not long after the new terminal opened, the city's newest skyscraper (and the tallest building in the entire Commonwealth), the Bank of Commerce Building on King Street West, opened for business and people were discussing the possibility of a municipal airport for Toronto. Quite a city, the Toronto of 1931.

While the city's Bay Street bus terminal was new in 1931, its owner, Gray Coach Lines, was in its fifth year of business, having been established on June 28, 1927 by the Toronto Transportation Commission as a way of joining together the financially lucrative bus charters and sightseeing operations that fell outside the TTC's prime area of responsibility.

Just two years earlier the Commission had taken over the assets of the Dominion Coach and Livery Company, a private enterprise that had been showing visitors around town for years in their huge "Charabanc" solid-rubber-tired buses. This sightseeing operation was subsequently turned over to the new Gray Coach when it was established in 1927, and with the purchase of White Star Transit later in the year Gray Coach obtained its first inter-city line, the run between Toronto and Hamilton, which was eventually extended through to Buffalo.

About a year later, Gray Coach purchased Metropolitan Bus Lines and took over that company's Toronto–Orillia service. This acquisition was followed almost immediately by another purchase, that of Red Bus Lines and the company's Port Credit run. In that same year, 1928, the Hill route, a special service between

*Gray Coach Lines had been in business for four years when the Bay Street
bus terminal opened on December 19, 1931.*

downtown Toronto and suburbs to the north of Eglinton Avenue, for which a double fare was charged, became a Gray Coach service.

The next year the Highway Queen, Maple Leaf–Markham, Del-Ray and Collacutt companies were absorbed by Gray Coach; and routes to Oshawa, Markham, Islington and Brampton came under Gray Coach jurisdiction.

But as busy as the new company was, it was forced to load and unload passengers and freight in makeshift terminals scattered around downtown Toronto until the company's new Bay Street facility was officially opened by the acting premier of the province, Attorney General Price, on December 19, 1931.

Over the following years, several other small bus companies were being purchased by Gray Coach and new routes established. Many of these routes started out as runs out into the suburbs surrounding Toronto, but as the city grew those suburban areas became highly populated communities like the Kingsway, Malton and Forest Hill. Gray

Coach eventually turned many of these routes over to either a local operating authority or Gray Coach's parent company, the TTC, to operate as part of the city system.

All the while, bus operations continued out of the Bay Street terminal that was now starting to show the strain of ever-increasing coach traffic.

Today, with more than 17 million Gray Coach, Greyhound, Voyageur and GO Transit passengers using the overcrowded building facility each year, major upgrading to improve both passenger comfort and vehicle efficiency is finally going to happen. Work on Toronto's new coach terminal, which will retain the historic 1931 Bay Street façade, will commence in 1989 and should be completed some time the following year.

[Since this story first appeared in 1988, Toronto's modern new Coach Terminal opened and on 13 November 1990, Gray Coach, formerly a subsidiary of the Toronto Transit Commission, has been sold to private interests.]

Sports Stadiums for Toronto Not New

June 12, 1988

The site of this post–First World War stadium was to be on reclaimed land south of Fort York. Its $150,000 cost was just too much for the electorate.

You know, it's funny how some ideas that appear to be brand new are, in fact, just a rehash of someone else's ideas that were presented years earlier. Take, for instance, the city's new SkyDome that's rising on the edge of Toronto Bay.

While it's true that the decision to use a fully retractable roof to cover the remarkable structure is a new concept, the idea of a sports facility on the waterfront is not. Now, before I hear from David Garrick, the new facility's PR guy, let me state that SkyDome will be much more than just a sports stadium with baseball and football occupying less than 50% of the time SkyDome is open, the rest of the time being devoted to public and trade shows, concerts, etc., etc.

Be that as it may, shortly after the end of the First Great War, a local orga-nization known as the Sportsmen's Patriotic Association was seeking the construction of a civic stadium or bowl (as it was then described) on the city's waterfront. The Association's spokes-man, P.J. Mulqueen, appeared before the city's Board of Control and spoke at great length about how the city, while spending millions of dollars on various public works, had neglected the sports-minded.

To quote Mulqueen, "Surely it is not too much to ask that you [the city fa-thers] consider the propriety of expend-ing a few thousand dollars in an effort to rehabilitate that greatest of all Canadian assets, its manhood."

(The fact there was no reference to womanhood was certainly a sign of the times, and please, dear reader, keep in mind this was not my quote.)

George Ross, the city's finance commissioner, was then asked to meet with the city architect and park's commissioner and, in concert, to develop a plan for a new sports stadium to be called War Memorial Stadium, which could be constructed on reclaimed land directly south of Fort York.

They came up with a plan to erect a 16,000-seat concrete structure, complete with a quarter-mile track, midway between Bathurst Street and Strachan Avenue, streets that had yet to be extended over the reclaimed land. Eventually, both Bathurst and Strachan would be extended southerly and connected with the newly constructed Boulevard Drive, a busy thoroughfare we now know as Lake Shore Boulevard West.

In their report, the officials stated, "The place proposed is a central and easily accessible one" (heard that before?) and went on to conclude that to provide such a stadium would require a city expenditure of ... wait for it ... $150,000 !!!

For various reasons, the proposal wasn't acted on immediately other than to change the stadium's name to "Flanders Field." Eventually, the whole idea just kind of vanished only to be resurrected a few years later by the Toronto Harbour Commission with the construction of their new horseshoe-shaped Maple Leaf Stadium at the foot of Bathurst Street in the mid-1920s.

This structure cost $750,000 and could accommodate 18,000 fans, though was capable of being expanded to 30,000. Actually, this "state-of-the-art" structure was the brainchild of entrepreneur and Maple Leaf baseball team owner, Lol Solman, whose team had been playing at Hanlan's Point. A mainland stadium would mean a lot more fans would pay to watch the Leafs play other international league teams. Maple Leaf Stadium opened on April 29, 1926, and for the next 41 years was Toronto's summer sports stadium. It was demolished in 1968, one year after the Leaf baseball team folded.

Since 1959, CNE Stadium has been home to the Argos with the Jays roosting there since the club's formation in 1977. Soon it'll all happen at SkyDome.

Toronto's magnificent SkyDome was officially opened on June 3, 1989, by Ontario Premier David Peterson. Two days later, the Blue Jays played their first game in the new stadium, losing 5-3 to the Milwaukee Braves.

Toronto's SkyDome was officially opened on June 3, 1989.

The Ubiquitous Rev. Scadding

February 14, 1987

Dr. Henry Scadding (1813–1901).

Tucked in between the massive Eaton Centre complex and the historic Holy Trinity Church is a three-storey structure that dates from 1857. Until recently, the old building had been officially referred to as simply #10 Trinity Square. That's now changed.

The old structure's best-known resident was Dr. Henry Scadding, without doubt this city's greatest history buff, and it's thanks to this gentleman that we know so much of our great city's early history. In tribute to Henry Scadding and his love for our city and its history, the building has been renamed Scadding House. Henry Scadding was born in England in 1813, the youngest son of John and Melicent Scadding. As a young man Scadding Sr. had worked for John Simcoe as property manager overseeing Simcoe's 5,000-acre estate near Wolford, in Devonshire. When Simcoe was appointed lieutenant-governor of the newly created Province of Upper Canada in 1791, his young assistant decided to accompany his employer to the "new world."

A few years later, Simcoe decided to establish a naval shipyard and a small community on the north shore of Lake Ontario (at a place that wasn't much more than a clearing in the dense forest), well removed from the American border. Simcoe's new townsite, which he called York, has evolved into today's modern Metropolitan Toronto.

John Scadding, along with others who had agreed to join the lieutenant-governor in developing the new townsite, was given a substantial land grant on the east bank of the Don River stretching from Toronto Bay north to the Second Concession, today's Danforth Avenue.

When ill health forced Simcoe to return to England in 1796, Scadding went with him and once again took up the position of estate manager in Devonshire, first for the ex-lieutenant-governor and, after his death in 1806, for his wife, Elizabeth.

It was shortly before John Simcoe died that Scadding met and married Melicent Triggs. She presented him with three sons, the youngest being Henry. When the youngster was but eight years of age, the Scadding family returned to Upper Canada, taking up residence on the same land grant given to Scadding Sr. by Simcoe 29 years earlier.

One of the original Scadding buildings that stood for years on the east bank of the Don, just north of Queen Street, was moved to the CNE grounds by the York Pioneer and Historical Society in 1879, where it can still be visited.

Three years after the family's return to Upper Canada, John Scadding was

In 1879, the Scadding cabin was taken apart, log by log, and moved to the Industrial Exhibition grounds (CNE) where it was reassembled by members of the York Pioneers. The historic structure is still maintained by this society.

killed when a tree he was cutting down accidentally fell on him. Nevertheless, young Henry was able to obtain the best primary education available in the young community and was the first pupil to enrol in the newly established Upper Canada College (UCC) that opened at the corner of King and Simcoe streets in 1830.

He completed his education at St. John's College, Cambridge, receiving his Doctor of Divinity degree in 1832. Scadding returned to Toronto six years later and was appointed a classical master at Upper Canada College. After being ordained a minister and serving a short stint as assistant minister at St. James' on King Street, he was appointed as the first rector of the newly consecrated Holy Trinity Church in the west end of town.

Scadding retired from UCC in 1862 and from Holy Trinity in 1875. Five years later he was elected president of the York Pioneer and Historical Society (still a very active organization), a position he held for the next 18 years. Henry Scadding died at his residence, 10 Trinity Square, in 1901.

One of the elderly gentleman's greatest pleasures was documenting his memories of an earlier Toronto. Scadding contributed descriptive text to John Charles Dent's *Toronto, Past & Present* (published in 1884) and Mercer Adam's *Toronto, Old & New* (1891) and both of these books are now much sought after by collectors. Recently, Dundurn Press of Toronto reprinted Scadding's own written work on Toronto's early history entitled *Toronto of Old* which was first published in 1873 (original copies are now worth in the vicinity of $100). In either its original form (now worth a great deal of money to collectors) or in the reprint version, *Toronto of Old* continues to bring the city of the early 1830s to life in the words of this accomplished writer/researcher/raconteur who wanders the streets of the little town and paints for the reader a vivid picture of York as it approached 1834, the year the small community was elevated to city status.

Cemetery Offers Visitors
Peaceful Look at Old T.O.

April 8, 1990

The modern Yonge/St. Clair intersection is one of the busiest in all of Metro. But, while hundreds of cars, trucks, streetcars, buses and (in the middle of it all) work-weary pedestrians wrestle with each other for space, just a few short steps away there's a heavenly oasis of quiet.

Nestled in behind a row of stores on the west side of Yonge Street, just a few steps south of St. Clair Avenue (and accessed via a short laneway beside a hardware store at 1418 Yonge Street), is the historic St. Michael's Cemetery, truly a quiet gentle surprise.

To discuss the history of this old cemetery, it's necessary first to look at previous Catholic cemeteries in Toronto. As early as 1822 (when Toronto was still the little Town of York), the community's first Catholic parish, the Parish of St. Paul's, was established in the northeastern outskirts of the town on the south side of a narrow, dusty pathway known in those days as Dundas Street. The street is now part of Queen Street East.

In those far-off days, land around the newly consecrated church was plentiful and it was not difficult to lay out a cemetery east and south of the little brick building to serve the needs of Catholics residing in and around the outskirts of the young provincial capital.

In 1848, St. Michael's Cathedral opened at the north-west corner of Church and Shuter streets and while a few prominent Catholics were buried in crypts under the church, most continued to be interred in the cemetery adjacent to old St. Paul's.

In 1852, the city's third Parish church opened on Bathurst Street, opposite Adelaide, and a small cemetery was established nearby. However, St. Paul's continued to be Toronto's major Catholic cemetery.

As the city's population grew (many of these new arrivals were Irish Catholics fleeing the recent devastating potato famine in their homeland), it became obvious to the church officials that a larger cemetery would be needed and a small committee was established to come up with a location. After much de-

The 1855 winter vault was recently restored by Summit Restoration as part of the 150th anniversary of the Archdiocese of Toronto, Catholic Cemeteries. Because frost in the ground during the winter months made digging graves difficult, if not impossible, bodies were stored in the vault until the spring.

36

liberation, it was decided that 6 acres of land would be purchased for 1,000 pounds (about $5000) and situated on the west side of Yonge Street just south of the Third Concession road, well out in the country in the small community of Deer Park, a name that was most fitting considering the multitude of deer that roamed this early Toronto suburb. An additional 4 acres were purchased in 1866 for 210 pounds (or $1,050) to permit enlargement of the cemetery to the south.

Many members of the church were upset that their new burial ground was to be so far out in the country, especially since the old St. Paul's Cemetery was almost in the heart of the city. In those days, a trip up a dusty unpaved Yonge Street to the new burial ground combined with an equally lengthy return trip would take almost a whole day, and if it rained, well, one can only imagine the mood of the travellers.

Nevertheless, on September 17, 1855, James Fitzgerald, age 59, became the first person to be buried in the new St. Michael's Cemetery. Two years later the burial ground next to St. Paul's closed. The old headstones in the latter cemetery were removed and the property eventually paved over. In 1933 a pieta and memorial stone were erected at the corner of Queen and Power streets as a memorial to the numerous, and for the most part anonymous, Catholics buried in the nearby churchyard.

Since that early fall day in 1855, almost 29,000 burials have taken place within the hallowed grounds of St. Michael's, including the grandparents of Toronto-born motion picture star Mary Pickford, Theresa Small (wife of Ambrose whose disappearance in December 1919 has never been solved), brewer/philanthropist Eugene O'Keefe and a young Irish immigrant, Matthew Sheedy.

This latter burial is most poignant, especially since Matthew was but 23 years of age when he was stabbed with a pitchfork during a St. Patrick's day parade through downtown Toronto in 1858. In the burial register poor Sheedy's interment notice is accompanied by the words "killed by an orangeman."

Today, burials in St. Michael's are rare occurrences, though on occasion members of pioneer Toronto families owning burial plots in the cemetery are laid to rest in the historic graveyard.

Since 1961 these sacred grounds have been administered by the Toronto Catholic Cemetery Association which encourages vistors to discover an earler Toronto just steps from the busy Yonge and St. Clair corner.

St. Michael's Cemetery is blanketed in snow in this 1990 view.

Sunday Laws Stripped Away
One by One

January 7, 1990

With all the noise about the legality of Sunday shopping, a newcomer to our community might think that all the controversy over what can and cannot be done on Sunday in Toronto is a new topic. In fact, there was a time when something as common to today's TTC travelers as getting from A to B by streetcar on a Sunday was against the law here in Toronto. On three separate occasions during the latter part of the last century, opponents of the anti-streetcar by-law were able to have a referendum put before the electorate, and twice the "no streetcars on Sunday" by-law was upheld, albeit with ever-diminishing majorities.

The Sunday cars proponents appeared to be "on track" when on May 15, 1897, the third vote to approve Sunday streetcars was held. To the delight of those proponents, exactly 16,273 said "yes," while 16,051 continued to say "no." Thus by a slim majority of just 222 votes, the existing by-law was overturned and it finally became legal to ride the city's trolleys on Sundays, whether that ride be to grandma's, a family picnic outing or, perhaps, even to church. The use of streetcars wasn't the only controversial subject when the Sunday "dos" and "don'ts" were under discussion. At various times throughout

"Cup Cake" Cassidy.

Toronto Telegram *photo.*

our city's history skating, tobogganing or the playing of sports on the sabbath were all frowned on as was the selling of milk, bread, candy or cigarettes.

Pity poor Alderman Harry Hunt, who ran the popular Hunt's bakery shops that could be found all around town. He even lost his bid for the mayor's chair when it was revealed that he sold chocolates and other confectionery goods on Sunday.

The next major change in the city's Sunday blue laws occurred in 1950 when the electorate, led by one of the feistiest politicians in the city's history, Alan Lamport, approved Sunday professional sports by a majority of 5,300 votes.

Eleven years later, another longtime Sunday blue law was cast aside when the majority of voters, who were asked on the 1961 municipal ballot "are you in favour of the City of Toronto seeking legislation to legalize the showing of motion pictures and the performances of concerts and plays in theatres and halls on Sundays?", answered with a resounding "yes."

To be completely accurate, the first Sunday movies ever shown in Toronto were seen by members of the armed forces, free of charge, in the spring of 1943 at the Imperial, now the Pantages theatre. Films were presented as a moral booster and tickets had to be obtained at the military camps or at the Landseair club located inside Union Station. In keeping with tradition and within the law, the theatre was not open to the general populace.

Following the voters' approval of the showing of motion pictures seven days a week, the citizens were all set to go to the show on Sunday, May 28, 1961, the day the law went into effect. But due to contract problems with the projectionists' union, only six of the smaller neighbourhood theatres were able to open that first Sunday. Those that did were the Centre, Christie, Paradise, Melody, Gay and La Salle theatres. Over at the staid old Massey Hall, Sunday performances were kicked off by folk singer and guitarist, Theodore Bikel.

Without doubt, the most talked about Sunday performance that spring day in 1961 didn't take place in a motion picture house or even at Massey Hall. It was the performance put on by the celebrated stripper "Cup Cake Cassidy" at the Lux Theatre on College Street. Incidentally, except for Miss Cassidy's performance, those first Sunday presentations proved to be, pardon the expression, a bust. Once the large chains had settled their financial differences with their union projectionists, the theatres, operated by Loew's, Famous Players, B&F and Odeon, opened a week later on July 2 with films such as "Windjammer," "Exodus," "The Last Sunset," "Parrish" and "Nikki, Wild Dog

of the North" entertaining the crowds.

Most of the suburban theatres would remain closed for another year and a half. Scarborough Council, however, didn't OK Sunday movies until March of 1963.

Toronto Telegram *photo.*

When Sunday entertainment became legal on May 28, 1961, seems all eyes were on stripper "Cup Cake" Cassidy doing her thing at the little Lux theatre on College Street. Oh, a few movie houses opened that Sunday too.

Waiting for a Streetcar

June 21, 1987

Following a parade led by work car #6 and the mandatory political speeches, the TTC–operated Rogers streetcar line in the Township of York opened on August 29, 1925.

With the Ontario Municipal Board's approval of the TTC's proposed new Harbourfront light rail transit (the modern day terminology for a grade separated streetcar line) project, Toronto will soon get its first totally new streetcar route in more than six decades.

It was away back in 1924 that the Township of York requested of the Toronto Transportation Commission that it construct 2 new streetcar lines to service the fast-growing parts of the township along Oakwood Avenue and Rogers Road.

The Commission responded by building two routes both of which commenced at St. Clair and Oakwood Avenues. Cars on the new Oakwood line went into service on November 19, 1924, and operated north on Oakwood and west on Eglinton to a loop west of Caledonia Road at Gilbert Street.

The Rogers cars, which also went into service on November 19, operated on Oakwood Avenue from St. Clair to Rogers Road where the cars curved west and ran to a loop a short distance west of Keele Street at Bicknell Street. Both these lines were of the conventional style with track down the centre of the street.

To be sure, in the intervening years the TTC has upgraded and extended a number of existing streetcar routes, but Oakwood and Rogers remain in the history books as the last entirely new streetcar lines built by the Commission.

One specific aspect of the new Harbourfront line that will differ greatly from the traditional city streetcar lines in Toronto is that the Harbourfront streetcars will operate on a protected right of way on Queen's Quay, thus permitting unobstructed movement of the streetcar and its complement of passengers through the vehicular traffic, no matter how congested. This right of way will be similar to, though not as conspicuous as, the one found on The Queensway on which Queen cars have operated with great success since 1957.

Protected right of ways in this city are certainly not new. Soon after the first horse-drawn streetcars began clip-clopping up and down Spadina Avenue in 1878, a centre reservation, complete with trees, was constructed by the city. It was later removed.

Commencing in the summer of 1913, cars on the St. Clair Civic streetcar line operated on a protected reservation along the centre of a wide St. Clair Avenue between Bathurst and Yonge streets. This reservation was removed during the darkest days of the Great Depression as a "make work" project.

Actually, the concept of streetcars running on protected "reservations" is extremely popular in Europe where many cities, large and small, use low-level curbs or other obstructions to permit transit vehicles easier movement through traffic.

In fact, some cities have transit malls down the main streets where pedestrians and streetcars interface in harmony. No cars or trucks are permitted except at certain times for delivery purposes. The idea of streetcars running on protected reservations on Bay and Queen's Quay as well as on Spadina Avenue (if and when the proposed Spadina LRT line goes into service), has evoked all manner of comments, both negative and positive. So too did the introduction of electrically operated streetcars nearly a century ago.

[Since this column first appeared in the summer of 1990, numerous meetings have taken place and it wasn't until March 13, 1992, that final approval for the new $128.6 million Spadina line (1983 estimates ranged between $28 million and $45 million) was given by the Ministry of the Environment, thereby permiting electric vehicles to replace diesel buses on this badly conjested downtown street. Depending on when actual construction starts, it is anticipated that the project, now (mid-1992) estimated at $141 million, will be ready in mid-1996.]

PCC 4502, the last streetcar on the Rogers route, July 19, 1975.

Mr. Lea's New Town

November 24, 1985

Town of Leaside, with a population numbering fewer than 50 and covering a little more than 1,000 acres of fertile countryside, was incorporated by a special act of the provincial legislature following the submission of a petition sponsored by the Canadian North Land Corporation, a subsidiary of the Canadian Northern Railway.

The Canadian Northern, which would soon to be assimilated by the government's own Canadian National Railways, had been created by Sir William Mackenzie and Sir Donald Mann several years earlier as the nation's third transcontinental railway. Officials of the company recognized the necessity for appropriate locomotive and rolling stock servicing facilities and saw the proposed new community fulfilling this need as the perfect railway town, complete with a roundhouse, marshalling yards, machine shops, offices and workers' homes, all within close proximity to each other.

To ensure that the new town met the optimum criteria, the Canadian Northern instructed American-born landscape architect, Frederick Todd, to lay out a townsite similar to his recently completed Mount Royal development in Montreal.

However, with the outbreak of the

William Lea (1815–93) built a brick farmhouse on the east side of the First Concession, East of Yonge (now Bayview Avenue) in the early 1850s and called it "Leaside."

First World War, develoment of the new 1,000-acre site (that had formally been named Leaside in honour of the pioneering Lea family that had settled the area in 1819) had set the railway back almost $2 million, putting it on hold indefinitely.

One thing that did go ahead, however, was the election of municipal officials, with Randolph McRae becoming the community's first mayor. Two of Leaside's main thoroughfares were subsequently named for this gentleman, and eventually the town's municipal office was erected at the corner of McRae Drive and Randolph Road.

While the residential portion of the new community had to wait until the allies could "hang out the washing on the Zeigfried line," industry was eager to put down roots in the new town. The first to do so was Canada Wire and Cable, consolidating its various Toronto plants into one sprawling factory on the east side of Laird Drive, opposite McRae Drive in 1914. Contracted by the federal government to manufacture 9.2-inch shells for the war effort, the company created a new subsidiary called the Leaside Munitions Company.

Although it was not an industry, the next major war-related activity to be developed in Leaside was an airfield, complete with hangars and ancillary buildings, on a 220-acre piece of property adjacent to and just north of the Canada Wire and Cable plant where training of Canadian pilots for the Royal Air Force would take place.

Canada's own air force would not materialize until well after the cessation of hostilities.

Not put into full-time use until the latter part of the war, the field was finally closed in 1931, though many of the buildings stood until the early 1970s.

Another early industry in Leaside was the Durant Motor Company where hundreds of Durant and Star automobiles and Rugby trucks were built until a financial crisis, brought on by the Great Depression, forced the company out of business. Many of their buildings were acquired by the fast-growing Canada Wire and Cable company next door.

Over the years Leaside grew both as an industrial centre and a community of hundreds of fine residences. In 1966, with the streamlining of Metropolitan Toronto, the legal entity known as the Town of Leaside disappeared into the enlarged Borough of East York.

To the locals, however, there'll always be a Leaside.

Airplanes and Durant motorcars were early products of the Leaside factories.

Historic Schoolhouse Turned Restaurant

September 25, 1988

Located at the south-east corner of Cherry and Front streets right in the heart of the proposed $1.4 billion St. Lawrence Square housing development, is a rather interesting looking building that is home to the Canary Restaurant, along with a couple of other businesses. This old building has a rather interesting history and hopefully will be preserved when the demolition company's bulldozers are let loose.

The sprawling building has actually grown like topsy over the years. Today, the building has a restaurant on the main floor and a music rehearsal hall upstairs, though it actually started off as the Cherry Street Hotel (so called for obvious reasons) that opened in 1906. The hotel was well patronized by the multitude of railway workers that once worked in the area when the hotel was surrounded by bustling rail freight yards. But of more interest is the southerly part of the old hotel, a structure that was actually built much earlier.

The story goes like this. In 1859, the newly organized Toronto Board of Education needed a replacement school for the small Enoch Turner schoolhouse which was a little further to the north on Trinity Street beside Little Trinity Church. This school had been built by wealthy brewer Enoch Turner in 1848 as a place where the children of newly arrived immigrants in the neighbourhood could get a free education. It should be remembered that in those days, education was something most parents had to buy for their children. Thus, Mr. Turner's gift was a blessing, pure and simple.

A replacement school, only slightly larger than the one Mr. Turner had provided, was erected on what was then called Palace Street (so called as the thoroughfare led to and from the Palace of Government, a rather grand title for the small Parliament Buildings erected near the foot of Parliament Street). Palace Street eventually became the easterly extension of Front Street. The Palace Street Public School, as this new building was to be known, was originally a simple, 1-storey, 2-room schoolhouse (1 room for boys, the other for girls ... an average of 170 students in 2 rooms!).

At some yet undetermined date the school was doubled in size by the addition of a second floor, and as the surrounding community continued to grow with the ever-increasing influx of immigrants it was again necessary to provide another larger educational facility. Thus, in 1887 the new Sackville Street Public School opened and the old Palace Street School closed.

Georgina Riches, principal of the Palace Street School and rumoured to be Toronto's first married female teacher.

Canary Restaurant at the south-east corner of Cherry and Front streets was once a hotel, and before that a school.

An interesting sidelight to the Palace Street School story occurred in 1882, when the Toronto Board of Education appointed Mrs. Georgina Riches as the school's principal and paid her the equivalent of what they were paying some male principals! This was one of the few occasions that the Board had ever paid a female on a par with men with the same responsibilities and qualifications. This move caused major disagreements throughout the Board with one trustee, male of course, remarking that it was an outrage that a female should receive $750 a year even though she was a principal, when his wife only received $250.

"Probably all she was worth," was Mrs. Riches sharp reply.

Thanks to Don Nethery, the Board's archivist, I have a copy of an article written by a group of 100 "lady teachers" that appeared in the Mail newspaper in February of 1882. In the letter the teachers complained about the pay discrepancy that existed stating "of course we know the world is yet adverse to putting women's salaries on a par with those of men, but surely in this 19th century, with its boasted culture and many improvements, it is time the common sense of the people decree that those who do equal work should receive equal remuneration, be their sex or age what it may."

In response to the letter, officials of the Toronto Board of Education simply suggested that those who didn't agree with the pay schedule should resign.

Interestingly, Mrs. Riches went on to become the first principal of the new Sackville Street School where she remained until her retirement in 1912. Also, there is an unconfirmed rumour that Mrs. Riches was the Board's first married female teacher!

Brickbats and Bouquets
for Old T.O.

March 29, 1981

York's shoreline near today's Front/Jarvis intersection as it appeared, c. 1800. The location of this early shoreline is still evident in the grade on Jarvis Street south of Front.

As we welcome thousands of visitors to our city this coming spring and summer, we're sure to hear many compliments, ranging from how clean the streets are to the efficiency of our public transit system.

The first traveller of note to Upper Canada did not bother stopping at York, but sent a couple of his followers over from Newark (Niagara-on-the-Lake) to report on the state of the new capital. But that did not stop his grace, the Duke de la Rochefoucauld-Liancourt, from writing about the city. He described York as an unhealthy place and said of the people:

"They do not possess the fairest character."

Isaac Weld dropped in for a visit in 1796 and immediately complained about the name York. He wrote:

"It is to be lamented, that the Indian names, so grand, so sonorous, should ever have been changed for others. Newark, Kingston, York are poor substitutes for the original names of the respective places, Niagara, Cataraqui, Toronto."

In 1882 John Howison arrived, stopped off for an hour's stroll about town and hurriedly re-embarked on the steamboat for Niagara.

"The land all around the harbour and behind the town is low and swampy and apparently of inferior quality. The town, in which there are some good houses, contains about 3,000 inhabitants. There is but little land cleared in its immediate vicinity and this circumstance increases the natural unpleasantness of its situation."

Capt. Thomas Hamilton, author of *Cyril Thornton* and one of the best sellers of the period, dropped in on York just after Howison and actually got a pleasant surprise:

"In passing through the streets, I was surprised to observe a sign indicating that ice creams were to be had within. The weather being hot, I entered and found the master of the establishment to be an Italian. I never ate better ices at Grange's."

But it is a different picture painted by the irate Dr. Tiger Dunlop in 1832:

"York on the banks of a lake and surrounded by a forest, is, not to say indifferently supplied, but positively without anything like a regular supply of fish or game; and when you do by accident stumble on a brace of partridge or a couple of wild ducks, you pay more for them than you do in almost any part of Great Britain, London alone excepted."

There were, apparently, plenty of pigeons, for in 1830 another traveller writes:

"A stream of wild pigeons took it into their heads to fly over York and for three or four days the town resounded with one continued roll of firing. Every gun, pistol, musket, blunderbuss and firearm of whatever description, was put in requisition. The constables and police magistrates were on the alert, and offenders without number were pulled up; among them were honourable Members of Parliament, the Executive and Legislative Councils, crown lawyers, respectable, staid citizens, and, last of all, the sheriff of the county; till at last it was found that pigeons flying within easy shot were a temptation too strong for human virtue to withstand,

Jordan's York Hotel, erected in 1801 and one of the most fashionable in the whole province, was located on the south side of today's King Street between Berkeley and Princess Streets (the site of the Toronto Sun building). In 1814, the parliament of Upper Canada met in the hotel following the destruction of the government buildings by the invading Americans the previous year.

and so the contest was given up."

And despite the lack of game which Dr. Dunlop complained about, Lieutenant Coke, in his *Subaltern's Furlough* writes:

"There are no places of amusement at York and the chief diversion of the young men appears to consist of shooting mosquito hawks."

In 1861, the famous novelist, Anthony Trollope, writes:

"Toronto as a city is not generally attractive to a traveller. The country around is flat; and though it stands on a lake, that lake has no attributes of beauty. The streets in Toronto are paved with wood, or rather planked as are those of Montreal and Quebec; but they are kept in better order. I should say the planks are first used in Toronto, then sent down by the lake to Montreal and, when all but rotted out, they are again floated off by the St. Lawrence to be used in the thoroughfares of the old French capital."

Canada's First Victoria Cross Winner a Toronto Boy

January 10, 1988

The year was 1854 and war had broken out between Great Britain and France and Russia. Known as the Crimean War, since most of the action took place on the Crimean Peninsula, the conflict was eventually won by the allies in early 1856.

Just days before the armistice was signed, Queen Victoria decreed that a new medal would be struck to pay honour to those who had performed extraordinary acts of bravery or gallantry, not only during the Crimean War, but during any future battle in which armed forces of any of the countries of the British Empire participated. Nor did recipients have to be high-ranking officers, as the lowliest foot-soldier was just as eligible to win the coveted Victoria Cross (VC).

The medal takes the shape of a Maltese Cross. On one side is the royal crest, below which appear the two simple words "For Valour." On the reverse is the date of the incident for which the medal was awarded. The cross is suspended from a bar on which the winner's name and military affiliation is inscribed. The bar and medal are in turn attached to a ribbon that originally was blue in colour for a naval recipient, and red for a member of the army. However, since 1920 all ribbons have been crimson in colour.

One of the first winners of this new Victoria Cross was a Canadian, a young man who was born in our city when it was still called York. Alexander Roberts Dunn was just 21 and a lieutenant in the 11th Regiment of Hussars when he took part in the now famous "Charge of the Light Brigade" at Balaclava during the Crimean War. It is said that because he was so tall, he had to use a sword longer than that normally permitted in the army. It was the length of his sword that enabled Dunn to drive off a phalanx of enemy troops thereby saving many of his comrades. For his bravery, Dunn was awarded the Victoria Cross. Dunn Avenue in Parkdale is named for the young man's father, John Henry Dunn, a pioneer property owner in the area.

In the years since Alexander Dunn won his medal, almost 100 Canadians have been awarded the Victoria Cross. Several, including Bobby Kerr, Fred Topham and David Hornell, were resi-

Captain George "Bobby" Kerr, who won his Victoria Cross during the First World War, died of carbon monoxide poisoning in his garage on December 8, 1929. Note the cross carved onto the memorial stone at his grave in Mt. Pleasant Cemetery.

Lying in an unmarked grave in St. Michael's Cemetery for more than a century, the final resting place of Private Denis Dempsey, VC, was marked with a commemorative plaque in the summer of 1992, thanks to the efforts of Paul Culliton and officials at the Catholic Cemeteries of the Archdiocese of Toronto.

Private Denis Dempsey, VC (1826–86).

---

dents of Toronto (the latter actually residing in suburban Mimico).

In addition to these fellows, there is another VC winner who, while not a native-born Canadian, was laid to rest in a Toronto cemetery, a cemetery that is as little known as is this Victoria Cross winner.

Denis Dempsey was born in Ireland in 1826 and as a young man of 18 sought to improve his prospects by joining the Grenadier Company of the 10th (Lincolnshire) Regiment, a crack British military troop that was to become heavily involved in the infamous Sepoy Mutiny of 1857.

On 2 separate occasions during the conflict, Private Dempsey risked his life to save brother soldiers. These actions were noted by his superior officers, and in November 1860 the young man was awarded the Victoria Cross by his sovereign at a special ceremony at Windsor Castle.

Dempsey's whereabouts following his discharge from the British Army in 1867 remained unrecorded (though it is suspected that he obtained a land grant in Canada) until the appearance of a death notice in the register of Toronto's old St. Michael's Cemetery, a small Catholic burial ground that nestles quietly behind a row of modern storefronts on the west side of Yonge Street, steps south of St. Clair Ave.

In the register it was recorded that on January 10, 1886, Denis Dempsey died from "congestion of the lungs" and was buried in a "poor grave" where he rests without even the simplest form of marker.

That is, until attention was drawn to the fact that this "soldier of the Queen" was a gallant recipient of the unique and highly respected Victoria Cross.

On June 14, 1992, during a special service honouring the 150th anniversary of the Catholic Archdiocese of Toronto, a commemorative plaque was unveiled at the grave site of Private Denis Dempsey, VC.

[The second part of this article, in which the previously untold story of Private Denis Dempsey, VC, is related, has been added to the original Victoria Cross story that appeared in the *Sunday Sun* in 1988.]

Suited for Tip Top Success

June 28, 1987

One of the most interesting buildings on the city's waterfront is the Tip Top Tailors structure on the south side of Lake Shore Boulevard just west of Bathurst. Recent restoration of the building has served to enhance this true city landmark.

Tip Top Tailors was the creation of David Dunkelman who was born in Poland in 1880. When David was still a baby, his family emigrated to Brooklyn, New York, and about a decade later, the Dunkelmans moved again, this time to Toronto.

The family patriarch, Elias, obtained work as a buttonhole manufacturer and eventually opened his own company. Son, David, tried his hand in his father's small factory, but soon decided to go out on his own and, in 1910, purchased for the grand sum of $1,500 the old Berger Tailoring Company, a wholesale manufacturing enterprise located on the fourth floor of a building at 73 Adelaide Street West.

On March 11 of the following year, David Dunkelman opened his new company's first retail store at 245 Yonge Street. The new enterprise needed a catchy name, so the young Dunkelman decided to hold a contest in which the person supplying the best name for the store would receive $25, cash.

There were numerous entries – $25 being a substantial sum in those days. Legend has it that an advertising salesman for the old *Telegram* newspaper suggested the phrase "Tip Top Tailors."

"I like it!" reacted Dunkelman. And so Tip Top Tailors it became.

The company soon outgrew the Adelaide Street premises and, in 1915, a new structure further along the street at number 256 was erected. A unique feature of the new building was a huge painted sign stretching from the roof to the sidewalk proclaiming that this was "TIP TOP TAILORS, HOME OF THE $14.00 SUIT."

As the years went by, Dunkelman's

EVERY 8 SECONDS Another Uniform For Our Armed Forces is Completed at TIP TOP TAILORS

TIP TOP TAILORS *Ltd.*

Newspaper ad from a wartime edition of
The Evening Telegram *newspaper.*

business prospered and eventually another new and more modern facility was needed. Thus it was that, in March of 1929, work began on a five-storey office–factory complex designed by Toronto architect Roy Bishop that was to be erected at a cost of $500,000 on land recently reclaimed from Lake Ontario on the city's western lake front by the Toronto Harbour Commission.

All tailoring operations, which at the time consisted of fabricating only men's wear, moved into the imposing new Fleet Street (now Lake Shore Boulevard West) building during the week between Christmas 1929, and New Year's Day 1930, so as to interrupt business as little as possible. In 1935, the company began fabricating women's cloth coats in addition to men's suits that, thanks to inflation, had now risen to $24.00!

With the outbreak of war in the fall of 1939, Tip Top Tailors began devoting more and more time to the production of uniforms for the three armed services. A news article of the period stated that "a military garment came off the production floor ready for dispatch every eight seconds."

Following the war, the demand for suits increased tremendously even though men's suits were selling for $49.50 in 1949. Two years later, the addition of a sixth floor added another 24,000 square feet of space to the complex.

Tip Top Tailors remained in the Dunkelman family until controlling interest was acquired by Dylex Diversified Ltd. in 1967.

The Tip Top Tailors factory on Fleet Street West (later Lake Shore Blvd. West), 1929.

Hero Called Coward

April 13, 1986

It was exactly 74 years ago tomorrow night, April 14, 1912, that the majestic RMS *Titanic*, the world's largest moving object, met her untimely end when she struck a mammoth iceberg in the North Atlantic. The resulting damage not only ended the life of this supposedly "unsinkable" ship, but the lives of hundreds of her passengers and crew as well.

On board *Titanic* that evening was well-known Toronto businessman Arthur G. Peuchen. Born in Montreal in 1859, Peuchen moved to Toronto while still a young man. In 1888, he joined the Queen's Own Rifles, being promoted to the rank of Major in 1904.

Portrait of Major Arthur Godfrey Peuchen (1859–1929), hero of the RMS Titanic *disaster, from* Greater Toronto and the Men Who Made It *published the year before the sinking.*

After holding a number of business positions with various Toronto companies, Peuchen became president and general manager of the Standard Chemical Company, an enterprise created to exploit Peuchen's discovery of a new method for the extraction of various valuable chemicals, such as acetic acid, acetone and wood alcohol, from the scraps of hardwood left to rot on the forest floor. This alternate source of these and other important chemicals made Peuchen both rich and influential.

One use of acetone was in the manufacture of munitions, and with war with Germany on the horizon, Peuchen was much sought after by the British government. It was while visiting Great Britain in early 1912 that Peuchen decided to book his return passage on the White Star's new ocean liner RMS *Titanic*.

Titanic had been constructed in the huge Belfast shipyard of Messrs. Harland and Wolff, the keel being laid on March 31, 1909. The $7 ½ million, 882-foot-long giant was launched on May 31, 1911, and fitted out over the next few months.

Passing her trials with flying colours *Titanic*, and her manifest of 1,320 passengers (including 416 women and 104 children) and 915 crew, departed Southampton, England, on April 10, 1912, for the scheduled eight-day crossing with expected arrival in New York harbour sometime in the afternoon of April 17, 1912. A first-class ticket on the new ship sold for $4,320, and it was this type of ticket that the Major purchased.

Everything went perfectly for the first few days of the trip. Then, at 11:46 pm on Sunday evening, April 14, *Titanic* narrowly missed a head-on collision with a towering iceberg. Actually, a head-on collision would probably have been far less fatal. As it happened, the veering ship came in contact with a huge underwater spur jutting out from the berg. The razor-like spur tore a wicked gash below the waterline along most of the vessel's port side. Tons of water poured in and the vessel's fate was sealed. There was no doubt that *Titanic* would sink.

Peuchen's grave in Mt. Pleasant Cemetery.

hundreds of others (women and children included) had not. Peuchen was to become the brunt of many unkind comments, and the nightmare of April 1912 was to follow him for years. In 1929, he contracted pneumonia and died.

As the passengers and crew prepared to abandon the stricken ship, it became obvious that there weren't nearly enough lifeboats for all on board.

"Women and children first," ordered Captain Smith.

As the 20 lifeboats began to fill with screaming women and bewildered children, it quickly became apparent that #6 needed an experienced seaman at the tiller. After some searching, Third Officer Lightoller requested that Major Peuchen, who had advised the ship's officer that he had experience in sailing as a member of the Royal Canadian Yacht Club in Toronto, Canada, take command.

This, the Major did, but only after obtaining written authorization from the officer. Peuchen and the others in his lifeboat survived as did about 700 others. More than 1500 did not.

When the Major testified at the hearings into the disaster, he spoke harshly about the poor conduct of many of the crew, including Captain Smith. He then returned to Toronto where for a time he was regarded as a hero for assisting in the rescue. But, as people realized that while the major had survived,

Advertisement for the return(!)
of the Titanic.

Those Floating Airports
in Our Past and Future

April 29, 1990

You know, with all the games the politicians are playing over the future of the Toronto Island Airport, I'm not so sure they shouldn't have just left the old amusement park at Hanlan's Point. At least then there would be a reason for all the games.

Long before anyone thought of putting an airport on the island (actually, it was even years before anyone thought of putting a plane in the air), the western end of the sandbar (for that's all it was) had been the site of a few rides and games and a small hotel.

Initially, the rides were fairly simple efforts and were scattered around the hotel of John Hanlan (the father of the famous sculler, Ned) as a kind of divertissement for his guests. But, as the 1870s came and went, so, too, did the small single-storey hotel and nearby playground, and in their place, a substantial hostelry and amusement park quickly appeared.

A few years later, 1897 to be precise, a stadium was built and soon the hotly contested home games of the popular Maple Leaf baseball team and equally popular Tecumsehs lacrosse team were just 2 more reasons to visit Hanlan's Point.

Coincident with the opening of Sunnyside Amusement Park near the foot of Roncesvalles Avenue in 1922 was the drop in the number of people crossing the bay by ferry boat to visit the Point. When the Leaf team got its new stadium at the foot of Bathurst Street four years later, even the baseball fans had no further need to fight the crowds to watch "the boys of summer." Travelers to the Island hit an all time low.

Just when it looked as if Hanlan's

A postcard artist's rather fanciful (and rather scary) representation of the Toronto Island Airport.

Point would be left to the birds, surveyors from the Toronto Harbour Commission appeared and in due course heavy earth-moving machinery began scratching out a pair of 3,000-foot-long runways, several taxi strips and a parking apron. In the spring of 1939, a new administration building (built from the same set of plans that was being used to construct a similar terminal building for another airport near the small farming community of Malton) opened and a small cable ferry was put into service to connect the new airport with the mainland just across the western gap.

The use of a ferry boat to provide access to and from the airport has been a problem ever since the first aircraft landed at the Island in February 1939. Obviously, as the number of flights in and out of the airport increases, that problem gets more and more acute. As early as 1935, four years before the airport opened, the Conservative government of the day under R.B. Bennett recognized the problem and agreed to

Sun artist Andy Donato sketched this floating airport concept for a March 1968 story in the Toronto Telegram.

construct a tunnel under the gap. This plan, however, was quickly thrown out by the newly elected Liberal government under Mackenzie King (with help from Island resident and city controller, Sam McBride).

Concerns about the development of airports to serve our city didn't just affect an earlier generation of citizens. As recently as 1973, several engineering firms, prompted by the anti-Pickering airport "People or Planes" organization, suggested that Toronto's second International Airport should take the form of a new $5 billion (in 1973 dollars) "floating" facility several miles out in Lake Ontario.

Anchored in 400 feet of water, passenger access to the 800-acre site would be by hovercraft, helicopter or a subway line that would operate through a tunnel suspended 50 feet below the surface of the lake. To keep some sort of control over the numbers traveling out to the new airport, all ticketing and baggage handling would be done at a downtown terminal.

The proposed floating airport's runways would be situated on top of a series of hollow concrete boxes, motorized so they could be rotated 180 degrees to permit into-the-wind landings. The problems posed by rough weather and icing conditions on the operation of such a facility would not be insurmountable, at least not to the engineers who wrote the report.

They also felt that a second, smaller floating airport should be built half-way between the city's waterfront and the new floating international airport (it too should be accessible by the rapid transit tube) to handle short takeoff and landing commuter aircraft. Presumably, once these new facilities were in operation, the existing Island Airport could then be shut down.

Now, if we're awarded the 1996 Olympics and the World's Fair for the year 2000 and we could start building these floating airports right away ...

What a pipe dream. Last week I couldn't even get a limousine out of Malton, oops Pearson.

The "Squirt" Makes Its First Toronto Appearance

February 23, 1992

In July 1910, Torontonians witnessed the first flight of a powered aircraft over their city. Thirty-five years later, citizens were equally spellbound when the first jet-powered aircraft flashed across a much different skyline. Here, then, is the story of what the papers dubbed "the squirt."

The idea of substituting an aircraft's piston engine with a jet engine was foreseen as early as 1930 by Frank (later Sir Frank) Whittle, a young student at the Royal Air Force Cadet College at Cranwell, who obtained a patent for a gas-turbine system of jet propulsion that year.

Whittle eventually formed his own company which he called British Power Jets Ltd., and on April 12, 1937, conducted the first successful test-bed run of the experimental "Whittle Unit," the world's first jet engine. The revolutionary engine was subsequently installed in a Gloster-Whittle E.28/39 aircraft which flew on May 15, 1941, thus becoming England's first jet airplane.

History would record, however, that Whittle's creation wouldn't be the world's first jet aircraft. That distinction was held by the German Heinkel 178 which had taken to the air some 21 months earlier. Its inventor was Dr. Hans von Ohain who, working independently of Whittle, had come up with his own version of a centrifugal-flow jet engine.

With the outbreak of the Second World War, both Great Britain and Germany concentrated their efforts on turning out better and faster variants of tried and true piston engine fighter aircraft such as the *Spitfire, Hurricane,* Ju87 and Me109. In addition, and under the strictest secrecy, both countries also

Gloster Meteor *in flight and on display at the airport soon after the historic flight over Toronto on November 1, 1945.*

began developing jet-powered fighters.

First off the ground was the German Me262 which performed its maiden flight in the summer of 1942. Production models of the 540-mph jet fighter entered service in June of 1944. One month later, the first jet to ever engage an enemy in combat occurred when an Me262 intercepted a de Havilland *Mosquito* over Munich. The shocked English pilot evaded five firing passes by the jet before being able to escape into a friendly cloudbank.

Meanwhile, back in England the people at the Gloster Aircraft plant were working on their model F9/40 that took to the air on March 5, 1943. The first 2 production models of what became known as the Gloster *Meteor* F Mk1 became operational in July, 1944. Interestingly, just days after the

"Mossie" was chased by the German Me262 jet fighter, England's first jet deflected and downed an incoming V-1 flying bomb.

While jets played a relatively minor role in the war, it was obvious to everyone that jet-powered aircraft were the way of the future. In fact, the war had been over less than a year when the Royal Canadian Air Force requested the loan of three *Meteors* (a pair of F.3s and a F.4) and a de Havilland *Vampire* F.1 for evaluation as possible additions to their roster of aircraft.

In the fall of 1945, the three *Meteors* were taken on a cross-Canada tour prior to cold-weather testing at the Winter Experimental Establishment at RCAF Station Edmonton. Inquisitive Canadians examined the jets at airports in Quebec City, Montreal and Ottawa. Then it was Toronto's turn.

About mid-morning on November 1, a Gloster *Meteor*, serial number EE361 (in case the question ever comes up in Trivial Pursuit), piloted by Toronto-born Jack Ritch, flashed over the city at 500 mph as thousands of citizens gazed skyward to witness the first jet aircraft to fly over their city. Actually, only a few saw the jet, most just heard the whoosh. Newspapers, attempting to describe the aircraft and its revolutionary engine, referred to it as the "squirt."

"Make no mistake," the papers reported, "the jet has arrived in Toronto and aviation will never be the same."

Some experts even prophesied that within a decade all commercial aircraft would be jet powered. And while Canada's Avro *Jetliner* was flying just four years later, the nation's airlines didn't get their first jet passenger aircraft, albeit the American-designed and -built DC-8, until the early 1960s.

Of the three *Meteors* loaned to Canada in the mid-1940s, one crash landed in a Northern Ontario lake, while a second (the one seen by Torontonians) was irreparably damaged in a landing accident out west. It didn't really matter, however, as those in command decreed that the single-engine de Havilland *Vampire* was to become the RCAF's first jet fighter. A total of 86 *Vampires* served with the RCAF until the last was "taken off strength" in 1956 to be replaced by a series of ever faster jets.

Courtesy of de Havilland of Canada.

The government opted for de Havilland Vampires *(similar to this Royal Navy variant seen over the* CNE *grounds during an air show) instead of* Meteors *for the* RCAF.

A Jewel at Yonge and Front

January 24, 1988

Anyone walking or driving past the intersection of Bay and Front streets will see that another mammoth downtown development is underway behind the hording on the north-east corner as huge earthmovers take gigantic chunks out of the ground and mighty pile drivers clang and bang. The project will be known as BCE Place (BCE standing for Bell Canada Enterprises) and when complete will give Toronto 2 more downtown office towers, one 53 stories, the other 43.

But with this project, there is an interesting addendum to the original BCE proposal that can be found in what's called City of Toronto Bylaw #44-88 passed by City Council several months ago. In exchange for increased densities, thanks to land transfers and other special provisions I'll never understand, the developer has agreed to, among other things, restore the facades of several old buildings around the periphery of the development site.

To the general public, the most obvious of the buildings included in this unique plan, though by no means the oldest, is the gracious structure at 30 Yonge Street, better known as the old Bank of Montreal building at the north-west corner of Yonge and Front Streets.

Erected in 1885–86, this little jewel has provided a startling contrast between what was seen as classic architecture a century ago and what is perceived today as our best towering over it. Interestingly, the Bank of Montreal, a company that started business in that Quebec city in 1818, opened its first Toronto branch in 1845 on the same Yonge and Front site, though in a much smaller structure.

As the Bank's business investments (especially those involving the newly established Canadian Pacific Railway) prospered, work space in the 1845 building became too cramped and the architectural firm of Darling and Curry was engaged to come up with plans for a new, larger facility on the same site.

One of the features of Frank Darling's new building was an immense 2-storey banking hall some 55-feet square, the largest of its kind in the entire country, even larger than any found in the Bank's hometown of Montreal.

Around the outside of the building modern-day passersby can marvel at the huge sculptures depicting both the arts (agriculture, music, painting and architecture) and industry (communications, railways and, of course, banking).

Crowning the little jewel is a huge stained-glass skylight manufactured by the Robert McCausland Company, a firm that would, several years later, create the magnificent stained-glass window inside the (then) new City Hall at the top of Bay Street. The McCausland people still do great work, including the recent restoration of the window in what is now lovingly called "old" City Hall.

Soon after the end of the Second World War, the Bank of Montreal opened a new Toronto Main Branch at the north-west corner of King and Bay streets, leaving the Yonge and Front branch to carry on in various less important capacities until 1982 when it was closed as a public banking building.

Word is that in the new BCE Place development, the landmark structure will revert to public use once again, only this time as the new home of the Hockey Hall of Fame. To retain the building's intimate connection with our city's

The historic Bank of Montreal is seen at the extreme left of this photo that captures Yonge Street north from Front, c. 1890. Note northbound Yonge horsecar (the line was electrified in the fall of 1892) and an early electric arc light suspended over the intersection.

history, I hope they use the banking hall to tell the story of hockey here in our city, the arenas, St. Pats and so on, but the history of hockey in our city is another story.

Back at the BCE Place site, some of the other structures that will have their facades, thus providing a somewhat more human streetscape along Yonge, are former warehouses at numbers 36 (built in 1844), 38 (1851), 40 (1851), 44 (1850) and the old Argyle Hotel at 46 (1844), remodeled in 1895 and becoming a branch of the Standard Bank. Around the corner on Wellington Street, warehouses at numbers 5, 7, 9, and 11 (the first and last dating from the 1850s, when the Dominion of Canada was still just an idea and only 40,000 people could call themselves Torontonians, and the middle 2 standing since 1871) will be preserved.

Hiding at number 15 Wellington Street West is another old bank builing,

the once proud Commercial Bank of the Midland District (later the Merchant's Bank) that was erected in 1845 when the City of Toronto had only been in existence 11 years. From 1913 to 1969, the well-known accounting firm of Clarkson Gordon occupied the old building, erecting an annex next door to obtain more working space. It is proposed that the Commercial Bank Building be moved to a place of prominence in an atrium setting within the BCE development.

[Since this column appeared, BCE Place has opened, the historic facades have been restored and the Commercial Bank taken apart, stone by stone, and rebuilt within the development. The old Bank of Montreal Building, which is still undergoing restoration, is expected to reopen as the Hockey Hall of Fame in the spring of 1993.]

A Historic Car Wash

December 13, 1987

It's interesting how peoples' names often become generic terms in our everyday language. For instance, the statement "going to Loblaw's" (after Alliston-born Theodore Loblaw) really means "going to the supermarket" or "doing some last minute Christmas shopping at Eaton's" (after the original Eaton, Timothy) is another way of saying "doing some last minute shopping at the big department store."

In the same way, there are thousands of car owners who used to say "gonna get the car washed at Farb's" meaning they were off to the car wash at the north-west corner of King and John Streets. Just as there was a real Mr. Loblaw and a real Mr. Eaton, there was also a real Mr. Farb; Saul Farb, to be specific, who operated a successful car wash in downtown Toronto for many, many years.

Recently, that "landmark" car wash at King and John streets was closed and

Courtesy of Don Farb.

A 1956 Buick and Meteor "come clean" at Farb's.

demolished, actions that sparked my interest in learning more about the Farb story.

So it was that I met with Saul Farb's son, Don, and together we chatted about an earlier Toronto when the now ubiquitous car wash was still a unique feature of the cityscape and getting one's car washed by someone else was a real adventure.

About the turn-of-the-century Saul Farb, his parents and six sisters and brothers emigrated to the "new world" from their native Poland and began farming near Pontypool, Ontario. Eventually, the elder Mr. Farb sold the property and moved his entire family to the big city of Toronto. Saul soon decided to get out on his own. Shortly after leaving home, the Great War broke out and Saul quickly signed up with the Canadian Army.

Following the end of hostilities, he moved to New York City, obtained work as a motor mechanic and married a native New Yorker, pretty Shirley Kornblum. In 1929, Saul was on the move again, this time northward many hundreds of miles to Kapuskasing, Ontario, where he took over the running of his late brother-in-law's men's clothing store.

After only a few years in the north country, the lure of Toronto again beckoned and in the early '30s, the Farb family moved back to the big city where Saul returned to the auto repair business opening the Bloor Motors Garage (later to become known as Bloor Motors and Visible Motor Tune-up), first on Bloor Street West eventually moving the business to 464 Bathurst Street.

But still, Farb hadn't found his ultimate niche in the auto business. At that time the idea of operating a mechanical car wash had been tried by a few local companies, including Ford dealer See and Duggan with a car wash at 10 Irwin Avenue, Max Starkman's Spee-D-Auto Wash at Victoria and Shuter streets, and Charlie Walsh's Ten Minute Car Wash at the south-west corner of University Avenue and Richmond Street. Each one was less than a rousing success and each operated only on an intermittent basis.

In 1941, Farb purchased Walsh's car wash and adjacent ESSO service station, both of which had been closed for several months, and within a short time, the business became known as the Ten Minute Car Wash. The concept of fully automated car washes was still many years in the future and, with the advent of another world war, Farb's labour-intensive business was soon put under great pressure.

However, those pressures were offset by government-imposed fuel and tire rationing that greatly decreased the number of vehicles on city streets for the duration of the war. Throughout this period, the cost of a car wash remained at a dollar.

It was three years after the war ended when the name Farb first appeared, when the name of Saul's business was changed to Farb's Ten Minute Car Wash. In 1949, to service the greatly increased number of automobiles now driving (and getting dirty) on the streets of a rapidly growing Toronto, Farb's was joined by a proliferation of car wash businesses scattered all over town.

Meanwhile, the number of cars being washed at Farb's Richmond Street operation was growing by leaps and bounds and frequently cars were lined up around the block (University, Adelaide and Simcoe, before the latter two streets became one way) waiting to enter the wash line. Alterations and improvements in the way cars were being washed put Farb's in the forefront of the Canadian car wash industry and soon a continuous flow of curious car wash people and prospective car wash operators from all over the continent

Peter Witt #2894 streetcar, operating on a special sightseeing route, passes Farb's car wash in the summer of 1975.

appeared at his Richmond Street door.

With increased prosperity, it soon became apparent that a new, more spacious location was necessary if the business was to continue to prosper. Wishing to remain downtown, the Farb family first looked at land at the south-east corner of Adelaide and John streets, but eventually acquired property on King Street West, the site of Toronto's first hospital (the York General) and later the site of the popular Arlington Hotel.

One day in the spring of 1953, Farb's Car Wash at the Richmond and University corner closed, and on the very next day a new Farb's Car Wash at King and John streets opened where some 90 people (earning 85 cents an hour) were kept busy washing more than 200 cars every hour at the new site.

Then, as the years passed, automation in the form of mechanical wheel washers, underbody sprays, and so on, arrived, and while the number of car washes remained high, the number of car washers dropped drastically. Farb's continued to operate as a family business for almost two decades with wife Shirley looking after the bookkeeping chores, sons Jerry, Stuart and Don looking after day to day activities and the founder, Saul Farb, supervising all aspects of what had become a true Toronto landmark.

In 1971, the long-time family business was sold. Saul died four years later. Several weeks ago, the last car proceeded through the Farb's wash line, and a few days later Farb's Car Wash was no more.

Throwing Drivers a Curve

June 28, 1992

Those of you who travel up and down Bayview Avenue in the vicinity of Lawrence Avenue may have often said to yourself "wonder why this street makes this crazy bend just before it dips under the Lawrence Avenue overpass?" Or maybe you've never even thought about it. Let's at least pretend you have.

For the most of its length, Bayview Avenue, which was laid out originally as a concession road by the early surveyors, is as straight as an arrow. But, in the vicinity of York University's Glendon Campus, the road kind of hiccups to the west.

The reason for this deviation is because of a pair of old residences, Glendon Hall and the nearby Chedington, the mansion at the north-east corner of Bayview and Lawrence that's presently being converted into expensive condos. Here's the story.

Eighty or so years ago, north Bayview Avenue was lined with the huge suburban estates of Toronto's rich and famous. People like the Kilgours of Sunnybrook Farm, Canada Packers' founder James McLean, T. Eaton company Vice-President J.J. Vaughan and the Wood boys, Edward and Frank, would drive, or more likely would be driven, from their offices in the busy city to their Bayview Avenue homes out in the countryside.

The bend in a two-lane Bayview Avenue north of the Lawrence Avenue intersection is evident in this 1952 aerial photo. The large stables adjacent to the Sifton residence (now the Toronto French School) can be seen at the left of the view.

Of particular interest amongst this distinguished group is Edward Rogers Wood who was born in Peterborough, Ontario, in 1866. He moved to Toronto in 1884 and joined the Central Canada Loan and Savings Company, soon to evolve into the extremely powerful Dominion Securities Corporation.

For a time, Wood lived on Queen's Park Crescent, but in the mid-1920s

62

The bend is still evident north of the Lawrence Avenue overpass, March 1990.

moved to a newly constructed residence he called Glendon Hall on Bayview Avenue, just north of Bob Kilgour's Sunnybrook Farm (now the site of Sunnybrook Hospital).

A few years later Wood's brother, Frank, built a house in which Crescent School is now located, a short distance to the north, just across the Don River ravine. When E.R.'s daughter, Mildred, married, the father built Chedington for her on property adjacent to his Glendon Hall.

But because his home and Mildred's new place were separated by a narrow dirt concession road called Bayview Avenue, Woods used his considerable influence to have a new stretch of Bayview constructed a few hundred feet or so to the west, a stretch that would carry traffic around the two Wood residences.

That's why, to this day, commuters continue to be moved by the actions of Edward Rogers Wood.

The First Airplane Over Toronto

February 16, 1992

Every day, hundreds of thousands of people all over the world climb aboard airplanes of all shapes and sizes to fly to and from innumerable vacation or business destinations. In fact, the idea of flying either here or there has become so commonplace that hardly ever do we turn our eyes skyward as another airliner soars overhead. But that wasn't always the case.

On July 13, 1910, an air meet was underway on the Weston farm of wealthy prospector, W.G. Trethewey. The farm straddled a private thoroughfare called Homestead Drive which, years later and after being deeded to the township by its owner, was renamed Trethewey Drive.

The Weston air meet had commenced some days earlier, but poor weather had limited flights to short hops around the muddy field. One of the participants was the affable Count Jacques de Lesseps, son of the late Ferdinand de Lesseps, the brilliant French engineer who had been responsible for the construction of the Suez Canal during the decade 1860 to 1869.

The young Count too was interested in engineering, but devoted his talents to the development of the newest wonder of the age, the flying machine. In fact, while all the world recognizes Louis Bleriot as the first person to fly across the English Channel, less well known is the fact that 26-year-old

Count Jacques de Lesseps (1883–1927), first person to fly over Toronto.

Jacques was the second.

So it was with considerable acclaim that the Count arrived at the small Weston airfield with his Bleriot No. 9 monoplane which de Lesseps had christened *La Scarabée*.

The weather continued unsettled on the 13th, but as evening approached the sky cleared. At approximately 8 pm, de Lesseps climbed into his plane, fired up the engine and bounced across a rutted, water-soaked field. After what seemed like an eternity *La Scarabée* finally lifted off the ground, banked and headed for the city.

At a height of 2,500 feet and traveling at 70 mph, de Lesseps was soon over Sunnyside where he again banked, flying over the Exhibition grounds, then out over the bay turning once again to pilot the little craft over the heart of the city. Below, bewildered citizens filled streets and sidewalks, and lined porches and roof tops as they gazed skyward for a glimpse of the first airplane to ever fly over their city. Torontonians were thunderstruck.

Eventually, as darkness descended, de Lesseps headed back to the little airfield where some of his crew had set fire to a drum of gasoline to act as a beacon. Following a bumpy landing, de Lesseps was wrapped in a tricolour and fêted as no visitor to the city had ever been before.

The following day, the Toronto

La Scarabée, *the aircraft in which de Lesseps flew over the city.*

newspapers were filled with photos and stories trumpeting de Lesseps's incredible accomplishment. Every detail of the aircraft, its wings, controls and engine, were described in minute detail. "The Vision of a Thousand Years," exclaimed one headline while another proclaimed that de Lesseps' flight was the "Greatest Sight of the Twentieth Century," a century that was not yet a decade old.

A prophetic editorial writer penned, "Toronto has seen the first great flight, the beginning of many others that shall annihilate our mighty distance and make the men of our city a neighbor with his brother on the wave-washed shores of the Pacific."

While a visitor to Toronto, the Count met Grace Mackenzie, daughter of Sir William Mackenzie, owner of the city's street railway company, President of the Canadian Northern Railway and prominent Canadian entrepreneur. Following their meeting Count de Lesseps would frequently be a guest at the beautiful Mackenzie mansion called Benvenuto, on the Avenue Road hill.

In the fall of the year, the Count traveled to an aviation meet at New York City's Belmont Park on board Mackenzie's private railway car accompanied by Grace and her two sisters. On October 25, 1910, Grace Mackenzie became the first Canadian woman to fly when she took a couple of circuits of the Belmont Park airfield with the Count in his famous *La Scarabée*. Exactly three months later the couple was married in St. James' Church, Spanish Place, London, England.

With the outbreak of the Great War, de Lesseps returned to France joining the aviation branch of the army. For service to his country in its time of need, he was awarded the Croix de Guerre and Cross of the Legion of Honor.

With the cessation of hostilities, de Lesseps returned to Toronto where he and his wife and their young family, Guy, Francois, Elisabeth and Katherine, lived for a time at 55 Ridge Road in north Rosedale. Then, in late May 1927, the Count traveled to the Gaspé to supervise an extensive aerial survey that was being undertaken for the Canadian government. The project required that 20,000 photographs be taken from 10,000 feet. Things went well until October 18 when word was received that de Lesseps's aircraft had crashed into the St. Lawrence River. Speculation was that engine trouble had caused the craft to plummet earthward at a tremendous rate of speed.

While traces of wreckage were found, there was no sign of the famed aviator or his mechanic. In fact, more than seven weeks passed before the bodies were located.

A cairn near the village of Gaspé commemorates the life of de Lesseps, the first person to fly over Toronto. The Count is buried in the local cemetery.

Small a Big Mystery

December 3, 1989

December 2, 1989, marks the 70th aniversary of the disappearance of one Ambrose J. Small, an occurrence that touched off this city's most extensive and baffling missing persons case, a case that has never been solved.

Ambrose John Small, to give him his full moniker, was born in Bradford, Ontario, in 1867. The family moved to Toronto obtaining lodging at 9 Herbert

Ambrose Small whose disappearance in 1919 has never been solved.

Street in the Queen and Sherbourne part of town. As a youngster, Ambie, as people called him, attended De La Salle Institute when the school was located on what we now call Adelaide Street East, though in Small's time the thoroughfare was still called Duke Street.

Ambrose's hard working father, Daniel, was employed as a saloon keeper at the old Grand Hotel on the south side of Adelaide Street West, steps west of Yonge, and just across a laneway from the popular Grand Opera House, one of the city's best-known playhouses.

Built in 1874, the playhouse had a seating capacity of more than 1,700 and had been completely rebuilt in just 51 days after a devastating fire gutted the building in 1879.

Daniel got to know O.B. Sheppard, owner of the Grand Opera House, quite well and was eventually able to talk him into giving his son, Ambrose, a job in the theatre. And what a lofty position it was, that of assistant treasurer. Before long, the teenager was made treasurer. Then,

with the promise of a hefty raise in pay, Ambrose quit the Grand and accepted a similar position at the competing Toronto Opera House, a few doors west along the street. There was little doubt in anybody's mind that the young Mr. Small was good at what he liked doing most, making money.

Eventually, the ambitious Small became part owner of the Toronto Opera House, and in 1890 was on the move again, taking out an option to purchase his first love, the old Grand. With a $50,000 down payment, the shrewd young businessman (he was only 24) acquired the theatre and was able to pay off the remaining $100,000 in less than two years. Not satisfied with one Grand Opera House Small then purchased several other theatres, all with the same name, in various cities across southern Ontario. In addition, he also became lessee of the Russell Theatre in Ottawa.

In 1902, Ambrose married Theresa Kormann, an accomplished musician and teacher who had taken graduate courses in Paris and Milan. She was also Small's stepmother's sister and the youngest child in the extremely wealthy Kormann Brewing Company family. The happy young couple moved into a 16-room mansion at 56 Glen Road in wealthy Rosedale.

One year later, Small's second Toronto holding, the Toronto Opera House, was destroyed by fire, to be replaced almost immediately on the same site by a new theatre called the Majestic. Eventually, Small sold this theatre, which had been allowed to degenerate into a "blood and thunder" melodrama playhouse, to the newly established Famous Players organization who completely remodeled the building, renamed it the Regent and turned it into the company's first motion picture house.

As the years went by Small became restless and in late 1919 decided to sell his theatre empire. During a brief business meeting in Montreal with several of that city's wealthy capitalists, he concluded a deal whereby he'd sell them all his Ontario holdings for $2 million, half to be paid by cheque, the remainder over the next few months. Ambie was rich.

On Saturday, November 29, 1919, Small returned to Toronto and the next day met with his staff to discuss the situation and express his hopes that they would find continued employment with the new owners.

Two days later Small deposited a cheque for one million dollars in his account at the main branch of the Dominion Bank at King and Yonge streets. At noon the following day, Tuesday, December 2, Small and his lawyer, E. F. Flock of London, Ontario, met at the theatre to put the finishing touches on the deal. After their meeting had concluded, about 5:30 in the afternoon, Flock left his client and boarded the Toronto–London train.

An hour or so later Small was seen buying a newspaper and then, poof! It was if he disappeared from the face of the earth. No one ever saw Ambrose Small again, dead or alive.

Several weeks went by before anyone really got concerned about Small's disappearance (word was he had a mistress and he had taken off before) so that by the time the police got on the case, all traces of the man were stone cold.

Over the years, numerous suggestions as to Small's fate were presented – he took his fortune and ran away to South America, he was fuel for the theatre's huge furnace, his body became landfill in a Rosedale garbage dump and the most intriguing, he was chopped up, becoming an ingredient in pig food for a piggery located near today's O'Connor Road–Greenwood Avenue intersection. In fact, a long-time Toronto police detective believed the inedible part of Small was mixed in with the gravel and sand that forms the base of little Linsmore Crescent.

Some people even pointed the finger at his wife, poor Theresa. On October 14, 1933, she died at her Glen Road home after a long illness brought on, some said, as a result of constant persecution by those who felt she had done the dirty deed herself.

Several days later after her death, Theresa was buried in St. Michael's Cemetery near the corner of Yonge and St. Clair. Her grave had no headstone. She was afraid the curious would chip away at it as they had done at her.

After 20 years of bickering and litigation involving Small's two sisters, Ambrose Small's estate was settled on March 31, 1935. The $2 million had dwindled to just $141,313, not enough to pay even the creditors.

To this day, the fate of Toronto's most famous disappearing person, Ambrose Small, is unresolved.

Small sold his Grand Opera House on Adelaide Street West shortly before his disappearance on December 2, 1919.

Meet Mr. Bloor – or is It Bloore?

August 14, 1988

I really don't know how to tell the city mapmakers, street-sign manufacturers and Bloor Street businessmen this except to tell them straight out ... Bloor is spelled wrong! That's right. It's not B L O O R , but B L O O R E , with that final "e." And how do I know that? Glad you asked.

While compiling the origins of Toronto street names for a proposed book, I discovered that Joseph Bloor, after whom Toronto's "Fifth Avenue" takes its name, was buried in the Necropolis. Desiring to learn more about this early Yorkville businessman, I began perusing the old burial records of the historic cemetery located on the west bank of the Don River just north of Gerrard Street.

I found that Bloor was indeed buried there and what was even more interesting was that inscribed right on his headstone is the statement "IN MEMORY OF JOSEPH BLOORE (complete with the final "E") WHO DIED AUGUST 31, 1862."

Now, if that isn't proof enough that we spell Bloor incorrectly or if people think that the spelling of the surname on the headstone may just have been a spelling error on the part of the chiseler, rather the stonecutter, a second line reminds us that buried alongside Joseph is "SARAH, WIFE OF JOSEPH BLOORE" (again with the final "E").

One misspelling on a grave stone, perhaps, but two mistakes on one stone? I don't think the marker maker would get away with that. More proof? Nearby are grave stones honouring "JOHN HELLIWELL, SON OF JOSEPH AND SARAH BLOORE" and across the way another stone reading "MARY ANN CLARKE, DAUGHTER OF JOSEPH AND SARAH BLOORE," both children having died years after their parents.

One final piece of proof can be found on the card filled out at the time of each death and subsequent burial and kept in the Necropolis file. Here all the Bloore surnames again appear with the final "e." I rest my case.

Now that we've established that the street is in fact spelled wrong (I suppose we'll have to live with the inaccuracy), perhaps it will be of interest to find out who this guy Joe Bloore was anyway. While most of our community's earliest street names were selected to memorialize the hierarchy in England, King for King George III, Queen for Queen Victoria, Yonge for Sir George Yonge, Dundas for Sir Henry Dundas (the latter two prominent English MPs) and so on, it turns out that Bloor (or Bloore) was named for an ordinary Joe, Joe Bloore to be precise.

Joe was born in Staffordshire, England in 1789, emigrating to Up-

Portrait of Joseph Bloor, Esq. (1788–1862).

Courtesy of Metropolitan Toronto Public Library

68

Bloore's grave marker (note spelling) in The Necropolis.

per Canada in 1818 and settling in the Town of York (as Toronto was then called) where he ran a small hotel called the Farmers' Inn at King and Francis streets, steps north of the town's busy St. Lawrence Market.

About a dozen years later, having made a little bit of money, Bloore moved out into the countryside north of town and established a brewery near the top of today's Sherbourne Street. Soon a small village began to evolve just to the west of his factory and north of the intersection of what today is called Yonge Street (then it was simply the "road to Yonge Street") and a narrow dirt pathway that had been laid out years earlier by the government surveyors exactly 1 1/4 miles north of the base line that has become today's busy Queen Street. That mile and a quarter between the two east-west thoroughfares was, in surveyor's terminology, a concession, giving rise to the northerly thoroughfare's original name, the Second Concession Line.

Before long a toll-gate was established at the intersection of the Second Concession and the "road to Yonge Street" and the east-west path became the Tollgate Road. Eventually, that name too was changed becoming St. Paul's Road after St. Paul's Anglican Church that was erected in 1842 on the south side of the concession road. And all the while, the nearby community continued to grow and soon took the name Yorkville.

Prominent in the emerging community was Joseph Bloore, the prosperous brewer who had decided to branch out into the land development business with his friend, William Jarvis. In fact, so involved was Mr. Bloore in his new business that for a time it looked as if Yorkville would be renamed Blooreville. Well, you can bet Mr. Jarvis had something to say about that and the name Yorkville was ultimately retained.

In time, Mr. Bloore erected a large residence on the south side of the concession road just east of Yonge, and it wasn't long before the thoroughfare was identified by another name and Bloore Street was born.

Then, somewhere, sometime, someone dropped that final letter in the word Bloore. But I won't tell if you don't.

New Uses for an Old Castle

April 6, 1986

Casa Loma, the "castle on-the-hill."

Perched high on the Davenport hill Casa Loma is, without doubt, one of our city's most intriguing landmarks. Built as a residence for visiting British royalty, the "castle on-the-hill" never fulfilled its destiny. As a matter of fact, the city itself almost had the structure demolished, claiming it was both an "eyesore and a financial drain on the beleaguered taxpayers of Toronto."

Construction of Casa Loma began in 1911 and two years later financier and "faithful servant of the monarch," Sir Henry Pellatt, was ready to move into his fantasy house. As a result of personal financial setbacks and ever-increasing property taxes (from $600 a year in 1914 to $1000 a month in the early 1920s) the elderly gentleman was forced to vacate his castle. Today we call what happened

to Sir Henry's real estate holdings market value reassessment.

Once Pellatt had abandoned Casa Loma the question arose as to what to do with a pseudo-castle stuck in the middle of a growing city. The place stood empty for years during which time there was no lack of ideas, some more practical than others; a club for millionaires or a mausoleum for millionaires, an Orange Hall, a home for the Dionne quintuplets, screen star Mary Pickford's Toronto home, a military museum and someone even had the nerve to suggest (as poor Henry had proposed years before) a Canadian residence for the King and Queen.

In 1926 a plan was put forward by prominent Toronto-born architect William F. Sparling (Metropolitan

Building, Adelaide Street East, Granite Club, St. Clair Avenue West, Masonic Temple, Yonge and Davenport, etc.) whereby he would personally invest more than $100,000 to convert the castle into what the newspapers described would become "one of the most plutocratic apartment hotels in North America." When asked his reasons for taking on the challenge of what to do with the castle, Sparling said that he simply wanted to give something back to a city that had been so good to him.

Unfortunately, his grand plan for the castle never fully materialized due in great measure to constant interference from municipal officials and many of the residents living near the castle who were concerned with the increasing number of cars cruising the sidestreets and the delivery trucks bringing supplies and, more particularly, the tons and tons of coal needed to feed the building's immense heating system.

Nevertheless, an undaunted Sparling opened a less-sumptuous Casa Loma Hotel in the spring of 1927, announcing a year later that he would soon erect a large addition to handle the influx of guests he foresaw arriving at the huge front doors.

Once again he was overly optimistic and in June, 1928, Sparling's hotel in a castle was forced to close.

Of historical interest is the fact that it was during the brief era of the Casa Loma Hotel that one of the most popular of the "big bands" got its start.

Sparling hired one of American band leader Jean Goldkette's many musical groups performing in the Detroit area to play at his new Casa Loma Hotel. After their Toronto stint, the Orange Blossoms returned stateside and decided to alter the business makeup, becoming a co-operative band instead, owned by the members. Their leader-cum-president of the new organization changed his name too. Spike Knoblaugh and his Orange Blossoms became Glen Gray and the Casa Loma Orchestra.

To be completely accurate, at first the new band was called simply the Casa Loma Orchestra, but modified the title slightly when members became fed up with dancers' requests to meet Mr. Loma.

No less an authority than George Simon wrote in his definitive book on the subject, *The Big Bands*, that "more than any other single musical organization, the Casa Loma Orchestra set the stage for the big band era."

Sparling was never the same after his hotel closed and he died, very much in debt, in 1940.

In 1937, the city turned the operation of the castle over to the Kiwanis Club of West Toronto who continue to operate this unique attraction with proceeds from admissions and bookings allocated to various club charities.

[Soon after the original version of this article appeared in the April 6, 1986 edition of the *Sunday Sun*, I was introduced to Sparling's son, Rand, who was good enough to give me further details about his father's attempt to operate Casa Loma. To make the story more complete, I have rewritten the 1986 article incorporating many of those important details.]

Toronto architect William Sparling (1885–1940) who operated the Casa Loma Hotel.

The Gardens on Mutual

January 29, 1989

Lost in all of the recent name-calling over whether Maple Leaf Gardens is or isn't a historic site, there is an unfortunate fact of life looming that will see our city lose another building that is only slightly less historic than the Gardens. However, this one will probably "bite the dust" without a whimper.

Interestingly, it, too, had the word Gardens as part of its original name, but rather than being built as a home for a hockey team, the Arena Gardens on Mutual Street was built to serve as both an opera house and public auditorium.

It was said that the building with its innovative use of huge steel trusses spanning the entire width of the structure was the first of its kind on the entire North American continent. It was also the largest indoor facility in Canada.

The half dozen or so men behind the mammoth project were among the "Who's Who" of the Toronto of the day with Henry Pellatt, who resided in the city's northern suburbs in a place called Casa Loma, serving as the organization's voluminous president.

The Arena Gardens which was built at a cost exceeding $500,000, a tidy sum in 1912, opened on October 7, 1912, with a highly successful six-day music festival. By the end of the year it could also boast that it was the new home of the city's professional hockey team, a team that was soon fittingly renamed the Toronto Arenas. The Arenas had another name change in 1919, becoming first the St. Pats and eight years later, under the guidance of the legendary Connie Smythe, the Maple Leafs. Interestingly, the team was to be known as the Maple Leafs while still playing in the Arena Gardens. The team's move to the "new" Maple Leaf Gardens up on Carlton Street didn't happen until November 1931.

The first professional hockey game at the new Arena Gardens between teams in the old National Hockey Association (the NHL didn't arrive until 1917) took place on Christmas night, 1912. And wouldn't you know it, the Canadiens from Montreal beat our guys, 9-5. Seems our Leafs come by it honestly. More than 4,000 fans witnessed that first game at the city's new hockey palace, though the game had actually been delayed several days owing to a problem in putting in a good, level ice surface.

In all, the Arenas/St.Pats/Leafs played a total of 19 seasons on Mutual Street before the team moved to "the house that Smythe built" on Carlton Street.

While the sport of hockey may have moved out of the Arena Gardens, or Mutual Arena as it was renamed, many other sports moved in: Torchy Peden and bicycle racing, Sammy Luftspring

A 1931 newspaper ad for a boxing match at the Arena.

72

The Arena on Mutual Street in the 1930s.

---

and boxing, Stan Stasiuk and wrestling, Pancho Segura and tennis and many more.

The "big bands" moved in too. In fact, the biggest of the "big bands," led by Glenn Miller, only played Toronto once in the leader's all-too-brief career. On January 23, 1942, Glenn, his 17-piece band and accompanied by songstress Marion Hutton, tenor Roy Eberley and the Modernaires Quartette had the 6,000 fans crammed into the Arena on Mutual Street, to quote the next day's papers, "really swinging it."

While the papers were all impressed by the "Miller sound," they were somewhat appalled by the ticket scalping that had the $1.50 tickets going for an exorbitant five bucks!

Six years later, a young crooner by the name of Frank Sinatra was signed up for a two-night stint at Mutual and was paid the incredible sum of $10,000.

The building's original name, Arena Gardens, had been changed to Mutual Street Arena in 1938 by its new owner, Bill Dickson, who had just purchased the historic old building from the City of Toronto, the city having acquired control when the previous owners, a Montreal-based group, got into financial difficulties.

The Dicksons introduced roller skating at Mutual in August of 1938 and during the war years several thousand skaters could be found gliding around the huge floor every evening. The popularity of roller skating waned in the 1950s, only to make a come-back in the early '60s.

Mutual Arena was also home to several kinds of trade and consumer shows, including the city's first Boat Show in 1954. Melody Fair, which went on to become a Toronto tradition, also got its start at Mutual in 1954, with a singer by the name of Robert Goulet meeting his public for the first time during that year's performances. Then in 1962, the building was extensively remodeled to the tune of $3 million with an 18 sheet curling rink, large parking garage, new front façade and restaurant added.

Virtually the only remnants of the original structure left intact were the north, south and west exterior walls. The building then reopened as The Terrace. Word is that this unique, yes even historic building, will soon be demolished and have some form of housing development erected on the site.

[Since this column appeared, The Terrace has been demolished and after a long period of inactivity, work has recently commenced on Cathedral Square, a condominium development, that will rise on the site.

A 1942 ad in the Tely.

The Aikenheads – Ironmongers Extraordinaire

January 17, 1987

One of my fascinations with the history of our city is the original derivations of words that over the years have become generic terms for common, everyday places like Loblaw's (after Theodore Loblaw) for grocery supermarket, Eaton's (after Timothy Eaton) or Simpson's (after Robert Simpson) for department store or, more recently, McDonald's (after Maurice and Richard McDonald) for fast food restaurant.

Then there's the word Aikenhead, for more than a century a word synonymous here in Toronto with hardware store and a company that lays claim to being the oldest retailing operation in the city.

The company's origins go back to the Town of York in the year 1831, three years before the little community was to be elevated to the status of city and given back its original name, Toronto. In that year, two brothers, George Percival and Joseph Davis Ridout, opened what in those far-off days was called an ironmongery in their newly adopted hometown. The business was located in a recently erected brick building at the north-east corner of Yonge and King streets, several blocks west of the town's business centre near Front and Jarvis and on the site of what had been a thriving plum tree orchard.

The Ridout boys were born in Bristol, England, and in 1820 emigrated to the United States with their father, George Sr. While living there the two boys were employed by Tarrat's, the well-known iron and hardware merchants of Wolverhampton, England. The two Georges, Senior and Junior, eventually moved to York, Upper Canada, while Joe remained with Tarrat's in the United States until 1831 when he too moved to York and rejoined the family.

The following year, George Jr. and Joseph opened a hardware store in York which was from the very start a huge success, serving the growing city's most prominent citizens. People, like the city's first mayor, William Lyon Mackenzie, industrialist and philanthropist Jesse Ketchum and hero of the attack on York in 1813, and later Bishop of Toronto, John Strachan, were all customers.

Following the elevation of the town to city status in 1834, the Ridout ironmongery also began providing hardware and fittings for use in the construction of most of the fast growing community's new buildings including the then "new" City Hall at the southwest corner of Front and Jarvis streets and the Rev. Strachan's church just east of their store on King Street, a small church that would eventually evolve into today's magnificent St. James' Cathedral. In 1847, James Aikenhead, about whom little is known, joined the company as a junior clerk and in 1866, following George Percival's retirement, became a full partner with Joe Ridout and Alexander Crombie (another longtime employee and no, he was not related to our tiny perfect Crombie) in the enterprise which then became known as Ridout, Aikenhead and Crombie.

In 1891, the company moved to 6 Adelaide Street East, a few steps east of Yonge Street. Two years later and soon after James' son, Thomas Edward Aikenhead, had taken command, the names Ridout and Crombie were dropped from the title to form, simply, Aikenhead Hardware Limited.

Thomas E. Aikenhead was born in Toronto in 1859 and had joined his fa-

The Ridout Brothers, Aikenhead and Crombie, hardware emporium is seen at the north-east corner of Yonge and King streets in this old photograph that was taken in the 1870s. Note the condition of Yonge Street, the horse and carriage parked on the wrong side of the traffic-free thoroughfare and an advertising sign projecting out over the street (now illegal).

ther's firm in 1873. It was under T.E.'s direction that the company really began to flourish, and by 1911 Aikenhead's had a staff of more than 100 employees and was, to quote from the 1911 book *Greater Toronto and the Men Who Made It,* "one of the most widely known hardware houses in Canada."

Aikenhead's was the headquarters for such important products as Valentine's Felt weatherstrip, Kasper's Oat Cleaner and the Coburn Patent Trolley Hanger "the best for barn, parlour or firehouse doors."

In 1905, the company moved again, this time into the former Comet Bicycle factory on Temperance Street, a building erected in 1895. Here the company remains (though no longer in the Aikenhead family) at least until the block is redeveloped by Simpson's/ Hudson's Bay people. In the meantime a new Aikenhead store has opened in another historic building on Front Street, just west of Church, and not far from James' first store at Yonge and King streets. Looks like the oldest store in town will be around for a while longer.

[Subsequent to the appearance of this article, the Temperance Street operation closed as did the Front Street store some time later prompting me to believe that Aikenhead's had gone out of business. However, the name Aikenhead lives on with the April, 1992, first of a series of new Aikenhead Home Improvement Centres in Scarborough.]

Canadian Tire Goes to Market

April 30, 1989

I'm sure that one of the best-known stores in the entire city is that of the Canadian Tire Company at the northeast corner of Yonge and Davenport in central Toronto.

No doubt some of you reading this article visited that store years ago, as I did, to buy things like seat belts. Remember when cars didn't come equipped with belts and you had to buy and install them yourself? And did you ever buy their "running lights" that attached to the grill and stayed on all the time, just like they're talking about now. Or maybe you just remember the sloping terrazzo floor or the counter people on roller skates?

Just prior to last Christmas, Canadian Tire vacated the old building, though they're still very much a part of the neighbourhood in a brand new building right next door. But, that's not to say the original building has gone. In fact, quite the contrary. It's now a large display area that, starting tomorrow night and running throughout the summer, will feature "Windows On Yonge," a nostalgic look at some antique cars, old automotive accessories and historic views of Toronto's main thoroughfare as the street looked over the half-century that Canadian Tire was located on the corner.

To be historically accurate, what we recognized for years as simply an old Canadian Tire store actually started out as the Grand Central Market, a creation of an organization called the Associated Development Corporation. While the project was announced in the fall of 1928, it became a victim of the depression that hit soon after. The Market didn't actually open for another seven years, on May 28, 1935, to be precise.

An introductory ad in that day's *Evening Telegram* newspaper invited every householder in the city to attend the official opening of the Grand Central Market that was to be performed by Mr. Duncan Marshall, the then provincial Minister of Agriculture, who included in his welcoming speech a comparison of this new market with the St. Lawrence Market, suggesting the new would serve the same purpose for those in the northern reaches of the city as the

historic old market had done for downtown folk for more than a century.

The ad went on to state that more than a million dollars had been spent on creating the Grand Central Market and that it would feature 80 merchants "ready to serve those seeking items for the dinner table."

"From the farm to the table" was this early Toronto shopping centre's slogan though it did incorporate as well a hair dressing salon, a shoe shine parlour, a gift shop and a linen store. But, for whatever reason (perhaps it was too far north of downtown) the market idea didn't work out. The building was soon vacated and it wasn't until 1937 that the erstwhile market building had a new tenant.

This time it was the Billes Brothers who had been looking for a new location for their cramped automotive accessory store that they had opened a few years earlier a few blocks to the south at the corner of Yonge and Isabella Streets. John and Alfred Billes had actually established their small but growing automotive accessory empire in a small garage at the corner of Gerrard and Hamilton streets across the Don River in 1922 with a total investment of $1900. In those days the boys specialized in supplying automotive and truck tires and called their place, naturally enough, the Hamilton Tire and Rubber Company. I guess it just as easily could have been called Gerrard Tire and Rubber, but it really doesn't matter because, before long, the company was renamed Canadian Tire.

The boys moved first from Gerrard Street East, to 557 Yonge Street, just south of Wellesley, and a couple of years later to 639 Yonge, just south of Bloor and at the corner of Isabella. They continued to expanded their product line to include an ever-greater array of automotive accessories.

When the depression hit in the late 1920s, it hurt most people, but it actually helped the Billes's enterprise. The public was forced to keep cars longer and repair them rather than to buy new ones. Canadian Tire had the things the public needed to keep mobile.

As a result, business boomed and eventually the old store at Yonge and Isabella streets soon became too small. So it was that in 1937 another move was made, this time a few blocks north to the former Central Market building.

It was here at 837–847 Yonge Street that Canadian Tire operated its main store for 51 years. Then late last year the company's new, ultra-modern store opened a few steps to the north. The façade of the old store has been recycled so if you get a chance, why not stop by the old store and take a look through the windows at a Yonge Street that used to be?

The Canadian Who Helped Build the Empire State Building

August 11, 1991

One day not too many weeks back I was driving north on Yonge Street and, as I approached Aurora, decided to pay a visit to my favourite bookstore in that part of the world, Ron Wallace's Book Barn.

Every author likes to check out the stock and move his or her books from the back row (where some other author has put them) to a front and centre location.

"Hey Filey," bawled Ron (who I've known ever since he had a real job editing the Aurora Banner newspaper and was always hitting me up for tickets to Canada's Wonderland when I too had a real job as the Public Relation's Manager), "your books are selling quite well up here. Surprised?"

"Not at all, I was always of the opinion that Aurorites (or whatever citizens of the fine town are called) had impeccable taste."

"Your Mt. Pleasant Cemetery guide is doing extremely well, all things considered," he went on.

Not wanting to consider what "all things" might be, I thanked him and resumed repositioning the books on his shelves.

"By the way," (he startled me ... I was allocating my SkyDome book a place of honour in front of a bunch of Berton's stuff), "we have an interesting

John William Bowser (1892–1956).
Courtesy of Margaret Bowser.

cemetery here in Aurora, you know."

Actually, I didn't know, but before I had a chance to ask what was so interesting about it, Ron zinged me with the proclamation that if I were to stand on the highest hill in the Aurora cemetery and look southeast, I'd be able to see the Empire State Building. Well, I'm nobody's fool and I was about to tell him just that when he suggested that I take a quick drive down Yonge Street and take a look for myself. As a matter of fact, he was pretty sure that what I'd find would make a good *Sunday Sun* story.

As the little cemetery was just a mile or so south of Ron's store, I figured I'd keep him happy (and my books in stock) and said I'd take a look, and off I drove.

Just south of the railway bridge, I turned east into the cemetery ... along a winding dirt path ... out of the car ... up the hill ... scan the horizon and Holy Smoke!! (probably not the best epithet to use in a cemetery) ... over there, between that pair of huge evergreen trees was ... the Empire State Building.

In fact, what I had discovered was a 10-foot high granite likeness of the Empire State Building serving as a massive headstone over the final resting place of a person named Bowser. Ron was right, I had myself a story.

Back at the Sun library, a quick look at a copy of the old *Telegram* newspaper published March 30, 1956, the date inscribed on the headstone, gave me a clue as to who might be able to help me track down the story behind this unique monument. While there was no hard news story, in the obituary section there was a listing for "Bowser, John William" and a reference to a surviving son, Jack. Assuming the family still lived in the Aurora area, I called the telephone information operator and after a few moments a synthesized voice gave me the number for Mrs. Jack Bowser. I redialed and after a few rings, Margaret Bowser, Jack's widow, answered. She turned out to be a real treasure. Revealing to her my interest both in the monument and the man for whom it was created, she quickly offered to provide me details on the Canadian who helped build the world famous Empire State Building.

John Bowser was born on June 2, 1892, in the Township of Whitchurch, north of Toronto. As a youngster he lived in a small house that still stands on the north side of Wellington Street East on the outskirts of Aurora and attended the old one-room Hartman School a mile or so to the east, close to the dusty intersection known locally as Hartman Corners after prominent landowners in the area. Today, Hartman Corners is the busy Wellington Street/Bayview Avenue intersection.

John was still only 11 when he quit school and set out on his own to experience the "cowboys and Indians" lifestyle the pulp magazines told him could be found throughout the vast and sparsely settled Canadian prairies.

However, it wasn't all fun and games and soon John was back home, hard at work on his father's Whitchurch farm. The years went by and again the youngster got the wanderlust. This time John headed north and he got work helping to build the country's third transcontinental railway, Sir William Mackenzie's now all-but-forgotten Canadian Northern.

Returning to Toronto in 1907, the 15-year-old obtained work in the construction industry. One of his first jobs was on the tunnel that connected the Eaton's downtown store with the nearby mail order and Annex buildings. He was assigned to the concrete pouring crew and soon became highly proficient at this relatively new facet of construction work.

Other major Toronto projects on which John Bowser worked included the new temple-like head office of the Bank of Toronto at the King and Bay intersection and the first phase of the University of Toronto's Royal Ontario Museum taking shape north of Queen's Park. Bowser's talents came to the attention of the executives of one of the largest construction companies in the United States, and in 1919 he was hired by the giant Fuller Construction Company.

Bowser soon found himself one of a trio of Canadians working on a massive project to help beautify the sprawling City of Tokyo. He personally supervised the construction of five large buildings in the heart of that Japanese city, all of which were completed on time and within budget. More importantly, all five withstood the massive September 1, 1923 earthquake that devastated much of the country. Of the approximately 100,000 people who died in the quake, not one person working in the various buildings constructed under the supervision of Bowser and his Canadian associates was even injured. Returning to the States, Bowser was then asked to supervise the demolition of the obsolete Madison Square Gardens in the heart of bustling New York City. At first he was upset with the company. "I'm a builder, not a wrecker," he growled.

But as it turned out, demolition was only part of this project. Bowser was also to supervise the construction of the magnificent 33-storey New York Life Insurance Company that was to rise from the rubble. This structure was one of the finest structures to ever grace the

New York skyline.

Not long after, a major shake-up within the hierarchy of the Fuller Construction Company led to the creation of Starett Brothers and Eken. Bowser decided to take his chances with the new company. On August 30, 1929, former New York State Governor Alf Smith and president of the newly established Empire State, Inc., announced plans to erect the world's tallest building, a 102-storey colossus that would, on completion, be the largest structure ever created by man. A few weeks later, the firm of Starett Brothers and Eken was appointed General Contractor. They quickly appointed the 37-year-old from Whitchurch Town ship, Ontario, as Project Construction Superintendent.

Interestingly, Bowser wasn't the only Canadian on the project. A member of the architectural team was a native of Nova Scotia, the specification writer was from New Brunswick while labour liaison was in the capable hands of a Montrealer.

Before actual construction of the new Empire State Building could commence, the time-worn Waldorf Astoria Hotel had to be demolished and the gigantic 2-acre footprint for the new building, that would front on 5th Avenue, cleared.

The old hotel was gone in less than

John Bowser's memorial stone in the Aurora Cemetery resembles a miniature Empire State Building.

six months. Then, under the watchful eye of John Bowser, work on the new building's foundation commenced on March 17, 1930. A short 410 days later (more than a month ahead of schedule and well within budget constraints that were made even more constraining with the onset of the Great Depression), official opening ceremonies were held.

John Bowser returned to Canada soon after the Empire State Building was completed and in the late 1930s acquired the Aurora Building Company that had been formerly owned by his brother-in-law. The company went on to build many of the industrial structures and private residences in and around Aurora and Newmarket, including Eaton Hall and barns (now operated by Seneca College), the Office Specialty offices (now home to York Region Police) and "Camp Newmarket," a post–Second Word War housing complex for returning veterans and their families that, in a much altered form, still provides accommodation for dozens of Newmarket citizens.

During the Second World War, Bowser directed his supervisory talents to the building of minesweepers when he was asked to join the engineering staff at the Redfern Shipbuilding concern on the quayside at the foot of Spadina Avenue here in Toronto.

For a time John, his wife Adaline and their son Jack lived in the former Timothy Roger's house on the west side of Yonge Street near Eagle Street in Newmarket. The house was located on 186 acres of property once owned by pioneer Quaker settler, Timothy Rogers, who had traveled more than 2,200 miles on foot from Vermont to settle this part of Upper Canada.

John Bowser lovingly restored the old house which still stands, though now sadly boarded up, near the Glenway Golf Club and adjacent to a non-descript strip plaza. A nearby small community street bears the name John Bowser Crescent.

John was in the process of building a

The world famous Empire State Building in New York City.

Courtesy of Empire State Building.

new log home for his family on 50 acres of land in Aurora when Adaline was tragically killed, struck down by a car driven by an impaired driver. Nevertheless, a heartbroken John completed the new house, eventually remarried and moved to another part of town.

On March 30, 1956, after suffering a brief illness, John William Bowser, age 64, died. Three days later he was buried in the Aurora Cemetery. A majestic granite likeness of "his" Empire State Building soars over this final resting place.

Incidentally, a recent call to the Empire State Building's public relations representatives revealed that they knew nothing about this talented Canadian's involvement with one of the world's landmark structures. Typical!

Postal History on Bay Street

January 3, 1988

Located at the north-west corner of Bay Street and Lake Shore Boulevard West in downtown Toronto (40 Bay Street to give it its official address) is the huge Postal Delivery Building, the construction of which commenced in 1938. With the outbreak of the Second World War the following year, the $2 million structure was used for military purposes and wasn't used by the post office until 1946.

Though now somewhat removed from a regular flow of pedestrian traffic, it's worth taking a walk past the building if only to inspect the beautifully sculpted scenes depicting the early days of postal delivery in our country.

One scene shows rampaging Indians chasing a Royal Mail coach, another a large Royal Mail steamship crossing the ocean and a third features a smiling postman having just delivered mail to a residence somewhere in Canada.

On the Lake Shore Boulevard side of the building adjacent to the truck entrance is a large carving of a huge four-piston engine flying boat, the "state-of-the-art" in aircraft design at the time the building was being constructed a half-century ago. Of specific interest to me as an "aviation trivia buff" was the name Canopus carved near the cockpit on the fuselage of the airplane.

A quick look in the dictionary revealed that Canopus is the name of a first-magnitude star in the constellation Carina, and the second brightest star in the heavens. It was also the name of a seaport city in ancient Egypt. But what do these references have to do with the Postal Delivery Building in downtown Toronto?

Historically the aircraft, depicted on the south wall of the Postal Delivery

The mythical flying boat, Canopus, *is carved in relief on the Lake Shore Blvd. side of the Postal Delivery Building at 40 Bay Street.*

Building, is typical of the flying boats designed and built by the Short Brothers. They were flown by Britain's Imperial Airways on transatlantic flights, carrying both passengers and the Royal Mail to and from Canada. Imperial Airways, established in 1924, became part of BOAC in 1939. BOAC, in turn, has evolved into today's British Airways.

Again, what does all this have to do with Toronto and the Postal Delivery Building? Well, in 1937, a year before the building under question was started, Imperial Airways embarked on a three-day, six-city tour of Quebec and Ontario with their flying boat, *Cambria*, in an effort to promote the company's transatlantic air routes. Imperial had a number of similar aircraft all of which bore astronomical names or ancient place names (*Cambria* being the medieval term for Wales).

Torontonians had never seen such a huge aircraft (it was 88 feet in length, an

The Evening Telegram photo.

Crew sit on the starboard wing of Cambria in an attempt to balance the stricken aircraft that had damaged a float while landing on the lake south of the CNE, *September 4, 1937.*

Air Canada 747 is over 230 feet in length) and as a result citizens turned out by the thousands to watch the Imperial Airways craft fly over the 1937 edition of the CNE and land on the lake south of the breakwall. Unfortunately, as the huge flying boat skimmed inches above the lake surface one of its pontoons caught a cresting wave or some half-submerged debris and snapped off, causing the aircraft to lean precariously to one side as it glided to a stop.

There were fears that it would turn over and sink before the craft could be secured to the Harbour Commission tug, the *Ned Hanlan* (now resting high and dry just west of the Marine Museum at the CNE), which had come to *Cambria's* rescue. After undergoing three weeks of repair work in the Ship Channel at the east end of Toronto Harbour, *Cambria* departed for Newfoundland and the British Isles on September 24.

Though not specifically recalling *Cambria*, there's little doubt that the artisan who carved the flying boat on the south wall of the Postal Delivery Building had the craft's near disaster in mind when he added the name *Canopus* to his work of art.

An Explosive Success

February 10, 1991

"America's Sweetheart," Toronto-born Mary Pickford, poses with women plant workers at GECO in 1943.

In last week's column, 3 February 1991, I wrote about a plan devised by the Canadian government shortly after the outbreak of the Second World War that would result in the country's largest fuze-filling plant being erected in the midst of rolling farmlands in rural Scarborough Township. This highly secret "Project 24," as it was dubbed, was made official on February 17, 1941. A contract was subsequently signed by the Hon. C.D. Howe, Canadian Minister of Munitions and Supply, and the Toronto-based General Engineering Company (Canada) Limited (GECO) authorizing the company to design, construct and equip a plant where fuzes, primers and gaines would be filled and assembled. Work on what became known informally as the GECO plant (a name that stuck) started almost immediately. Canada would again do her bit.

The war in Europe was almost 17 months old when land surveyors began the initial work of laying out the roadways and building sites for the huge complex that would soon cover the frozen farm fields on the south side of Eglinton Avenue between Warden Avenue and Birchmount Road.

It had become painfully obvious during those 17 months that the allies needed an endless supply of ammunition to help defeat the enemy. Through-out Canada, more than 130 companies had become involved in the manufacture of the numerous components that went into the various types of ammunition required by the Allied armed forces.

Some factories manufactured the chemicals that would be converted by others into explosive materials. Other plants fabricated the various types of shell casings, while still others produced internal timing and detonating mechanisms that gave the larger shells and bombs their specific characteristics.

Following extensive deliberations, it was decided by the experts that the new GECO complex in Scarborough would be devoted exclusively to the assembly and filling of fuzes. The initial production output of the plant was to be 1,500,000 units per month, but as hostilities intensified that number was more than doubled to a monthly output of more than 3 million units.

Throughout the early months of 1941 and under the capable leadership of GECO president Robert Hamilton, work proceeded at a furious pace to get the new plant up and running. And while the buildings and interconnecting tunnels (to ensure that an optimum environment was maintained throughout the complex and to protect against the spread of fire) were being built, the search was on for people to staff the plant.

Fuze-filling courses for supervisory personnel were begun at Danforth and Northern Technical Schools, while at the same time employment offices were opened at strategic locations around the city where recruiters sought out the hundreds of people needed to work on the assembly lines.

Sun reader Warren Evans (with original GECO sign in hand) stands in front of one of the company's buildings that's now occupied by a food company, March, 1991.

In addition to the pride workers could take in helping "win the war," the job paid approximately $20 for a 51-hour work week. Stylish uniforms were supplied and laundered free of charge. To complete the ensemble, metal-free "arsenal shoes" were provided to protect against sparks that could prove to be disastrous in a plant where so much explosive material was kept. Free transportation to and from the plant on specially chartered Hollinger buses was also furnished. With gas and tire rationing in effect, this apparent convenience was a necessity for most plant workers.

Full-course meals in the company cafeteria (supervised by the unforgettable Mrs. Ignatief (who had been in charge of feeding hundreds of employees at Eaton's downtown store and had been seconded by the government for the new GECO plant) were available for 25 cents, while hot and cold drinks could be purchased during breaks (two 10-minute "rest pauses" per shift) for a nickel. Coincident with the construction of the GECO complex, and while staffing quotas were being filled, experimental fuze-filling techniques were underway in the concourse building at 100 Adelaide Street West.

For obvious reasons it was thought best not to talk publicly about what was going on in the basement of the downtown Toronto skyscraper.

As the first of the munitions workers began arriving at the new Scarborough complex, a routine had been developed to ensure that the employees (of which there came to be nearly 6,000, the vast majority female) carried out their assigned tasks in complete safety.

Upon arrival at the plant, workers would enter change buildings and exchange street clothes for special uniforms which included head coverings and "arsenal" shoes. To guard against static electricity and sparks, no rayon, silk or steel-ribbed garments of any kind were permitted in the work areas. In fact, after changing into the company uniform, workers had to be inspected, then asked to step over barriers before entering the plant proper.

Thanks to the company's intensive safety program, there was never a serious accident at the plant. (The most serious accident actually occurred outside the plant when, on January 26, 1945, the company bus was hit by a transport truck on Eglinton Avenue. Several workers were seriously hurt, one of whom died a few days later.)

As the war in Europe dragged on, GECO's output continued to increase dramatically. Originally filling and assembling just 11 different kinds of ammunition, this number had quickly grown to 41. By war's end, the sprawling complex, now consisting of 131 buildings connected by nearly 5 1/2 miles of tunnels, had assembled and filled more than a quarter of a billion ammunition units for the Allied war effort. Each and every unit was proudly inscribed with the initials "SC/C," short for Scarborough/Canada.

Pioneer Industry Packs It In

August 26, 1990

On the last day of this month, August 31, 1990, the city's oldest industry will close its doors forever and the ancient distillery at the foot of Trinity Street, which has been operated by Gooderham and Worts for more than a century and a half, will be no more. The reasons for the firm's demise here in Toronto are both financial and political. Regardless of the cause, or causes, the bottom line is that within days another Toronto tradition will have gone the way of the dodo (the bird, not any specific politician).

The Gooderham and Worts story here in Toronto, a story that actually started as the Worts and Gooderham story, began in the year 1832 when James Worts and William Gooderham established a flour mill on the edge of the bay, between the east boundary of the Town of York (as Toronto was then called) and the river Don.

Worts had arrived in the little town the previous year from Suffolk, England, and began erecting a flour mill in a forest clearing east of today's Parliament Street. In 1832, he was joined by his brother-in-law, William Gooderham, who had also decided to emigrate to the young province of Upper Canada from his native England.

Accompanying Gooderham on his voyage were members of both the Gooderham and Worts families, several of their servants and a clutch of 11 children. Thus with the arrival of Mr. Gooderham and his retinue, the town's population of 3,969 was increased by 54. Gooderham invested 3,000 pounds (approximately $15,000) in the new partnership which soon became known throughout the area as Worts and Gooderham.

Their mill was unique in that it had a 70-foot high windmill constructed of red brick that stood on the edge of Toronto Bay. The windmill's large vanes were turned by gusts of wind that raced over the open expanse of water. Through a series of gears, this wind was used to turn the grinding stone which in turn pulverized the grain that had been brought to the mill by local farmers.

As most farmers were used to paying for goods and services with quantities of grain, Messrs. Worts and

Gooderham and Worts employees pose for this historic photo as the last barrels of product (rum spirits) leave the Toronto plant on August 3, 1990. The plant, in business for 158 consecutive years, closed forever four weeks later.

Courtesy of Canadian Illustrated News.

"The distillery of Messrs. Gooderham & Worts, Toronto" from a sketch in the Canadian Illustrated News, *April 25, 1863.*

Gooderham decided to convert quantities of this so called "payment" into alcohol which they then sold. It wasn't long before the production of spirits overtook the milling of flour and in 1845 a new business called the Toronto Steam Mills and Distillery was born.

Unfortunately, one of the partners wasn't around when the new business came into being. In February of 1834, James Worts had committed suicide by throwing himself down the distillery well after receiving word that his beloved wife (Gooderham's sister) had died in childbirth. Gooderham was now faced with the responsibility of not only running a very busy distilling business, but also had to look after his own children, of which there were 13, plus those of his late brother-in-law.

In 1845 Gooderham brought his nephew, James Gooderham Worts, into the business as a full partner and the company name was changed once more, this time to the well-known Gooderham and Worts.

As the years went by the enterprise continued to grow and, in 1877, it was proudly announced in the local press that Toronto's Gooderham and Worts distillery was now the largest in the world.

Then, in 1923, the entire operation left Gooderham family control when it was sold to Canadian-born businessman Harry Hatch who merged the distillery with his Hiram Walker operation in Windsor, Ontario. In more recent years, this Hiram Walker/Gooderham and Worts conglomerate came under the control of the Britain's Allied Lyons who have determined that the Toronto operation is redundant. As a result, at the end of this week, all operations at the 158-year-old plant, Toronto's oldest, will cease. Men will be reassigned or laid off and the doors locked.

The future of the site and its numerous historic buildings is uncertain.

[This column appeared in the August 26, 1990 edition of the *Sunday Sun* and while numerous studies on what to do with the property have been undertaken, the future of the unique complex of buildings still remains uncertain.]

Airport Fury Flies

February 25, 1990

One of the hottest topics around town is the never-ending discussion about the inadequacies of Pearson International Airport.

And discussions get even hotter when the subject of Toronto becoming an "Olympic City" in 1996 creeps into the conversation.

To be sure, a few things are being done to try and improve some of the intolerable situations that plague the airport. In fact, if everything goes according to schedule, we'll be getting a third terminal sometime this year and that should relieve some of the pressure. But, there's still nothing in the works that would see the airport connected with the city by a rapid transit line that's been proposed on countless occasions. Oh well, maybe next century.

Actually, if the truth be known, all the horror stories about overcrowding, accessibility, lack of sufficient runways and noise problems are nothing new when describing an airport that many of us native-born Torontonians will probably always refer to by its old name, Malton.

In an apparent contradiction of the reasons for today's problems, when the decision was made in the mid-1930s to build an airport for the fast-growing City of Toronto, one of the reasons cited by those opposed to building it out near the little farming village of Malton was that it would be too far away from the city and no one would use it.

And, even if people wanted to use the new airport, the lack of good roads to and from the remote site was going to pose another problem. Once the Malton site was approved and after some head scratching and buck passing, a few minor improvements were made to Brown's Line, Highway 27 and the Sixth Line (now Airport Road).

And while all this was going on, the Toronto Harbour Commissioners finally agreed to construct and operate both the Malton field, as well as a second facility at Hanlan's Point on Toronto Island on behalf of the city. It was always believed that the Island Airport would be Toronto's prime airport, with the one out at Malton for use only when fog en-

The Passenger Terminal and Administration Building at the new Malton Airport, c. 1940.

veloped the waterfront.

One year and three days after the agreement was signed, on August 29, 1938 (to be precise), Toronto's new Malton Airport was in business. The facility consisted of a pair of paved runways, a single grass strip and a combined passenger terminal and operations centre.

The first arrival that hot summer day was an American Airline's DC-3 that, as the newspapers of the day reported, "rocketted in" (at 180 mph) from Buffalo, New York.

An American Airlines DC-3 was the first plane to land at the new Malton Airport on August 29, 1938.

In 1939, Malton got a new administration building, the design of which can be seen to this day at the Island Airport. Both these buildings were constructed from the same set of blueprints.

But, while the airport got a new building, the bureaucrats and politicians were still arguing over who should pay to have the roads leading to and from the airport paved. Things were so bad that in the spring of 1944, Brown's Line was, again to quote the papers, "virtually impassible."

However, things were looking up (so to speak) with the opening of the new Malton Road later that fall.

A full 10 years passed before a new, larger terminal, described as the "Empire's finest," was ready for the thousands of travellers flying the still-wide open skies. I especially remember this particular terminal with its long observation deck on the roof that was accessible up a flight of stairs after depositing a dime in a turnstile. Like lots of other kids, I'd ride my bike out to the airport and spend hours watching the comings and goings of dozens of prop-driven North Super Constellations, Viscounts, Vanguards and, in early 1960, something new they called a jet.

To be historically accurate, Malton Airport officially entered the jet age on March 1, 1960, when a British Overseas Airways Corporation Comet 4 passenger jet made, what was described by a *Telegram* newspaper reporter as, a "silent debut."

That was 30 years ago but, even then, people living near the airport were concerned about noise problems. In fact, when word was received that a jet passenger plane was about to land at the airport, members of the Etobicoke planning board adjourned their regular meeting to witness the comet's landing firsthand, just in case they got calls.

And while the landing was whisper quiet, the same couldn't be said for the takeoff as nose meters registered levels three times those recorded for regular piston-engine passenger aircraft.

But, while queried about potential jet aircraft noise problems in the vicinity of the airport (and this in 1960 remember), Sir Gerrard Erlanger, the Chairman of BOAC stated, "People here will get used to it." Oh, ya?

[This column appeared in the February 25, 1990 edition of the *Sunday Sun*, and while we aren't going to get the 1996 Olympics we did get Trillium Terminal 3 which opened February 21, 1991.]

"Heart" of the City

February 2, 1992

Earliest known sketch of the House of Providence on Power Street, 1857.

Throughout our community's long and fascinating history (which as the Town of York, and after 1834, as the City of Toronto will span exactly two centuries in 1993), there has always been a conscientious effort to administer to the needs of the ailing and less fortunate in our society.

Today the Scott Mission on Spadina Avenue, City Mission on Yonge Street, Fred Victor Mission on Queen Street East, and Seaton House on Seaton Street are taxed to overflowing, as are the facilities of the Salvation Army and various other organizations that attempt to look after the less fortunate in our midst.

As difficult as times may be these days, concern for the well-being of the community's poor, destitute and troubled is not characteristic only of today's citizens.

In *Toronto, Past and Present* published in 1884, an entire chapter entitled "The Heart of the City" is devoted to the numerous benevolent and charitable organizations established in the energetic young city of 105,211 souls to help alleviate the suffering that has befallen many of Toronto's citizens, both young and old.

Included in the chapter are brief descriptions of the Infants' Home on St. Mary's Street, the Boy's Home at 281 George Street, the Girls' Home at 189 Gerrard Street and the Newsboys' Home at 42 Frederick Street. In addition, the House of Industry at the intersection of Elm and Elizabeth Streets, the Toronto Dispensary where a "free supply of medicine to the necessitous" was available and the Smallpox Hospital on the east bank of the Don River just north of Gerrard Street which boasted of "ample accommodation to cases of this dread disease," are also listed.

The chapter also describes, in somewhat greater detail, the Asylum for the Incurable (now the Queen Elizabeth Hospital) in "pretty, suburban" Parkdale, the Andrew Mercer Eye and Ear Infirmary at Sackville and Sumach streets, the nearby Burnside Lying-In Hospital and Toronto General Hospital (the latter on Gerrard near the zoo), the Lunatic Asylum out Queen Street West (today's more enlightened populace refer to it as the Queen Street Mental Health Centre) and the Hospital for Sick Children at the south-east corner of College and Elizabeth streets.

Incidentally, this latter building was quite small and was replaced by the larger, more modern Victorian Hospital for Sick Children, a structure which is presently undergoing extensive restoration work.

The author pays special attention to "one of the most noteworthy of Toronto edifices ... an extensive range of buildings in the form of an irregular quadrangle on Power Street (adjacent to St. Paul's Church) ... with a corridor worthy of Versailles or Windsor ... and, deservedly, a favorite with Toronto architects."

Sister Osmund serving the needy who flocked to House of Providence during the Great Depression, c. 1932.

The author continues, "The object of the House of Providence is the relieving of the aged, the orphans, the sick and the destitute of both sexes without distinction of creed. No charitable institution of our city more deserves the aid and sympathy of all who desire the good of their fellow creatures."

Established in 1857 by the Sisters of St. Joseph, four of whom had arrived in Toronto from Philadelphia just six years earlier to take over the running of a small Catholic orphanage on Jarvis Street, the House of Providence was a much needed addition to the list of charitable institutions in Toronto. In fact, just eight years after its opening, a staff of 10 Sisters were administering to the needs of more than 450 residents. This number was to eventually increase to 700.

About the turn of the century, the Sisters purchased a farm out Queen Street East in the Beach (now incorrectly referred to as the Beaches) where fresh produce was grown and shipped to the Power Street institution. In 1906, this farm was sold and a larger property was acquired in Scarborough Township at the north-west corner of a pair of dusty trails we know today as St. Clair and Warden Avenues.

The farm continued to supply provisions for the House of Providence until the early 1960s when construction of the the present Providence Villa and Hospital complex commenced. These new facilities were sorely needed for a couple of very good reasons. First, the ancient structures on Power Street were falling into disrepair and even if the money could be found to remedy the situation the Adelaide Street extension connecting with the new Don Valley Parkway were to be constructed right through the House of Providence property. Seemed like a good time to move.

On January 28, 1962, more than 600 residents of the old Power Street facilities were whisked to their new home in Scarborough thanks to Metro, Diamond, Oxford and Co-Op taxi companies, and Reliable, Hallowell, Klinck, Bell and City of Toronto ambulances (this was before ambulance service became the responsibility of Metro in 1975).

In 1990, to better describe the services provided by this long-time member of the Metro community, Providence Villa was renamed Providence Centre.

Trolly Buses Trundle into the History Books

January 19, 1992

There's been much discussion recently amongst the management and staff of the Toronto Transit Commission and from the public at large about the future of the trolley bus in our city. Should this unique type of transit vehicle be kept, scrapped or replaced by some other form of non-polluting conveyance, perhaps like the natural gas or propane powered buses? The controversy goes on.

One of Toronto's pioneer trolley buses on Merton Street. Its route was along Merton from Yonge to Mt. Pleasant, then north to Eglinton Avenue and then returnd. This service lasted from 1922 until 1925

Courtesy of TTC Photo Archives.

Perhaps a little history behind the evolution of the electrically-powered trolley bus, a kind of hybrid between the fixed rail electric streetcar and the diesel bus, might be appropriate. The first experimental trolley without tracks was a vehicle built by the electrical firm of Siemens and Halske in Germany in the early 1880s and over the ensuing years various companies attempted to perfect the idea of operating a free-wheeling omnibus using electricity obtained from overhead wires via poles and cables.

Several North American cities experimented with bus-like vehicles equipped with electric motors borrowed from streetcars with some success, but it wasn't until the late-1920s that buses with rubber tires and equipped with specially designed electric motors designed to run on power obtained from two overhead wires began to appear on the streets of Salt Lake City, Utah. The modern trolley bus was born.

Two overhead wires are necessary with rubber-tired trolley buses instead of a single wire as with streetcars, as the second or negative wire is used as a return for the 600 volt DC electric current. Steel wheels running on steel tracks form part of the return circuit for streetcars which also use 600 volts DC.

Our city saw its first electric trolley bus less than a year after the TTC was formed in 1921. These so-called "trackless trolleys" went into service on the Mt. Pleasant route that operated from Yonge and Merton streets to Mt. Pleasant Road and Eglinton Avenue. This new kind of transit vehicle didn't last very long, being replaced by the St. Clair streetcar when this route was extended up Mt. Pleasant Road from St. Clair Avenue East in 1925.

Several decades went by before a newly designed trolley bus, known as a Brill and built by Canadian Car and Foundry Company in its Fort William, Ontario factory, was introduced to Torontonians in 1947 on the Annette, Lansdowne, and Ossington routes. One year later similar buses began operating on the Weston route and in 1954 on the Nortown route.

For a short time following the opening of the Yonge subway in the spring of 1954, there was a Yonge trolley coach operating between the Eglinton subway station and the City Limits at Glen Echo Avenue.

Coincident with the subway opening, the Bay streetcar line was converted to diesel bus operation and then changed back to an electric route with the introduction of trolley buses a few years ago.

However, by 1967 it was evident that the aging trolley bus fleet of 152 vehicles would either have to be scrapped or, if the retention of trolley bus service was desired (sound familiar?) some sort of replacement vehicle would soon be necessary. The TTC then took the extraordinary step of rebuilding, at a cost of $5.5 million, their entire trolley bus fleet at the Western Flyer bus plant in Winnipeg, Manitoba. Interestingly, while the new buses certainly looked more modern, under the skin the electrical propulsion equipment remained essentially the same as that used on the buses built several decades earlier.

Now, the trolley bus question is with us again. I'd be willing to bet that the electric trolley bus, with all its benefits, will continue to be a component of the TTC fleet for the foreseeable future.

[Since this article appeared, the controversy over whether to keep or get rid of the city's trolley bus fleet is still very much unsettled. The most recent plan, put forward by a slim majority of TTC Commissioners, resulted in the leased Edmonton Transit trolley coaches to be put back into service on the Bay and Annette routes on September 6. 1992. The truth is, however, the future of Toronto's trolley buses is still very much undecided.]

Toronto Telegram *photo.*

A modern new trolley bus enters service on the Lansdowne route after appropriate ceremonies led by Toronto Mayor Robert Saunders, June 17, 1947.

Summertime Streetcars

July 26, 1987

Courtesy of TTC Photo Archives.

A bobby-helmeted constable keeps a close eye on things as young passengers board one of the TTC's "free bathing cars" on Bathurst Street. This summertime tradition lasted from the 1890s until August 9, 1950. That day just eight children showed up to ride the cars and the service was terminated.

Several weeks ago, I wrote about the Toronto of yesteryear when one sure way of cooling off was to take a trip on Lake Ontario on board one of the many lake steamers that sailed out of the Port of Toronto. Just thinking of recalling some of their names, *Cayuga, Chippewa, Turbinia, Macassa,* and so on, was enough to drop the temperature at least 10 degrees ... Fahrenheit!

But a lake cruise wasn't the only way to get away from the city heat. There were picnics in the countryside around Toronto and with some of the most popular picnic grounds being owned by the operators of the big,

green, electric radial cars.

These radial cars were in reality large, high-speed streetcars operating on tracks that radiated out from the city (thus the term radials) and were extremely popular modes of transportation in the early years of this century.

One of the best known of the so-called radial parks was Bond Lake Park, located on the shores of the lake of the same name just east of Yonge Street between Richmond Hill and Aurora. The park had become accessible by electric streetcars about 1907 when service was inaugurated between the Toronto's northerly boundary at the CPR crossing

Eager crowds alight from a fleet of big, green Metropolitan Division radial cars at Bond Lake Park north of the city, June 20, 1924.

on Yonge Street and the Town of Newmarket.

The privately owned Toronto and York Radial Railway Company, which operated what was known as the Metropolitan Division up and down Yonge Street, was taken over by the TTC in 1927. One result of this take-over was that now church and social groups could travel to Bond Lake Park by streetcar from anywhere inside the city without the need to change cars at the city limits.

TTC service to the park lasted only another two years, eventually succumbing to the ever-increasing popularity of the family automobile.

And if you didn't have the where-withall to venture out into the country-side to beat the heat, there were the "free bathing cars." Every summer commencing in the latter years of the last century, the streetcar company would put a number of vehicles in service that would roam the city streets gathering up children, each of whom would be clutching a swim suit and towel, and take them, free of charge, to the Island ferry docks at the foot of Bay Street or, after 1922, to the newly created Sunnyside Beach out near the Humber River for a day of fun in the cooling and unpolluted (or so it seemed) waters of Lake Ontario.

Then, at an appointed hour, the cars would return to retrieve the children returning them to where they had boarded the streetcar earlier in the day.

Interestingly, this Toronto tradition continued until changing attitudes and other forms of diversions (air conditioned theatres, park wading pools and the like) forced an end to the "free bathing cars" in the summer of 1950.

Trillium Flowers Again

June 17, 1990

Eighty years ago tomorrow, June 18th, 1910, at precisely 12 o'clock noon, a small crowd led by Toronto Ferry Company President, E.B. Osler, and his general manager, Lawrence ("Lol" to his friends) Solman, gathered in the old Polson Iron Works yard at the foot of Sherbourne Street and cheered as the latest member of their Toronto Island ferryboat fleet slid sideways into the Sherbourne Street slip.

Christened *Trillium* by the president's young niece, Phyllis Osler, the new paddle steamer was well and truly launched that sunny Saturday 80 years ago. Interestingly, the fact that the ferry company's modern new $175,000 vessel could be christened *Trillium* was only possible after officials of the company had pretty well exhausted the list of floral names that hadn't already been applied to the other vessels in their fleet.

Already running to the three Island ports were the new vessel's older sister *Blue Bell* (launched in 1906) and the much older *Mayflower* and *Primrose*, each of which had given faithful service since the summer of 1890. With the arrival of the fourth ferry, it was only natural that the tradition of using the names of flowers be extended.

As required by law, the Toronto Ferry Company made application to the Lloyd's Registry people in England to have their new craft insured, and the form contained the vessel's proposed name, *Arbutus*, of the trailing variety.

However, a reply was soon received from the London agency notifying the ferry company that the name *Arbutus* was being rejected since some ship, somewhere, was already using that designation.

Nothing daunted, the company next tried Hawthorne.

"Nope," came the reply. That too was being used.

"Well how 'bout Golden Rod?" company officials wondered.

"Sorry. Try again."

The company's fourth selection was the name of a flower that was indige-

Trillium *and the Toronto skyline, 1987.*

One of the earliest photos of Trillium *is this postcard view of the vessel at the Hanlan's Point dock. Note the merry-go-round, one of numerous rides at the Point, in the background, c. 1912.*

nous to the Province of Ontario, but was such an obvious choice that nobody had given it much thought, up until now, that is.

"Can we call our new paddle steamer *Trillium*?" was the request contained in the fourth envelope sent to the Lloyd's people.

"No problem" was the answer, or whatever the similar expression was back in those days.

So it was that when Toronto's new ferry boat went into service for the first time on Dominion Day, July 1, 1910, the city's new Island ferry boat had the name *Trillium* emblazoned on her paddle boxes. Another 27 years were to pass before official recognition of the trillium as Ontario's provincial flower was given.

We now jump forward in time almost a half of a century. In late 1955, after 45 years of faithful service to her Island ports of call, *Trillium* was taken out of service, towed to a secluded Island lagoon where she was left to rot.

More years went by. Finally, in 1973, the Council of Metropolitan Toronto voted to have the historic craft saved from total and absolute destruction. A few months later, under the guidance of marine engineer Gordon Champion, work began on *Trillium's* rebirth. In time for the 1976 season, *Trillium* returned to the Island ferry boat fleet where she joined the more modern *Sam McBride, William Iinglis, Thomas Rennie* and *Ongiara*.

Auto Heritage May Hit the Road

June 29, 1990

By the time you read this article, it may already be too late to save another piece of our city's vanishing heritage. But this time it's not a building. It is, however, something just as important. The Russell Knight has been described by experts as the first truly successful Canadian-designed and -built automobile. And the tragedy is that even as you read this piece, one of the few remaining Knights in existence may well be on its way out of the country and we'll have lost another piece of our heritage.

Thomas Alexander Russell (1877–1940).

The car was the brainchild of Thomas Alexander Russell who was born in Exeter, Ontario, on April 17, 1877. Russell received his early education in the local school system, after which he moved to Toronto, eventually obtaining an arts degree from the University of Toronto, followed by a fellowship in political science in 1899.

In 1903, after a short stint with the Canadian Manufacturers Association during which time he established the influential magazine, *Industrial Canada*, Russell was hired as manager of the thriving Canada Cycle and Motor Company (CCM).

CCM had been founded four years earlier as a way of bringing together a number of small semi-successful Canadian bicycle manufacturing companies thereby creating one extremely prosperous enterprise.

Shortly after the turn-of-the-century, the USA-based National Bicycle Company invaded Canada, and the sales battles that followed saw CCM repeatedly wave the Union Jack and use patriotic rhetoric as a means of enticing Canadians to buy Canadian-built bicycles. CCM was the eventual victor. As part of that victory, the Canadian company purchased the National Bicycle Company. Included in the package were the rights to the increasingly popular Locomobile steamer that was being assembled in Hamilton, Ontario.

After experimenting with the Locomobile and an electric car called the Ivanhoe, and offering a number of American-built vehicles such as the Ford, Autocar and Stevens-Duryea, Russell decided to build and distribute a totally Canadian creation. It was called the Russell Model A. Almost from the start, the various Russells that emerged from the company's Weston Road factory were a hit throughout the American-dominated automobile world.

In 1910, the revolutionary Knight sleeve-valve engine was installed in the Russell models for the first time. Over the next few years, car production at the

Tommy Russell (behind right-side [!] steering wheel, auto left of photo) leads a group of motorists in Model A Russell cars on a visit to Toronto City Hall, 1905.

West Toronto plant continued to expand as more and more Canadian motorists switched to the Russell. Unfortunately production costs continued to mount and a national recession began to cut into the firm's fiscal bottom line. Russell made changes and things began to look better with the introduction of the 1915 models.

With the outbreak of the first great war, a patriotic Tommy Russell ordered that many of the factory production lines be converted to the manufacture of much needed munitions for the allies. The Russell automobile became almost a sideline as the entire country mobilized in a desperate attempt to help "Mother England" defeat the dreaded "hun."

One vehicle that did come off the line before car production was cutback was a 1914, four-cylinder Russell Knight, serial number 969. Little is known of the car's early years. However, thanks to Jean-Pierre Lefebvre of Drummondville, Quebec, I've discovered that in the early 1950s the car appeared on a used car lot in Montreal. It was purchased by a builder and subse-

quently sold to a road contractor, both of whom were collectors. In 1966, the late Gaetan Trottier acquired the relic.

It's his estate that is now selling the car through Mr. Lefebvre. The asking price is $29,000. Early enquiries indicate that the Toronto-built piece of Canadian transportation history many soon be on its way to Belgium. Any guardian angels of Canadian history out there?

[Two days after this article appeared, I received a call from Tommy Russell's daughter who wanted to know who she might speak with to learn more about the car. I gave her what details I had and she indicated that she would definitely call me back to report any progress in keeping the car in Canada. As it turned out, not only did she buy the car, but she is also having it restored to 1914 condition. Thanks, Betty.]

A Cruise into History

February 17, 1991

Happy Heritage Week, folks! To be sure there's a lot of bad news around but, after all is said and done, we still live in the best place in the world. For the next seven days, from February 17 to 23, I encourage you to spend some time exploring and reading about those things that have made our country, province and city great. Why not call the Toronto Historical Board for some ideas on how to celebrate the week. Or stop by your local library and borrow something from their "local history" collection. We've got a mighty interesting place here.

Here's another suggestion on how we might spend part of Heritage Week. Let's leave the ice and snow behind for a few moments (at least in our mind's eye) and take an old-fashioned boat ride, just the way thousands of Torontonians would have taken back in the good old summertime of yesteryear.

Ever since the first pioneering steamboats arrived on the great lakes more than a century and a half ago, dozens and dozens of passenger vessels have called at the Port of Toronto (*Chippewa, Chicora Corona, Dalhousie City,*

Northumberland, Toronto and *Kingston*, to name just a few). But few will argue that the best loved lake boat of all was the sleek and graceful *Cayuga* that for nearly 50 years operated faithfully between Toronto and Niagara River ports.

When the 305-foot-long craft slid into the water adjacent to the Bertram Engine and Machine Works at the foot of the old Bathurst Street one cold March day in 1906, the $200,000 craft was still without a name. A contest to select a designation for the new vessel was held by the ship's owners, the Niagara Navigation Company. The only stipulation was that the new name had to fit in with the existing fleet roster consisting of the steamers *Chicora, Cibola* and *Chippewa.* Thus the new craft's name had to start with the letter "C" and end with an "A."

In all, 233 entries were submitted with *Cayuga* the winner because, as the judges pointed out, it was euphonious, met the contest rule about first and last letters and was an Indian name, as were the others.

After many months of fitting out at

Scheduled for the scrap yard, Cayuga *got a new lease on life thanks to dedicated shareholders of the new* Cayuga *Steamship Company. The historic craft is outbound through the East Gap in this June 3, 1954 photo.*

the Bertram dock, the new vessel departed on her maiden voyage to the Niagara River ports of Niagara-on-the-Lake and Queenston on June 8, 1907. A reporter assigned to cover the event was impressed with both the ship's interior fittings and the fact that *"Cayuga* was exceedingly comfortable to sail in." That first trip was the start of what would become 44 long seasons of faithful cross-lake service.

At the conclusion of the 1951 operating season Canada Steamship Lines (CSL), who many years earlier had taken over the assets and franchises of the Northern Navigation Company and three other steamship operations, decided that passenger service was no longer "cost effective." In future, CSL would only be in the freight business. Interestingly, this decision was made just months after the company had spent many thousands of dollars replacing *Cayuga's* old, inefficient Scotch marine boilers with a modern new oil-fired power plant. And, in response to new regulations brought about by the "Noronic" disaster in September of 1949, *Cayuga* also received the best fire detection and suppression equipment then available. After all that, the faithful craft was now to be scrapped.

But, not so fast. According to several enterprising Toronto businessmen, led by future Governor General Roland Michener and the late marine historian Alan Howard, there was still a flicker of life in the proud vessel.

It wasn't easy to raise the $100,000 purchase price placed on the vessel by CSL. Nevertheless, 700 shareholders invested an average of $185 each with the result that not only did the enthusiasts meet the purchase price, $30,000 was left over to buy fuel and other necessities to get *Cayuga* back into service.

It was like a miracle come true. On June 5, 1954, the proud vessel was back on her Niagara run. But times had changed.

Cayuga could no longer compete with the automobile and soon she was

The Canadian Shipbuilding Company ran this advertisement in the trade magazines soon after the company launched Cayuga at its Toronto shipyard at the foot of Bathurst Street in 1906.

in financial trouble again. Unfortunately, *Cayuga* was unable to obtain a liquor license which many felt would have greatly enhanced her chances of survival. The company lost thousands over the next few seasons and in the fall of 1957, *Cayuga* was once again destined for oblivion.

Sure, lots of ideas to keep her afloat were tossed around, but nothing ever gelled. In the fall of 1961, the once-distinguished craft was reduced to bits of scrap.

Today, one can revisit *Cayuga's* wheelhouse which was preserved intact and presented to the Marine Museum of Upper Canada by Greenspoon Brothers, the wrecking company that had the unhappy chore of dismantling a treasured piece of Toronto's past.

Summers Past in Old T.O.

July 5, 1987

Nattily attired crowds linger in the shade of the Jackson's Point waiting room for the departure of the Toronto-bound Toronto and York radial car, c. 1905.

Well, here we are in the dog days of summer. Sometimes the heat and humidity makes us wish for the ice and snow of the Canadian winter ... but that soon passes. Actually, we have it lucky in this day and age for when it gets too hot we simply turn on the air conditioner in the house or car, or make for the nearest shopping centre or movie house where things are usually much more comfortable.

In the Toronto of not too long ago, the heat of summer usually meant it was time to get out the picnic basket and start planning either a trip over to the coolness of the Island or to one of the various waterfront parks strung out along the lake's edge or, if you were really lucky, to an all-day outing to one of the many lush green pleasure parks that surrounded the steamy city. In all cases, the trip started out with a ride on one of the Toronto Transportation Commission's big red and cream-coloured streetcars. At some point in your journey to Ward's, Centre or Hanlan's, a ride down Bay Street on one of the Commission's new Witt cars, identified with the words "BAY-DOCKS"

high up on the front of the shiny red and cream coloured vehicle, was a necessity.

Crawling through the newly opened railway underpass south of Front Street, the outside temperature was at least 10 degrees cooler (that's Fahrenheit, Centigrade was only for scientists). The car soon broke out into the blazing sun, picked up speed, then slowed for the Fleet Street crossing (Fleet is now called Lake Shore Blvd.), on passed the big Simpson billboard on the corner, then Bayside ball-park on the left.

In the distance we could now see thick black smoke pouring from the stacks of the lake boats like the *Cayuga*, *Northumberland* and *Dalhousie City* moored at the Bay and Yonge Street wharves. (Too bad the gigantic *Noronic* left last evening for the Thousand Islands. She's a beauty).

The big car slowed to a crawl as it curved west along Queen's Quay gliding to a stop opposite the ferry docks, east of York Street where the streetcar would turn around to head back up into the city heat.

"Last one off the streetcars a ... "

"Where do you think you're going? Take my hand and watch the traffic," cried mom.

All of a sudden, one of the ferryboats lets go with a blast from its whistle and everyone jumps. But you pretend like nothing happened though your heart's racing so fast it's sure to burst any second.

"Last one on the ferry is a ... "

"And where do you think you're going? Calm down," bellowed dad.

If the Island wasn't on your family's itinerary this outing, perhaps one of the city's many lovely parks was.

How 'bout the eastern Beaches south of Queen Street East, or the lush green of High Park out Bloor West where the streetcars would let you off at the main entrance at the foot of the beautiful tree-lined High Park Boulevard. If you were lucky, you might see (and hear!) one of the Peter Witt cars, complete with a trailer, turning around in the loop near the park entrance.

Interestingly, when Mr. Howard offered us his park way back in the 1870s, several city council members refused his offer cause they thought that the proposed High Park (that's what Mr. Howard wanted it called) was too far out in country for anyone to visit. Ah, the wisdom of some politicians.

A ride on a different streetcar would take you out over the old steel bridge at the foot of Roncesvalles Avenue and along the Lakeshore Road to Sunnyside Beach, just this side of the Humber. Remember all those fabulous rides and the bathing tank and the red hots and the Vernor's ginger ale and the smell of chips and vinegar and, and, and ...

Probably the neatest day trip one could take way back then was an outing on the big green electric radial cars that took you from the end of some of the city lines into the countryside around Toronto. To places like Birch Cliff and Scarborough Heights east of the city, or the beaches at Port Credit and Long Branch to the west. But for a real excursion, you just couldn't beat a run out to Eldorado Park near Georgetown. Or, come to think of it, perhaps the most exciting trip in the world was the ride up Yonge Street from the City Limits. Picking up speed after departing the old station on the east side of the street, the car would soon be rocketing down the Hogg's Hollow hill, past the Jolly Miller Tavern, then over the steel girder bridge across a small branch of the Don and up the long hill, along the brow of which the far too utilitarian Highway 401 would slice years later.

Swinging from the side to the centre of the dirt road called Yonge, the radial (so called because the various lines radiated out from Toronto) rumbled, with frequent stops, through outposts like Willowdale, Newton's Brook, Steele's Corners, Thornhill and Richmond Hill, eventually stopping to disembark thousands each summer at the entrance to the picnic grounds at Bond Lake Park.

But the ride wasn't over yet.

After traversing a long laneway in behind Aurora's main drag, the radial car took off through fields to the north of town, rattling across concession roads, its piercing whistle screaming warnings to people and animals to keep off its track. Eventually the car emerged from the long

The immensely popular Lake Ontario, steamer Dalhousie City *at the Port Dalhousie dock that was located adjacent to a small picnic ground and amusement park, c. 1900. Though Port Dalhousie is now part of St. Catharines, the old Lakeside Park merry-go-round still offers rides for a nickel.*

waving grass at a spot near the south shore of Lake Simcoe. It then climbed up onto a private right of way (now called Metropolitan Road) to continue its Orient Express-like journey.

For years the big radial cars of the Metropolitan Division of the Toronto and York Radial Railway company carried vacationers, their bags of groceries, a summer's worth of reading material, a vast collection of swim suits and even the family pet to summer communities, stretched out in the sun along the south shore of Lake Simcoe.

When the car finally reached the end of the line in Sutton, the motorman would pull down one trolley pole, walk around to the other end of the car and put up the other, then flip the wicker seats over and the car would head off on its return journey to the big city buried in the steamy haze far to the south.

Red's Back in Town

March 12, 1989

On March 17 and 19, one of my favourite comedians will be here in town at Roy Thompson Hall. In fact when I read that Red Skelton would be coming to Toronto, I was immediately taken back in my mind's eye to June 2, 1953, when the Filey family, having become the third family on our street in North Toronto to acquire "one of them new" television sets (in our case a 17" black and white RCA Victor), played host to a bevy of neighbours who had dropped in to watch the Queen's coronation on our new set.

A young Red Skelton.

CBS in 1953 (seen locally on Buffalo's Channel 4, WBEN) fared much better. Within four years he had a number one show.

Obviously, when you're a kid the course of history doesn't really play a big role in your life. But Red's arrival in Toronto via invisible television signals and those obtrusive television antennas was by no means his first visit to our city. In fact, it could honestly be said that Red underwent his show business "baptism of fire" both here in our city and in Montreal, the other end of the CPR's passenger line which was Red's way of commuting between the two communities more than a half-century ago. (You know it was a long time ago because CPR was still in the people-moving business.) And why was Red such a frequent commuter between these two Canadian cities, you ask? Read on.

In those days there were no satellites to relay the event instantaneously around the world, with the result that the ceremony had been taped and the cans of film flown across the ocean to the CBC'sMontreal studios in a Canberra jet bomber.

What does all this have to do with Red Skelton? Well, as a kid, one of the few programs on television that would suspend a street hockey game out in front of the house or an "American" baseball game using our concrete steps as the batter (remember?) was the Red Skelton Show.

Red's first TV series started on NBC on September 30, 1951, and while it was less than a roaring success, his efforts for

Born Richard Red Skelton (no quotation marks around Red, please) in Vincennes, Indiana, July 18, 1913 (or was it 1906 as some in the know have suggested), Red left school while still in grade three. He joined a medicine show where he performed as a midget singer, eventually winding up in a succession of minstrel shows and one-night vaudeville stands, then as a comedian on-board the *Orange Blossom*, one of those legendary Mississippi showboats. During the Great Depression Red was able to earn a few dollars as a combination stand-up comic/master of ceremonies in a seemingly endless series of dance marathons in Kansas City.

It was during one of these competitions that he met his wife-to-be (the first of three), Edna Marie Stillwell. She was the winner in a dance marathon that had lasted 1,872 consecutive hours. The last thing she wanted following her win was to argue with the MC about whether she would date him or not. It was easier, and quicker to say yes. Within a few short weeks the couple was married, even though Red was so broke he had to borrow the $2 for the marriage license.

After what seemed an eternity of danceathons, in 1936 the young comedian eventually found himself on the stage of the old Loew's Princess Theatre in Montreal. Here for the very first time he enjoyed top billing, not to mention a $300 a week paycheck. On the same vaudeville circuit as the Montreal theatre was Toronto's Shea's Hippodrome on Bay Street, just across the street from City Hall.

For a full year, he alternated between the two vaudeville houses, depending on his fake drunk routine to get him on the train and into a supposedly much-needed washroom. The conductor, who was trying very hard to stay out of the boozer's way, simply waved him on. Red claimed that one ticket lasted more than a year.

It was while performing in Toronto that the comic took some time off and visited the CNE. While strolling the grounds, Red observed a spoiled youngster giving his mother a tough time. Then and there, his now-famous Junior, "the mean, widdle kid" was born.

Skelton returned to the EX many years later, though this time as headliner of the CNE Grandstand Show. Actually, his first appearance was scheduled for the 1960 CNE for which he would receive $55,000 for seven performances, the highest figure ever paid a CNE headliner. Once the figure got out though, Red canceled his Toronto appearance saying it wasn't a good idea to perform for people who know how much you're getting paid.

Following his successful Montreal/Toronto stint, Skelton was booked into the Capital theatre in Washington, DC. Interestingly, appended to his name in the ads and on the playbill were the words "the Canadian Comic." Red was on his way.

At Shea's Hippodrome on Bay Street opposite "Old City Hall" during the week of September 14, 1936, John Boles, the world's greatest singing star" warbled "in person" while a young comedian by the name of Red Skelton, "back by popular demand," acted as master of ceremonies.

When a Huge Snow Storm Paralyzed T.O.

January 20, 1991

As I sat at my desk a week or so ago getting ready to write this column, the radio announcer was telling everyone that the storm warnings were out. Toronto was about to be inflicted with the worst storm of the season. Up to 15 cm of snow along with high winds and a period of sleet were on the way.

Wow! Fifteen centimeters with winds and sleet. All that and Brian too! Well, at least the storm will give me the subject material for another "The Way We Were" column.

The weather report on page five of the early edition of the Monday, December 11, 1944 *Evening Telegram* newspaper reported that there was a good chance that Toronto would get snow that day and again on Tuesday along with a period of sleet accompanied by fresh to strong winds. It was a pretty straightforward forecast, nothing really out of the ordinary for that time of the year.

Another article on the same page in-

Heavy snowfalls weren't unusual in an early Toronto. This Harbord streetcar appears buried in the "white stuff" at Adelaide and Bay streets on March 7, 1931.

Courtesy of TTC.

dicated that it looked like "junior would get that long-awaited blanket of snow as a pre-christmas gift."

"We expect a few inches of snow to fall this time," was the official statement from the weather office. A few inches?? That statement turned out to be the weather prognostication understatement of the century.

Snow began to fall, lightly at first, early in the evening of the 11th. As the hours passed, the snow continued to fall with the weather department eventually revising its forecast and now predicting that between 25 and 30 cm (described as 10 to 12 inches in those pre-metrification days) would fall before the storm ended near daybreak.

Sensing potential trouble if the streetcar lines weren't kept clear throughout the night (the storm hit a decade before Toronto's first "storm-proof" subway opened), the TTC sent out its sweepers and plows. This equipment, though well-maintained, was old with some pieces dating back to the 1890s. It wasn't long before several of the sweepers became disabled and were taken out of service just when they were needed the most. And still the snow kept falling. Now the order went out from TTC control to rouse sleeping operators and get as many streetcars out on the various routes as possible in an attempt to keep the tracks clear and the lines open. Once the tracks were buried, it wouldn't be long before the line would become impassible.

As the morning approached, out went the buses to get ready to pick up the morning commuters. It was still snowing heavily and many of the vehicles got bogged down long before they even made the start of their respective

During the record snowfall of December 11–12, 1944, an old-style wooden streetcar split a snow-packed switch at Queen and Mutual streets and fell on its side. Officials estimated that the car was carrying 140 passengers when the derailment occurred, one of whom was killed in the accident.

routes. With the unprecedented snowfall now blocking virtually every thoroughfare, the TTC was almost at a standstill. Records indicate that the worst-hit streetcar lines were those servicing the city's outskirts. The Long Branch car from 18th Avenue to the loop opposite the Small Arms war plant at the end of the line was out of service from 7:40 in the morning of the 12th until 4:45 the next morning.

To the north, the wide open fields between Finch's Corners (today's Finch and Yonge) and Richmond Hill allowed the snow to drift creating impassible snow banks that knocked the North Yonge car out of service from 10 o'clock Tuesday morning until 10 the following night.

To the east, the Kingston Road car ceased operating east of the Bingham loop all the way to Birchmount Road from 11 o'clock Tuesday morning until well past noon the following day.

In the city proper every route, save the Yonge and St. Clair lines, suffered disruptions of varying durations. To help crews clear the lines, private automobiles were prohibited from operating on streets where there were streetcar tracks, which back then meant almost every major thoroughfare was automobile-free.

Of course, the TTC wasn't the only service in trouble. Bread and milk wagons couldn't get through the drifts and it became necessary to have supplies dropped off at the various fire halls. Citizens were advised by radio to trudge through the snow to pick up their supplies and to please bring back their empty milk bottles, as supplies were running short.

Torontonians were also requested to form groups of "block snow fighter commandos" and clear neighborhood sidewalks and remove snow from around local hydrants so that in case of fire, firemen wouldn't waste valuable time looking for hose connections.

Coal companies also asked customers to clear a path from the street to the coal chute so that the delivery man, with the ponderous sack of coal over his shoulder, would have a slightly easier time of it. Those customers on sidestreets where only one lane was plowed were asked to clear a spot in front of the house where the truck could layover while the driver made his delivery. For days following the unprecedented storm railway schedules were disrupted, funerals had to be postponed (16 Torontonians died as a result of the storm), fruits and vegetables became scarce at the corner stores, school classes were shortened or curtailed altogether and mail service was erratic. Malton airport was closed for more than 24 hours.

When the snow finally stopped falling on December 12, 1944, the worst snowstorm in the city's history had dumped more than 20 inches (50 cm) of the white stuff on an unsuspecting city.

Final Curtain for Famous Theatre

January 1, 1989

Downtown parking was only 20 cents an hour in the lot beside Shea's Hippodrome, a Bay Street theatre popular with Toronto movie-goers for nearly 43 years. The site is now occupied by part of Nathan Phillips Square.

On Tuesday, December 27, 1956, one of Toronto's most famous movie houses closed its doors for all time. In a letter addressed to the many thousands of its patrons published in the Toronto dailies that day, Ken Bishop, long-time manager of Shea's Hippodrome on Bay Street, just north of the Queen Street intersection, announced that the old building "would soon be torn down to make way for Toronto's new Civic Centre."

In fact, while the doors did close permanently on the 27th, actual demolition didn't occur for some time. The Civic Centre referred to in Bishop's statement became the site of Toronto's New City Hall, that was officially opened September 13, 1965, by Governor-General Georges Vanier, and the adjacent Nathan Phillips Square.

Shea's Hippodrome, built by the Shea Brothers, Mike and Jerry of Buffalo, New York, opened on April 27, 1914. It was located on the west side of what was then called Terauley Street, a name that commemorated two pioneering Toronto families, the Hayters and the Macauleys. The street was renamed Bay when the jog at the Bay/Terauley/Queen intersection was removed in an effort to improve the north-south flow of traffic.

In *the Evening Telegram* of April 28, 1914, the day after Toronto's newest theatre opened its doors to an eager public, it was reported that the Hippodrome can "well nigh be called a perfectly built theatre. It is larger than any other amusement house in Toronto seating 2,700 persons and is fitted with the most up-to-date novelties in the world. No other theatre in Canada can compare with it in size and construction. The decor is in the Renaissance style with Empire features and a handsome set of allegorical paintings by George Brant of Chicago decorate the sounding board before the proscenium arch. The ceiling is studded with electric light."

One of the novelties described by the reporter was an orchestrion, a large mechanical instrument that took the place of a full orchestra. Built in Germany, the Shea's orchestrion was the largest in the world and was operated by punch tapes that enabled the machine to emulate orchestras with as few as 30 instruments to one of 150. Sounds like what today we call an electronic synthesizer. The orchestrion was eventually replaced by a massive theatre organ that can still be heard at Casa Loma.

Another unique feature of the Hippodrome was a candy dispenser built into each theatre seat so "munchers" could pop in a dime to satisfy his or her sweet tooth without ever having to visit the candy bar in the lobby.

Shea's Hippodrome was originally built as a vaudeville house and until 1927 was part of the Family Time circuit. In that year, the theatre joined the larger Super Time circuit and featured such well-known performers as Kip and Kippy, Olsen and Johnson, LeRoy and Harvey and the Karnos Comedy Company. Others who appeared on the huge Hippodrome stage in supporting roles in those early days included Jack Benny, Bob Hope, Fred Allen, George Burns and Gracie Allen, Edgar Bergen and Charlie McCarthy.

In 1929, the theatre reluctantly added sound equipment enabling it to present the "new fangled talkies," though many were sure that sound with movies would never last. The first talking picture presentation was entitled *The Studio Murder Mystery* starring Neil Hamilton, Warner (Charlie Chan) Oland and Florence Eldridge.

Shea's Hippodrome remained essentially a vaudeville house until the early '40s, long after almost all the other Canadian vaudeville houses had either reverted to sound films or simply closed their doors. The Hippodrome continued to import talent from the States, paying the wages out of the receipts from the first-run movies that accompanied the live acts. Eventually, the Monday afternoon performances became a "must see" event for critics, press agents, hookey-playing students and just plain

Ad for the Elvis Presley movie Love me Tender *that played at Shea's late in 1956.*

vaudeville buffs from all over Ontario and upper New York State.

Ironically, though vaudeville was the heart of Shea's, it was a motion picture that was the biggest "hit" ever seen at the old theatre. *Buck Privates* with Abbott and Costello ran for 14 weeks with every performance sold out. A few years later, Elvis Presley movies had the teenagers literally knocking down the doors. But even when the movies had replaced vaudeville altogether, Shea's still presented frequent public appearances on its well-trodden stage by movie stars such as Jack Webb and Kim Novac.

Celebrating a Christmas Tradition

December 20, 1987

At this time of the year, it's interesting to reflect on the numerous traditions associated with the holiday season here in Toronto, traditions like giving a few dollars to the Salvation Army people out in front of Simpson's, buying a turkey at the old South St. Lawrence Market, open-air ice skating at a neighborhood park, giving the paper boy his annual "special" tip, a drive out into the countryside to get a freshly cut, real Christmas tree and the fun of trimming it (after having spent an hour trying to get the darn thing to stand straight in the tree stand).

The fourth St. James' Church and first Cathedral, 1839.

One of the oldest traditions in our city is the celebration of special Christmas Eve and Christmas Day services at many of our Metropolitan Toronto churches. And the church that has celebrated more Christmases than any other is the beautiful Cathedral Church of St. James at King and Church (the latter street so named because it led to this house of worship) streets in the heart of our city. Actually, the building that today towers over the intersection is a relative newcomer, having been erected in the middle of the last century. In fact, it is the fifth house of worship to stand on the corner. But let's go back to the start of the St. James' story.

In the beginning, religious activities in the predominantly Anglican Town of York were probably confined to services held for the men of the Queen's Rangers at Fort York. Then, as the town became better established, a newcomer, the Reverend Thomas Raddish, conducted religious meetings in the Government House near the Don River at the east end of town. Mr. Raddish left after only a couple of years on the job and in 1800, the Reverend George Okill Stuart arrived to take over, with part of his annual salary of £150 coming from the Society for the Propagation of the Gospel in Foreign Parts.

In 1803, some of the town's most prominent citizens sought to erect the community's first church. As most of York's population of 400 souls were originally from England, it was only natural that this new church would represent the Church of England or Anglican faith. While it was hoped that the new structure would be of brick, there were insufficient funds available to the townsfolk, and as a result, a small, unimpressive-looking wooden building was built on a 6-acre site bounded by King, Church, Newgate (now Adelaide) and New (now Jarvis) streets, a site that had been set aside for church purposes by the government of Upper Canada years before.

Interestingly, pews in that first church which opened in March 1807, were rented to citizens for £35 annually, and it wasn't until two years after church services were inaugurated that a special gallery was erected where poorer citizens, visitors and soldiers could sit while attending services.

Strangely, it appears that neither this church nor the slightly larger wooden one that followed it on the same site in 1818 had names. They were simply know as "the church at York." It wasn't until 1828 that Bishop Stewart of Quebec bestowed the title "Church of St. James," that our community's first house of worship had a name at all.

Four years later plans were drawn up for another new church, this time to be built of stone. The third church opened late in 1832 and was totally destroyed by fire just seven years later. Quickly a new and still larger structure was on the drawing board, this one opening on December 22, 1839, with the Reverend John Strachan, recently consecrated Bishop of Toronto, in the pulpit. During his tenure in our city, Strachan was one of the community's most influential citizens.

A short 10 years after the third

The fifth (and present) St. James' and second Cathedral, 1853, spire completed in 1874.

church opened a fierce conflagration that had erupted near the corner of King and George streets late in the afternoon of April 7, 1849, reduced this, the first St. James' Cathedral, along with numerous other structures in the small city, to ashes.

Nineteen months later, the cornerstone of Toronto architect William Cumberland's magnificent new building was laid by Bishop Strachan and on June 19, 1853, the present Cathedral Church of St. James, less its imposing bell and clock tower, was consecrated.

In 1865, a 35-foot tower was added inside of which were placed nine bells weighing a total of 17,555 pounds. (A 10th bell was added in 1928.) The original peel of bells was played for the first time on Christmas Eve, 1865. A decade later, Torontonians of all denominations helped fund a new clock for the church. Whenever the clock breaks down, the public still pays for its repair.

The present spire, which reaches 324 feet into the heavens, was finally completed in 1874 and in the following year, the 1873 Vienna Exhibition prize clock, purchased for and presented to the Cathedral by the citizens of Toronto, irrespective of faith, was installed and illuminated on Christmas Eve, 1875. To this day, repairs to the clock are performed at the taxpayers' expense. Money, I'm sure most taxpayers will agree, is well spent.

Santa Claus Comes to Town, Thankfully

November 15, 1987

One of the first Santa Claus parades wasn't much of a parade at all. It consisted of just the jolly old elf on horseback and a few helpers.

Today's the day that good old Santa Claus comes to town just like he has for the past 81 years. Well, not exactly just like he has for 81 years since back in 1905, the year of the first Santa Claus parade (the term "parade" is a bit of a misnomer as Santa was the only real participant), the bearded gentleman arrived in Toronto by train at the old Union Station.

In those far-off days the station was located on the south side of Front Street between York and Simcoe streets, well west of today's Union Station.

Santa then transferred to an open automobile and made his way through the crowds to the department store operated by the parade's sponsor, the T. Eaton Company on Queen Street.

The following year, Santa arrived in a tally-ho coach drawn by four huge white horses. In 1913, Santa drove down Yonge street in a real sleigh drawn by, what else, eight tiny reindeer who weren't too wild about the whole thing and nipped at any one who came within range. So much for using real reindeer.

It was also in 1913 that the parade idea first evolved as groups of children began to follow jolly St. Nick along his route stopping periodically to sing Christmas songs to the delight of the crowds gathered on the sidewalk.

By 1917, there were seven hand-drawn floats constructed out of wallboard, plywood and even papier mâché in the parade and as the years went by, more and more floats were added and soon some were even motorized.

Ever since that first parade in 1905, there has never been a year go by when there hasn't been a Santa Claus parade. Through two world wars, a seemingly endless depression, a devastating

In later years thousands watched and cheered as the "jolly old elf," on board his very own float, arrived at Eaton's main store at 'Yonge and Queen. Note Eaton's Annex in the background right and "old" City Hall in background left.

influenza outbreak in 1918 and various other low points in our history, the one constant has been the annual Toronto Santa Claus Parade. It has never missed a year.

But we came very close to losing it back in 1982 when, for economic reasons, the Eaton people were forced to drop sponsorship of the parade. However, before the idea of the Santa Claus Parade became just a memory, a group of influential Metro movers and shakers, led by then Metro Chairman and now Toronto Sun President, Paul Godfrey, came to the rescue and 20 corporate sponsors (including Canada's Wonderland where I worked as Public Relations Manager at the time) were secured, each of whom came up with $25,000 to sponsor a float in the newly restructured Santa Claus Parade.

Every year since, the Santa Claus Parade has returned to the streets of our city to continue the tradition of entertaining the child in all of us.

Some Super Highway History

June 4, 1989

The first cloverleaf interchange in Canada was located at the junction of the new Queen Elizabeth Way and Highway #10, just north of Port Credit. This June 10, 1939 view looks east toward Toronto.

Courtesy of Ontario Archives.

Today, June 4, 1989, marks the start of National Transportation Week, a time when the industry takes a moment to salute itself, and a week when we, the public, should also give a vote of thanks to the men and women that move people and goods from place to place across this great country.

It's interesting to note that right in the middle of this special week, which is being held for the 20th consecutive year and runs through to June 10, one of the major lifelines that keeps transportation alive and well in the Metro area will also be celebrating a special event.

Our very own Queen Elizabeth Highway will be 50 years old this coming Wednesday, June 7. To be historically accurate, it's only the name that will celebrate its Golden Anniversary, since the highway itself didn't officially open for another 15 months. The concept of today's "Queen E" was actually advanced by the old Toronto–Hamilton Highway Commission as far back as 1916. Their idea for a new highway, which didn't have a name at that time, was seen as a way of improving the deteriorating traffic conditions on the two existing roads that connected those two Ontario cities.

Running parallel to Lake Ontario, old Highway 2, the first paved highway in the country, was reaching capacity while to the north Lieutenant-Governor Simcoe's pioneer highway from York to Dundas, Upper Canada, now numbered Highway 5, was also becoming severely overcrowded.

The proposed new highway was to be located somewhere between the other two, and as the idea was being developed on paper it became known as the "Middle Road." Actual construction, however, didn't start on the thoroughfare until the Great Depression struck in the fall of 1929 and the road was initiated as part of the province's labour-relief program.

In the initial stages, the road was to simply be a four-lane highway connecting Hamilton and Toronto and would follow the alignment of two existing rural roads that would be widened from 66 to 86 feet. With the change of governments in 1934, the whole "Middle Road" concept changed too. Premier-elect Mitch Hepburn's new minister of highways, Thomas Baker McQuesten, saw a chance to construct a highway that would be unique in many ways. In fact, the thoroughfare that emerged from the drawing boards would become North America's first "superhighway."

One of the first changes McQuesten made to the original drawings was to relocate the thoroughfare's western terminus from Hamilton by swinging the highway around the west end of Lake Ontario and extending it through to Fort Erie, a small Canadian city just across the Niagara River from Buffalo, New York, and the lucrative American tourist market.

In addition to changing the routing of what was to be known as the New Niagara Highway, McQuesten also adopted some revolutionary engineering modifications that would improve "driving efficiency" and "automobile transportation safety." In doing so the "limited access, divided highway" was born in Canada and while a few parkways south of the border already had similar features, never before had they been in use over such a distance.

To accomplish the limited access aspect, Canada's first cloverleaf was constructed at the intersection of the New Niagara Highway and Highway 10, just west of Toronto, at a cost of $81,172. A partial cloverleaf was constructed at Burlington, while the Stoney Creek interchange remained a dangerous traffic "round-about" until it, too, was rebuilt as a cloverleaf.

Where possible, the width of the highway right of way was increased to 132 feet allowing for a pair of two-lane pavements divided down the middle by a central median bracketed by gravel shoulders and drainage ditches.

In addition, the entire route would be illuminated at night. Another first.

Almost as important as the engineering components were other factors such as landscaping and the design of bridges, overpasses and even the lighting standards. Not only were traffic engineers assigned to work on McQuesten's project, but so, too, were architects, landscape experts, artists and planners.

The expropriation of land for the new thoroughfare was not without its own serious problems, especially when

The same intersection after a major highway widening project in the early 1970s.

Courtesy of Ontario Archives.

property through the fruit belt was required. In fact, in the *Telegram* newspaper of July 7, 1937, a story was filed from Grimsby under the headline "Road Through Fruit Belt Compared to Invasion of Belgium by Kaiser." Whew, strong stuff.

Almost two full years after highway construction began, King George VI and Queen Elizabeth embarked on their first visit to Canada and, as part of the Royal couple's tour of the Niagara area, it was decided to officially name the route the Queen Elizabeth Way. In a brief ceremony on June 7, 1939, the Royal car drove through an electric beam causing twin Union Jacks to part as the couple drove across the Henley Bridge over Twelve Mile Creek at St. Catharines.

Work to complete the four-lane highway all the way to Niagara Falls was completed in the summer of 1940, and on August 23 of that same year McQuesten officially opened the Toronto to Niagara Falls section of the new Queen Elizabeth Highway.

And now for a bit of QEW trivia: When the Americans began pouring across the border to travel the new route, they thought the initials "E.R." on the light standards strung along the highway were those of their own Eleanor Roosevelt. They, of course, stood for Elizabeth Regina, but we didn't tell them.

Hotel Fit for the Royals

June 11, 1989

One of the city's most easily recognized landmarks is also one of its largest. When it was officially opened exactly 60 years today, June 11, 1929, the immense new Royal York Hotel was proudly portrayed as the largest hotel in the British Empire. Built at a cost of $16 million by the Canadian Pacific Railway, the Royal York was described as having "1,100 guest rooms as well as a floor completely dedicated to convention and banquet halls, talking picture equipment and a thousand and one comforts for its patrons." Work on the huge structure had started many months before with the demolition of a number of old buildings on the site starting as early as the fall of 1927. This was followed by weeks of excavating for the massive foundations.

Records indicate that the first owners of the present Royal York Hotel site, William Dummer Powell and his family, were granted what was then simply described as "a wooded site" in 1798. Because the land was so far outside the

Town of York, 14 years went by before the Chief Justice finally built any kind of structure on his property, and then it was a simple log building which was later covered in clapboard. In more precise terms, the Powell residence was located on the east side of York Street, well secluded from Front.

In 1843 Captain Thomas Dick, a well-known local mariner, built a row of four brick houses along the north side of Front Street, a little to the east of Powell's place. Called, rather grandiosely, "Ontario Terrace," these buildings were leased in 1846 by the newly organized Knox College and used for school purposes until the college moved uptown in 1853.

The buildings were then remodeled and the first of a succession of hotels, the first being called Sword's, opened. It changed names in 1860 becoming the Revere House. Within a couple of years, Captain Dick was back on the scene as the new hotel manager, and once again the converted school buildings got

A Sherbourne horse-car glides past the Queen's Hotel on the north side of an unpaved, tree-lined Front Street, c. 1880.

The Royal York Hotel had only been open a short time when this aerial view was taken. An addition to the east end of the building opened in 1959.

a name change, this time to the Queen's Hotel. The Queen's soon became one of the province's best known hostelries and introduced many new amenities to its customers.

For instance, it was the first hotel in the entire country to use a hot-air furnace in place of conventional fireplaces and wood stoves placed in each room. The Queen's was also the first to use a passenger elevator and was the first business establishment in the entire city to install a telephone. Of particular interest is the fact that The Queen's also pioneered hot and cold running water in each room as well as bathtubs. It's said that guests from the more remote townships would regret that part of their visit to the hotel wouldn't take in a Saturday night so they could avail themselves of a bath.

For a number of years during the latter part of the last century Toronto's first zoo, run by an interesting fellow by the name of Harry Piper, was located just west of the Queen's, with its covered entry and ticket booth about where the main Front Street entrance to the Royal York is now situated. Piper's Zoo

had the decaying remains of a large whale on display for a period of time, but the arrival of the warm weather put an end to that. Ancient newspaper clippings reported that the carcass and bones were used as landfill across the street where a new shoreline was being created.

An interesting feature of Mr. Piper's whale is that during recent excavations for the Harbourfront streetcar line tunnel under lower Bay Street, a whale's vertebrae was unearthed. No doubt it's all that remains of the pride of Piper's Zoo.

All these memories of an earlier Toronto were just that, memories, of when the country's 13th Governor-General Viscount Willingdon officially opened the Royal York Hotel at 12:45 pm on June 11, 1929. One of the unique features of the new hotel was its Roof Garden, described in the brochures as "overlooking the lake from the upper edge of the skyline."

The Roof Garden was formally opened the following evening, June 12, 1929, and guests enjoyed the music of one of the most popular American dance bands, Ben Bernie and his Originals.

[Soon after this column appeared in June of 1989, more than $100 million was spent on renovations that have made the Royal York the gem of Toronto hotels.]

The Alexandra Palace

September 9, 1992

Four young ladies out for a spin stop in front of the Alexandra Palace on the west side of University Avenue. Note the car has right-hand drive and snow chains on the rear wheels, c. 1907.

Torontonians were certainly filled with pride when the city's newest and most luxurious hotel opened on King Street East in 1903. Called the King Edward in honour of the reigning monarch, King Edward VII who had ascended the throne of just two years earlier, the hotel was the brainchild of industrialist, George Gooderham, who was determined to keep the business heart of the fast-growing city east of Yonge Street.

Four years went by and Torontonians' chests again swelled when what was described by those "in the know" as "the finest theatre on the North American continent" opened its doors, again on King Street, though this time on a site several blocks to the west of Yonge. Built at a cost of $750,000 (astronomic by 1907 standards) by the city's youngest millionaire, Cawthra Mulock, the Royal Alexandra was named in honour of Edward VII's wife.

Having described the two Toronto landmarks that honour the Empire's King and Queen from 1901 until 1910, does anyone remember the other elegant building here in town also named in honour of Edward's wife, a building that has long since vanished from the city's streetscape?

Erected in 1904 on the west side of University Avenue (opposite and a little to the north of where today's Gerrard Street intersects University Avenue) and designed by Toronto architect, Francis Baker, the Alexandra Palace was not only one of the tallest buildings in the city, it was also Toronto's first large apartment house. To be sure, there were other apartment buildings in Toronto, but with its seven floors, imposing façade and proximity to the new Legislative Buildings just up the street, there's no doubt that the "Palace," as it became known, was the city's most impressive apartment building.

In 1904, the year the "Palace" opened, Toronto was struggling to recover from the devastating fire that had destroyed much of the heart of the city in April of that year. Almost 125 buildings lay in ruins and 6,000 of her citizens were out of work. Nevertheless, even while the economic centre of the city was still smoldering, several prominent Toronto businessmen, including Dr. Oronhyatekha, the remarkable Six Nations Indian who became supreme chief ranger of the Independent Order of Foresters, and the Hon. George E. Foster, vice-president of the Union Trust Company, were overseeing final details prior to the official opening of their new Alexandra Palace apartment building.

The University Avenue of the turn-of-the-century was vastly different to the

University Avenue of today. Back then, in place of the insurance and office towers and numerous hospital structures that now line the thoroughfare, small cottages, and one and two-storey residences flanked the west side of a much narrower street that continued to be called by many, "the College Avenue." That name came about when the street was a private drive to and from King's College (the forerunner of the University of Toronto) that stood about where the Parliament Buildings stand today.

Slightly to the east of the College Avenue, and separated from it by a row of trees, was another street, this one publicly owned, with the rather pretentious name, Park Lane. It, too, was lined with simple one and two-storey homes with a smattering of institutional buildings like Osgoode Hall, the Armories and Drill Hall and the University Avenue Synagogue.

Both streets started at Queen and came to an abrupt termination at College Street. Eventually, College Avenue and Park Lane became one and were officially renamed University Avenue.

Even the small side streets in and around the "Palace," Orde, Caer Howell, Elm, McCaul and the like, were very much residential streets. Perhaps the only other large building in the neighborhood was the McCaul Street public school at McCaul and Caer Howell. This, then, was the neighborhood in which the imposing Alexandra Palace was built and where, for almost half a century, some of the city's best-known citizens resided; people like Sir Adam Beck, chairman of the Ontario Hydro (Hydro's head office was built next right next door in 1915), Ontario Premier Howard Ferguson, prominent lawyer Herbert Lennox, Toronto Mayor Reginald Geary, Charles McCrea, president of the Toronto General Trusts Corporation and many others.

For as long as anyone could remember, a uniformed Oriental doorman greeted visitors at the main entrance to the "Palace" and the entire staff of porters and chambermaids were Japanese. The main entry was always locked nightly promptly at 11 pm. The "Palace" never sought nor was awarded a beer or wine license. The place exuded class.

But things were changing in Toronto. In 1925, the residential apartment was converted into a residential hotel and while the six-room furnished suites continued to be rented for about $250 per month, transients could now stay over for about $5 or $6 a night. With the end of the Second War, those changes continued. New buildings were planned for the once tranquil and tree-lined University Avenue and in 1952, the Alexandra Palace was forced to close its doors. The 48-year-old structure underwent extensive remodeling, inside and out, reopening the following year as a modern office building. Space was immediately rented by the Hydro whose buildings to the north at numbers 620 and 640 were full to capacity.

But there was little doubt that the Alexandra Palace's days were numbered. Finally, in December 1968, demolition crews moved in, and within a few months the landmark was no more. Soon thereafter, work commenced on a new Mt. Sinai Hospital that has occupied the site since its opening in 1974.

A 1956 view of the Alexandra Palace after its conversion to an office building three years before. Note the lack of parking meters on University Avenue. That would soon change.

"Little Norway" Trained Airborne Force in Exile

December 9, 1990

I received an interesting letter the other day from reader Ron Simmons in which he described his childhood years growing up in a place called "Little Norway" at the foot of Bathurst Street on the Toronto waterfront. In fact, Ron's letter was so interesting that it'll form the basis of next week's column. While Ron remembers "Little Norway" as the small community where he and his family lived in the years shortly after the end of the Second World War, the Norwegian Air Training Establishment, to give it

The future King Olav V of Norway, accompanied by the Crown Princess, visit "Little Norway" in 1941.

Courtesy of Toronto Harbour Commission.

it's official name, actually came into being several years earlier. In this week's column I'll focus on the war years at "Little Norway." Next week, Ron will take us on a tour of the postwar version of his "Little Norway."

When Norway was invaded by German forces in the early spring of 1940, a gallant fight to rid the country of the invaders was to no avail. In June, all members of the Norwegian fighting forces were ordered to evacuate their homeland and regroup in Great Britain. After assessing the situation, it was decided by the Norwegian and British governments that the best way for the members of the Royal Norwegian Air Force (RNAF) and

Royal Norwegian Naval Air Force (RNNAF) to get back into the fight was for them to reorganize and develop a training program that would turn out pilots and ground crew that could help the allies defeat the enemy. Extensive discussions with the Canadian government followed and although all of Canada's military air bases were being utilized to the maximum as part of the massive British Commonwealth Air Training Plan program, it was agreed that the small airport at the west end of Toronto Island could be made available as the RNAF's new airfield.

Constructed and operated by the Toronto Harbour Commission, the year-and-a-half-old "Port George VI Island Airport" (to give the facility its official name) was turned over to the Norwegians in the summer of 1940. Along with airport, a small piece of property on the north side of the Western Channel was also made available, rent-free. This would become the site of a military camp affectionately called, by airmen and Torontonians alike, "Little Norway."

It didn't take long before the once-barren land behind the old Maple Leaf

Stadium became interlaced with roads and walkways. Numerous structures were erected some of which served as officers' and NCO's living quarters while others were used for administrative purposes, mess halls, training schools and the like. The camp even had its own hospital. Consisting of almost 20 buildings, "Little Norway" was officially opened on November 10, 1940. Norwegian personnel who had initially found temporary shelter at the old Lakeside Hospital on Toronto Island and onboard the S.S. *Iris,* a small steamship moored in the harbour that had transported the newcomers to Toronto from England, soon found more comfortable accommodation in their newly constructed quarters.

Access to the Island Airport on the south side of the channel, where a fleet of Fairchild PT-19 trainers, Curtiss *Hawk*s and Northrop N3PB patrol bombers was located, was via a small double-ended ferry that used a wire rope to pull itself across the gap.

As the months went by, more and more young Norwegians arrived at "Little Norway." Eventually, with almost 1,000 personnel packed onto the

site, it became obvious that expanded training facilities and increased accommodation space were needed. As a result, in the spring of the following year 430 acres near Gravenhurst were purchased to which most of the flight training activities and associated personnel were relocated. Flight training was done at Muskoka's Dominion Airport.

A few Norwegians remained in the Toronto area to carry on specific war duties, one of which was to dispose of their waterfront camp. In early 1943, "Little Norway" was sold to the RCAF who occupied the camp until war's end. "Little Norway" was officially closed as a military installation in mid-February 1945, but as we will see next week, "Little Norway" continued to live on for many Torontonians including Sun reader, Ron Simmons.

Just a year has past since the end of the Second World War and "Little Norway" has already been converted to a post-war housing complex to help alleviate the chronic housing shortage faced by Torontonians. Maple Leaf Stadium at top of photo.

A Prince of a Gate

July 12, 1987

The Prince of Wales cuts the ceremonial ribbon to officially open the Princes' Gates while his brother, Prince George (in the light suit and the other half of the duo identified in the term Princes'), looks on in the company of CNE President, Sam Harris, August 30, 1927.

Next month, our very own Canadian National Exhibition will open for the 109th time. (Actually it's only the 104th as the EX wasn't held during the period 1941–46 when the grounds were devoted to military uses.) This year there will really be something new at the fair, but visitors are going to have to look up high to find it. Near the foot of Strachan Avenue is a massive entrance leading into the east end of the grounds that was originally to be called the Diamond Jubilee of Confederation Gates, so named as the year of construction of the structure, 1927, coincided with the 60th anniversary of the birth of our country.

This impressive entrance was the first step in a much-needed expansion of the Exhibition grounds of the day which had become a congested gathering place

for more than one and a half-million visitors during the annual fair. The directors of the Exhibition felt that only something really spectacular would suffice as the new grand entrance to "the show-place of the nation," as the EX had become known far and wide.

In late 1926, Toronto architect Alfred Chapman (who had just completed the Ontario Government Building at the west end of the grounds) was assigned the task of creating the EX's new entrance. He came up with the concept of a 300-foot-long, 18-column structure (these columns were made up of two sets of nine, each set representing the nine Canadian provinces of the day) with a massive 41-foot-high central arch surmounted by a majestic 12-ton sculpture, 24 feet in height with immense wings outstretched high above the happy crowds and the lamp of learning in one hand and a laurel wreath in the other.

Winged Victory, and all the symbols that surround her, represent progress and advancement, two characteristics that were very much in the minds of all Canadians back in the 1920s. The Gates were constructed in slightly more than four months by the Sullivan and Fried Construction Company of Toronto and officially dedicated by Edward, the Prince of Wales and his brother, Prince George, during their visit to our city on August 27, 1927.

As almost an afterthought the original name selected for the structure, the

122

The original and badly damaged, poured concrete
Winged Victory, *was replaced with a replica*
constructed out of space-age plastic material.

Diamond Jubilee of Confederation Gate, which was quite a mouthful, became the simpler and more pleasing Princes' Gates in tribute to the two boys.

Recently, and as a result of the ravages of six decades of time and weather, the original 12-ton poured concrete figure of *Winged Victory* has been removed to soon be replaced virtually by an identical sculpture fashioned out of 1200 pounds of light-weight, ultra-high strength advanced plastic composite material developed by the Engineered Plastics Corporation of Mississauga.

The entire project, which comprised the removal of the original sculpture, the creation and placement of the new sculpture and major restoration work to the rest of the Gates, has been the responsibility of Summit Restoration of Etobicoke.

It is anticipated that our new *Winged Victory* will be hoisted into place on August 8, and rededicated on the opening day of this year's CNE, August 19, 1987.

Procession of Grief

October 9, 1988

The papers described it as one of the largest funeral processions in Toronto's history. All the way from St. James' Cathedral on King Street East, along King and up Yonge Street to Mount Pleasant Cemetery, crowds lined the sidewalks to pay their respects to the five firemen who gave their lives the morning of July 10, 1902. The conflagration at the McIntosh

Fred Clarke and Fred Russell, two of the five Toronto firemen killed in the McIntosh blaze.

The Evening Telegram *photo.*

feed warehouse would enter the record books as the scene of the heaviest loss of life in the history of the Toronto Fire Department.

The P. McIntosh and Son building stood at the south-west corner of Front and George Streets, just east of the recently renovated south St. Lawrence Market. The actual date of construction of the company's three-storey brick building is unknown though many of the older inhabitants of that day recalled that the builder was Lionel York, who also built the Parliament Buildings in Queen's Park and the three-year-old City Hall at the top of Bay Street.

Some of the more perceptive Torontonians also remembered that the structure had first been used as a distillery before it had been converted into a stable, boarding many of the horses that pulled the streetcars of the old Toronto Street Railway Company. In fact, the half-dozen or so horses assigned to pull the city's last horsecars on the McCaul route eight years before were stabled there.

After all the horses were retired and the street railway system electrified, Peter McIntosh and his son, James, had used the building to store oats, straw and hay. The building's proximity to the busy St. Lawrence Market and civic weight scale near the Front and Jarvis Street intersection made it an ideal site for McIntosh's busy animal feed business.

Dawn had just broken on the morning of July 10, 1902, and in the tower of the nearby Central Fire Hall on Lombard Street, a lonely fireman on look-out duty noticed smoke pouring from what appeared to be the powerhouse at Frederick Street and The Esplanade. Minutes later, the real source of the smoke became known when an alarm was rung in by McIntosh's foreman who discovered the interior of the old building enveloped in a mass of flames. In spite of the valiant efforts of the first firemen to arrive on the scene, the building was soon fully engulfed. A stiff breeze from the north didn't help matters, fanning the flames and carrying burning debris south across The Esplanade where a large ice house owned by the Knickerbocker Ice Company soon caught fire.

Then the wind shifted to the east and began to carry burning embers and smoke towards the market. Things were getting serious and at 6:20 am, a general alarm went out, bringing almost the entire city fire brigade to the scene. At 6:35 am, without warning, the entire

lapsed and the lives of two more fire-fighters were snuffed out beneath huge piles of bricks and sections of roof.

It was another half-day before the flames that had consumed three large buildings were totally extinguished. By then the full force of the tragedy had finally sunk in. Five young Toronto firemen were dead.

An Evening Telegram artist sketched this view of the McIntosh Feed building enveloped in flames at the height of the July 10, 1902 inferno.

The Evening Telegram *photo.*

Three days later, on Sunday, July 13, the bells of St. James' Cathedral tolled mournfully as thousands gathered to pay their last respects to the 5 young men. Outside the church, huge crowds stood in hushed silence, while inside religious leaders and civic officials took turns eulogizing the dead men.

Following the service, five black caskets were placed in separate hearses and one of the longest funeral processions in the city's history began – west along King to Yonge, then northward to Mount Pleasant Cemetery. Leading the procession was a large contingent of marchers and bandsmen representing the Orange Order to which three of the firemen had belonged. There followed members of the Toronto Railway Company Employees' Union, the Sons of Scotland, the Knights of Labour, the Veterans of the African War and the "G" Company of the Royal Grenadiers.

All along the route, hundreds of citizens gathered to pay their last respects while just inside the cemetery's Yonge Street entrance, hundreds more gathered to witness the burial rites as Fred Clarke and Adam Kerr, close friends as well as brother firefighters at the Central Hall, were buried beside each other. A short distance away Walter Collard, Fred Russell and David See were also laid to rest.

east wall of the McIntosh building collapsed onto George Street burying beneath the tons of brick and mortar firemen David See, who had recently returned from the Boer War, Harry Clarke, who was working his regular day off and Adam Kerr. All three firefighters worked out of the Central Hall on Lombard Street.

Without hesitation, dozens of their co-workers quickly rushed to the scene of the collapse and began digging frantically for the three men, but to no avail. Slowly, one after the other, the three lifeless and broken bodies were dragged from the smoldering debris.

Then, not five minutes later, it became obvious to Chief Thompson that two other firemen were missing, Walter Collard and Fred Russell, both from the Yonge Street Hall. They had been directed by the Chief to take a hoseline through a narrow laneway that ran westerly from George Street. While carrying out their orders, another wall col-

A Taste of History
at the Market Gallery

March 5, 1989

Exhibit floor at Market Gallery, South St. Lawrence Market.
City of Toronto Archives.

Tomorrow marks a very special day in the history of our city for it was on March 6, 1834, that the little Town of York was, as the official document stated, "erected" into the City of Toronto. The town itself had actually been around since 1793 when the province's first lieutenant-governor, John Graves Simcoe, decided to establish a small community near the mouth of a pristine river that his wife, Elizabeth, subsequently named the Don after the Don River in the northeast of England.

Though the area of the newly established Province of Upper Canada that Simcoe had selected for the new community had been known for decades as Toronto, the good Governor, not being a fan of Indian names, changed the new community's appellation to York in tribute to King George III's second eldest son, Frederick, the Duke of York, who, rumour had it, had recently defeated the French in a battle in Flanders. There's

little doubt that the decision to rename was a wise move on Simcoe's part, considering that Fred's father had a lot to say about the Governor's future activities and responsibilities.

Originally, the Town of York embraced just 10 small blocks tucked along the shoreline on the north-east corner of Toronto Bay. Over the next four decades York grew sufficiently, both in size and population, to require the enactment of a statute with the impressive title "4 William VI, Chapter 23" that, when enacted and signed, elevated the community of 9,254 souls from town to city status.

Now it was possible for civic leaders to finally introduce property taxation in order that a few of the necessary civic improvements, things like sidewalks and sewers to serve the growing community, could be financed.

An easy and entertaining way to learn more about Toronto's fascinating history is to stop by the Market Gallery down on Front Street East. Ever since its opening back in 1979, the Gallery has featured a variety of interesting exhibitions, each of which has focused on a specific aspect of Toronto's fascinating past.

Located over the historic South St. Lawrence Market, the main exhibit hall of the Gallery occupies the Council

Chamber of Toronto's "old, old" City Hall (not to be confused with "old" City Hall at Queen and Bay streets).

It was in this room that successive City Councils from 1845 through to 1899 met to discuss matters of civic importance; matters like the plans by several pioneering railway companies to fill in massive areas of Toronto Harbour so each could lay track and operate passenger and freight trains right into the heart of the young city. And what if the city fathers had the nerve to refuse their demands? The railways threatened to run their trains right down the middle of Queen Street, a threat that was very real. In fact, if the city fathers hadn't backed down and let the companies fill in part of the bay and lay their rails on the reclaimed land, the rumble of steam trains along several busy downtown streets would have been commonplace.

Or on a happier note, the old Council Chamber was also the location of exuberant meetings at which preparations were finalized for the visit to Toronto by Queen Victoria's son, the Prince of Wales, who was to arrive by boat from Kingston on September 7, 1861. The Prince, who was to become King Edward VII in 1901, came ashore almost exactly where SkyDome is now being rushed to completion.

When City Hall was constructed at the corner of Jarvis and Front streets in the mid-1840s, it was located right in the heart of the young city. Over the years, the city centre slowly shifted westerly, and in the late 1880s, civic officials decided to erect a new, larger and more modern hall at the top of Bay Street.

With the removal of the municipal offices from the Jarvis and Front corner in 1899, the old building became part of the St. Lawrence Market that had its origin across the street more than three-quarters of a century before.

Over the ensuing years, various parts of the former City Hall structure, including the stately old Council Chamber, were relegated to various market purposes, storage rooms, cold storage and the like.

Then, in the summer of 1978, a young alderman for Ward 4, Arthur C. Eggleton, suggested that an exhibition centre for the City Archives be established in the building housing the South St. Lawrence Market. The old Council Chamber was selected as the main exhibit gallery, while other areas of the building were earmarked for smaller exhibit halls, public gathering places and areas for conservation and exhibit preparation activities. In addition, a special storage vault for the safe storage for the city's most treasured and irreplaceable archival paintings and sketches was built on the uppermost floor.

Toronto's new Market Gallery opened on March 7, 1979, with an exhibit devoted to the life of John George Howard, architect, engineer, artist and one-time landlord of High Park. Since that first show a decade ago, there have been a steady stream of entertaining and educational exhibitions in Toronto's Market Gallery.

A Sign of the Times

March 26, 1989

Soon, one of those familiar gasoline station signs we all instantly recognize as we walk or drive down our city streets will vanish forever. And as the sign vanishes, so too will the company behind the sign and Texaco Canada will be no more.

While the name Texaco is a relative newcomer here in Canada, having first appeared on gas stations in 1947, the forerunner of the company goes back more than a century to the year 1873. In that year Canada was but six years old, John A. Macdonald was defeated at the polls, Prince Edward Island joined Confederation and Torontonians, John McColl and Isaac Anderson, pooled their resources and expertise and formed a company called McColl and Anderson. It became McColl, Stock and Anderson when George Stock joined the duo a few years later.

The company built a small processing and storage plant on the west bank of the Don River, a short distance north of the Queen Street bridge, where they processed American petroleum products into patented mixtures with impressive names like "Globe Machine Oil" and "Challenge Lubricator."

A few short years later, Stock and Anderson left the organization and McColl's brother, Angus, joined the firm which was subsequently renamed McColl Brothers and Company. It was to remain a family-owned business for the next 42 years.

Initially, this pioneering Toronto enterprise was primarily interested in the manufacture and sale of a variety of paints, varnishes, greases and oils, with their customers being the steamship and railway industries. As the railways moved west so too did the brothers who established offices and plants in Winnipeg, Regina, Calgary and Vancouver.

As the automobile became a more and more prominent fact of life, it was only natural that the company would decide to expand their product line to include automotive greases and lubricants. By 1916, McColl Brothers and Company was also retailing gasoline that they had imported from the United

The McColl, Stock and Anderson processing and storage facility on the west bank of the Don River, north of Queen Street, 1877.

States, eventually putting their own gasoline refinery "on stream" in 1925. It was also located on the company's property on the west bank of the Don.

Two years later, McColl Brothers merged with the Montreal-based Frontenac Oil Refineries Limited forming McColl-Frontenac and by 1940, thanks in part to the acquisition of smaller gasoline companies plus major cash investments in the McColl-Frontenac Company by The Texas Company, some 4,000 "Red Indian" gas stations were selling "Red Indian" brand motor oil, "Cyclo Gas" motor fuel and "Marathon" gasoline coast-to-coast.

The Texas Company, which had been established south of the border in 1902, was a wholly owned subsidiary of the Texas Company of the United States, and by 1948 controlled 35% of the McColl-Frontenac Company.

In 1941, McColl-Frontenac introduced the now-familiar "Sky Chief" line of products, and within six or seven years the once-familiar "Red Indian" had been totally replaced by Texaco signs, Texaco brands of oil and automotive products right across the country.

In 1950, the old McColl plant on the Don River closed to eventually be replaced by the Port Credit refinery of Regent Refining (Canada) Limited, a company that had, in turn, been acquired by The Texas Company some years before. Then in 1959, the name

McColl-Frontenac ad in
The Evening Telegram, *June 17, 1929.*

McColl-Frontenac was replaced totally by the new Texaco Canada Limited designation. Now, with the impending take-over of Texaco by Imperial Oil, even the Texaco name will disappear from the list of familiar corner gas stations.

"Five-Pin" Ryan Bowled Us Over with New Game

June 18, 1989

It's amazing the number of people who bowl as a way to pass their leisure time. Organized bowling is not a new sport, by a long shot. The game will soon enter its second century as a popular activity, though those early competitions were strictly of the 10-pin variety.

Bowling, in its simplest form, can be traced to 5200 BC, thanks to the discovery of artifacts in an Egyptian child's tomb. As can best be determined, nine pieces of stone were set in a specified pattern at which a stone "ball" was rolled, having first passed through a marble arch.

Tommy Ryan (1872–1961), inventor of 5-pin bowling.

Several thousand years later, people in the Italian Alps began tossing stones, underhanded, at various objects, originating the beginnings of a game we now know as boccie.

More recently, in the 16th century, "bowling at pins" was the national sport of Scotland. The early immigrants to the New World brought their games and soon 9-pin bowling was being played throughout the Americas.

Then in 1841, the state of Connecticut passed a law prohibiting playing the game and eventually other states joined the ban. Bowlers are a resourceful lot and someone added an additional pin, thereby creating 10-pin bowling. No law against that game – and the "new" pastime flourished.

The first regulation 10-pin bowling alleys here in Canada were introduced in 1905 by the multi-talented Thomas F. Ryan, or just simply Tommy to his many friends.

Tommy was born in Guelph, Ontario, in 1872. Back then, the "Royal City" was home to the Maple Leaf baseball team, one of the best on the entire continent. Tommy loved the sport and developed into an extremely talented ball player, eventually turning down an offer to turn professional with the Baltimore Orioles, south of the border.

When he was still only 19, Tommy moved to the bustling City of Toronto where he obtained employment in the office of Gowans & Kent, china, glassware and antique dealers. But sports were Tommy's real interest and eventually he opened his own billiard parlour on Yonge Street.

The years went by and in 1905 Tommy decided to invest $2,000 of his own hard-earned money in the nation's first regulation 10-pin bowling alley emporium over the Ryrie brothers' jewelry shop at the south-west corner of Yonge and Temperance streets. The old building is being demolished as you read this article.

Bowling was an inexpensive and popular sport during the war years. These ladies represented the three services at the Canadian Bowling Association annual championship held at Karry's Teraulay Street alleys, April 17, 1943.

He dressed up the place with a slew of imported potted palms, hired a nattily attired string orchestra and added a huge lunch counter. Admittance to his Toronto Bowling Club was by membership only, a restriction that history tells us was begun in order that management could keep some sort of control over the dreaded roughnecks about town.

It wasn't long before many of the city's most prominent citizens were whiling away their leisure hours bowling a few lines at Ryan's place. About three years went by before it suddenly dawned on Tommy that many of the larger citizens who hadn't used some of their muscles in years were having problems with those heavy bowling balls and all those pins. And, coincidentally, they were also spending too much time bowling and not enough time eating at the food counter.

The enterprising Tommy got together with his father who whittled down 5 of the large 10-pins into slightly smaller versions while at the same time fashioning a slightly smaller bowling ball. The younger Ryan then devised a new scoring system and, presto, 5-pin bowling was born.

Unfortunately for Tommy, he was so busy developing his brainstorm that he forgot to patent his idea. The young man never made a nickel from his idea, except from those who came to play at the Toronto Bowling Club.

In later life, Ryan was one of the city's best-known art and antiques dealers and for many years had his shop and residence in what today is the Keg restaurant on Jarvis Street, just north of Wellesley. In fact, it was Tommy who leased part of his place to a brand new radio station in town and on February 19, 1927, Ted Rogers' CFRB went "on the air" from studios in Ryan's Jarvis Street art gallery.

Tommy's death at his Jarvis Street home in 1961 was mourned by thousands.

Grandiose Transit System
Certainly Not New Idea

July 9, 1989

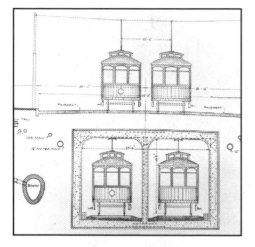

A 1911 transit improvement plan for Toronto suggested operating streetcars in "tubes" under the main streets, a concept that was the prototype of today's Yonge, Spadina and Bloor-Danforth subways.

In a recent statement issued by Minister of Transportation, Ed Fulton, it was revealed that the province would be spending more than one-half a billion dollars on public transit improvements over the next five years. Of that amount, GO Transit will be getting $400 million and the TTC, something in the vicinity of $150 million. Not much when you say it fast, eh?

The Minister's announcement prompted me to delve into a large collection of newspaper stories about earlier plans for transit improvements for Toronto. One of the most interesting is a comprehensive account of a report issued November 22, 1911, by Charles Rust, the city engineer, on a proposed "tube railway" for the city.

Earlier that year, the Toronto Board of Control directed that Rust, in concert with the city's Railway Engineer E.L.

Cousins, prepare a report on the construction of a series of "tube lines" (today they're called subways) to serve Toronto's 342,000 citizens. In his report, Cousins suggested that the city build several underground rapid transit lines emphasizing an early start on the all important Bay/Teraulay (as Bay Street north of Queen was then called) Yonge tube that would have terminals Bay and Front streets to the south (Union Station was 16 years in the future) and a point just north of St. Clair Avenue to the north. Rust estimated that 50,000 passengers a day would use this line each paying a 4-cent fare. A simplified version of this "tube" idea opened on March 30, 1954.

Integral with the Bay/Teraulay/Yonge line was a surface streetcar route west along St. Clair as far as today's Caledonia Road, with provisions to extend the line "if and when" needed all the way to West Toronto. Cousins and Rust also proposed a tube under Bloor Street and Danforth Avenue from Keele Street in the west to Coxwell in the east.

The first section of today's Bloor-Danforth subway opened in 1966.

Feeding these terminals would be surface lines on Coxwell and Keele, connecting with a third tube under Queen Street that would run between High Park in the west and the Woodbine race track in the east.

This line resurfaced in the late 1940s only to be rejected, though one station was roughed in under the present Queen station on the Yonge line.

In addition, Rust and Cousins produced drawings showing electric surface lines on Pape, Bloor Street West, Annette, Runnymede, St. Clair West, Vaughan Road, Forest Hill Road (!!), St. Clair East, Broadview, O'Connor, Woodbine, Danforth and Gerrard.

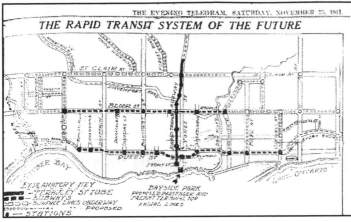

THE RAPID TRANSIT SYSTEM OF THE FUTURE

EXPLANATORY KEY
— TERAULEY ST TUBE
— SUBWAYS
□ □ □ — SURFACE LINES UNDERWAY
········ PROPOSED
■ — STATIONS

BAYSIDE PARK
PROPOSED PASSENGER AND
FREIGHT TERMINAL FOR
RADIAL LINES

Map outlining some of the improvements proposed in the 1911 transit plan.

One fly in the ointment was Engineer Rust's grand concept of building diagonal streets from downtown out into what he called the "suburban downtown" under which he believed extra deep subways could be built.

Cousins, on the other hand, felt the cost of constructing diagonal subways at $1,350,000 a mile was prohibitive. So while diagonal subways were in the report, little attention was paid to the concept by Cousins.

Another special feature of their comprehensive plan to serve the transit problems facing the Toronto of the teens was the interfacing of the streetcars and subways with the highly successful electric radial network then in place. At the east and west ends of Queen Street were the West Hill and Mimico radial lines of the Toronto and York Radial Railway. At the top of Yonge was the T&Y's Metropolitan Division that ran as far north as Sutton and Jackson's Point. Serving the Junction part of the city from Keele and Dundas Streets were the radial cars of the Toronto Suburban Railway connecting the city with Woodbridge and Guelph. Called "radials" because they "radiated" out from the city, the radial cars were actually large, non-polluting electric streetcars capable of handling immense volumes of people, moving them through the sparsely populated regions around the city proper on private right-of-ways at speeds of 60 mph.

One additional feature of the radial part of the Rust-Cousin plan was the inclusion of a large underground terminal at Bayside Park (a park that was located on the waterfront between Bay and Yonge streets north of today's Queen's Quay). It was visualized that in the not-too-distant future, the radial lines from the east and west would be extended underground into the waterfront of the city where passenger cars would connect with the subway during the day and goods carried into the city on radial freight cars could be delivered around town at night using the same subway system. Radial service in and around Toronto was eventually phased out as people turned their attention more and more to their automobiles. Highway improvements and widenings paved over much of the radial trackage with the Lake Simcoe line service ending in 1930, though Richmond Hill was still accessible by streetcar until 1948.

The timing of the Rust-Cousins proposals would see construction started in 1913 with many of the improvements in place within the incredibly short span of just three years, including several new streets; the modern Queen's Quay, Harbour Street and Lake Shore Boulevard, to name just three, would be constructed on the 266 acres of land that were to be reclaimed along the edge of the bay.

One final note. The estimated cost of implementing this comprehensive report would have been almost $23 million, a lot of money in 1911, but a mere 15% of what the TTC was recently promised by the provincial government.

Canada's First
Airmail Delivery – Late

June 24, 1990

Partially hidden from view near the front entrance to a small apartment at 970 Eglinton Avenue East is a provincial plaque that describes a Canadian transportation milestone of epic proportions that occurred on June 24, 1918, but went down in the history books with the wrong date.

As the awful days of the First World War passed into history, one thing was becoming more and more obvious. Aerial warfare had come into its own. And in an effort to attract more aviators, the Royal Flying Corps, with the aid of the Canadian government, leased 220 acres of flat land north of the Canada Wire and Cable plant on Laird Drive in early 1917.

A proper drainage system was installed, a number of hangers and workshops were built and soon the new Leaside aerodrome, home of Number 83 Canadian training squadron of the 43rd Wing, Royal Flying Corps, was in business.

But, as the "war to end all wars" dragged on, the number of young men signing up to become pilots dwindled alarmingly. So, in an effort to promote the Royal Flying Corps, Captain Bryan Peck and Corporal E.W. Mathers were authorized to fly to Montreal where they would put on an aerial demonstration in hopes of enticing some would-be flyers to sign up.

The flight to Montreal was uneventful, as was the air show. However, just as Peck was getting ready for the return flight, he was handed several large duffle bags, each full of an assortment of letters that several Montreal politicians and businessmen had talked government officials into letting Peck take with him on the return flight to Toronto.

With the unexpected cargo of 145 pieces of mail, each carefully hand canceled with a special stamp that recorded the words "via Air Mail, Montreal" and the day's date, June 23, 1918, off zoomed Peck and Mathers at precisely 10:12 am, June 23, 1918, in their Curtiss "Jenny" bound for Toronto with the country's first shipment of air mail.

A few miles out of Montreal, the weather closed in and the bad weather, combined with a load of bad fuel picked up in Montreal, forced the young flyers to land, first at the small Kingston airfield and later at a smaller field near Deseronto. There'd be a slight

Captain Brian Peck (left) enjoys some conversation with a brother office at Camp Leaside, c. 1918

Courtesy of National Postal Museum.

delay in making history.

Early the next day, June 24, the little "Jenny" again took to the air and a few hours later an historic cargo that had been painstakingly and officially dated June 23, 1918, finally arrived at the Leaside field, one day late.

Once on the ground, Peck jumped into a waiting army vehicle and he and his cargo were whisked downtown to the city's main post office on Adelaide Street East where Canada's first airmail shipment was finally handed over to the postmaster.

Weather and bad fuel are part of the official story as to why the country's first airmail delivery was late. The unofficial story features a slightly different set of reasons for the lateness of the "Jenny's"

arrival. Seems, someone on the Leaside base was getting married and with prohibition in force in Ontario, liquor with which to toast the young couple was nowhere to be found, locally.

However, liquor was easy to procure in Quebec. The story goes that Peck's aircraft was laden down with something other than just hand-canceled letters and packages and that something gurgled. Seems the weight of all that extra liquid cargo was what really made all those unscheduled landings necessary and Captain Peck a day late in the history books.

The House that Mary Built

February 19, 1989

Situated on the east side of Glenwood Crescent in the O'Connor Drive/St. Clair Avenue part of East York is a sprawling bungalow that looks like many other residences in the neighborhood. While it looks like many of the others, this one is special.

In May of 1943, during the darkest days of the Second World War, members of the District "A" branch of Lions International joined forces with the Gerrard Business Men's Association and constructed a rather unique bungalow in East York.

Many neighborhood companies donated building materials like electrical wiring, roofing shingles and the like while a major downtown store offered a selection of house furnishings. One-dollar raffle tickets were then sold by members of the service club with all the money thus raised donated to the *Telegram* newspaper British War Victim fund, the Lion's British Child War Victims fund and the Island of Malta War Relief fund.

But what made this particular house so special was the fact that it's construction had been made possible by an initial cash donation of $5,000 from "America's Sweetheart," Toronto's own Mary Pickford.

It's difficult for people today to appreciate the impact that "little" Mary's participation in this project had on the citizens of Toronto those many years ago.

Mary was born Gladys Marie Smith in a small house at 211 University Avenue in 1893. She was but four when her father, who worked on the old Niagara steamer *Chicora*, suffered a serious injury as a result of hitting his head on a hanging block and tackle on board ship. A short time later he died of a blood clot on the brain.

His young wife quickly realized that she and her young family, two daughters and a son, were in for a tough time if a new source of income wasn't found. Because the eldest daughter, Gladys, showed a remarkable flair for theatrics, she was allowed to join the Valentine Stock Company, making her professional stage debut at the old Princess Theatre on King Street West when she was only five. Soon after, the Smith family ventured into the United States to seek work. Nothing much happened and the family eventually returned to Toronto where they obtained lodging in a house at 13 Orde Street, in behind today's mod-

Mary Pickford and husband, Douglas Fairbanks, during their 1924 visit to Mary's hometown. They returned in 1931 and were divorced three years later.

Mary Pickford's birthplace,
211 University Avenue.

Newspaper ad for Mary's week-long
personal appearance at the Imperial
(now Pantages) Theatre on May 11, 1934.
She was in Toronto to help celebrate
the city's centennial.

ern Ontario Hydro building at University Avenue and College Street.

Eventually the pull of the Broadway
stage became too great and again the
family of four headed back to New
York. As fortune would have it, little
Gladys crossed paths with producer/
impresario David Belasco. Impressed
with the child's obvious talents, he
offered her a small part in his new play
"The Warrens of Virginia," but not
under her real name.

"Gladys Smith is too mundane," he
said. "Pick a new one for yourself."

Little Gladys thought for a moment,
then selecting Mary (from her middle
name Marie) and Pickford (her maternal
grandfather's middle name), Mary Pickford was born.

It wasn't long before Mary graduat-
ed from live stage performances to the
motion picture screen where she quickly
became the world's first screen starlet.

Mary Pickford returned to her
hometown several times, once during
the city's centennial in 1934 and again in
1938. Her 1943 visit to Toronto was part
of a promotional tour to raise funds for
the war effort. The highlight of this visit

to Toronto occurred on May 24 when
she officially unlocked the front door of
the newly constructed Mary Pickford
bungalow.

In a recent interview with the present owners of the house, I was told that
the winner of the raffle was a milkman
who couldn't afford the taxes and
upkeep of the bungalow. As a result he
sold it to the present owners who have
lived there ever since. Interestingly,
scratched in the paint on the front door
one can still discern "little Mary's"
signature, the one she signed when she
officially opened the house almost a
half-century ago.

A "Sweetheart" of a Deal

January 27, 1991

Some time ago I wrote about the "Mary Pickford Bungalow" that still stands on Glenwood Crescent just a few steps south of O'Connor drive in the Borough of East York. Using details gleaned from various stories in the old *Evening Telegram* newspaper, I attempted to explain how the house was built and subsequently raffled off in the summer of 1943 with the proceeds going to a number of charitable wartime projects.

What details I found were sketchy and I was pretty sure that with the passage of time the more obscure facts concerning this particular fund-raising effort had been lost forever, or so I thought.

Not long after the column appeared, I received a letter from David Peters who was closely involved with the project. In the letter, he asked if I'd be interested in more details about how the whole thing got started, Mary's involvement and so on.

"I sure would be," was my reply, "and I'm sure my readers would be too." Here then is, as they say, "the rest of the story."

The Second World War was in its fourth year and all over Canada groups and organizations of every description were actively engaged in a multitude of fund-raising projects. One day, David Peters, in his capacity as President of the Gerrard Business Men's Association, received notification that screen actress and native Torontonian, Mary Pickford, had offered to donate a house on Dewson Street, once owned by her

mother, in hopes of having it raffled off and the proceeds turned over to the Canadian Red Cross.

While the generous gesture was received with great enthusiasm, Peters felt that more money could be raised by selling the $4,000 house and applying that money to the construction of a brand new structure. And if Mary would lend her name to the endeavor and people in the construction, furniture and appliance industries persuaded to join the project, then they would have a real prize to raffle.

Peters subsequently met with Miss Pickford in New York City and after discussing the revised plan, obtained her complete approval. In fact, she would even come to her hometown and officially open the new house to the public, kicking off the ticket-selling campaign at the same time.

The Lions Clubs of District "A" and The Gerrard Business Men's Association request the pleasure of your presence at the opening of The Mary Pickford Bungalow Monday, May 24th, 1943 at 3 p.m. by Miss Mary Pickford O' Connor Drive and Glenwood Crescent This invitation will admit you to the Reserved Section

Invitation to the opening of the "Mary Pickford" bungalow, May 24, 1943. Raffling the house raised $45,508 for the British War Victims' Fund.

Courtesy of David Peters.

Now the work began in earnest. First East York Township donated a vacant lot, then a builder was engaged who agreed to erect the house at no cost. To spruce up the place, the Burroughs Furniture people loaned a large selection of interior furnishings while the Canadian General Electric Company donated $1,800 worth of appliances.

To ensure that draw tickets would get the widest possible distribution, the business association joined forces with the Lions Club of Toronto. Everything was set. It was time to go after the public.

But, suddenly there was a hitch. Back in the '40s lotteries of any kind were against the law. It didn't matter whether the proceeds went to deserving charities or into some individual's pocket, lotteries were illegal and that's all there was to it!

Unwilling to go against the law no matter how absurd that law was, the Red Cross reluctantly backed out of the project. Undaunted by this impasse, and believing the project too good to discard, the Mary Pickford Bungalow Committee sought out another charity and a way out of the dilemma.

Seems that while lotteries were against the law, the Corporations Act permitted shareholders, who were joint owners of a property, to decide by lottery a sole owner. So by making each person who purchased one of the raffle tickets a shareholder, then selecting a sole owner from the list of shareholders by a draw, the problem was solved.

With that problem out of the way, the committee then decided to split the proceeds from the sale of shares, 50% to the Lions British Child War Victims' Fund, 40% to the Evening Telegram British War Victims' Fund and the remaining 10% to the Malta War Relief Fund.

The bungalow, valued at $17,300, was officially opened to the public by "America's Sweetheart" on May 24, 1943. The opening also kicked off the sale of $1 shares that were available at outlets all over the city. The draw for the sole owner of the bungalow was held on August 26 in Riverdale Park where the huge "Fair for Britain" was in full swing. The fair had been developed as an alternative to the Canadian National Exhibition which had been canceled after the grounds were turned over to the military in 1940.

The winner of the bungalow was George Ellis, a Consumers' Gas employee who, needing money to solve a personal crisis, promptly sold the house for $10,000. According to David Peters, the "Mary Pickford Bungalow" project raised more money for charitable work than any other project in the entire country.

"Mary Pickford" bungalow in East York as it appears today.

Memory of a Disaster

May 13, 1984

About a year ago I wrote an article on the tragic streetcar-truck accident that occurred at Bloor and Bathurst Street late in the afternoon of May 3, 1946. Several passengers were killed and many injured. I received the following "first-person" letter from reader Doug Head.

"I had recently returned from overseas, been discharged from the RCAF and had obtained temporary employment at Simpson's. On this day a coworker, named Mary, and I were homebound on the ill-fated "red rocket" and seated just behind the centre doors. In retrospect, a location that proved to be a mighty wise choice.

"The westbound Bloor car had stopped at Bathurst Street to discharge and take on passengers. I recall very clearly that the car was absolutely packed and I'm sure the driver's view up Bathurst was completely blocked due to people standing at the front doors.

"The light turned green, the car accelerated and then came a tremendous crash. The impact drove #4076 off the track towards the south-west corner of the intersection, with its nose buried in the saddle tank of the tractor position of the huge machinery-moving vehicle.

"Immediately, flames from the tank shot through the streetcar, aided, no doubt, by a west wind. It sounded like a blow torch.

"The driver must have reacted very quickly because he jumped out of his seat and made his way along the main aisle.

"Two or three of us tried, unsuccessfully, to pry open the centre doors. The front doors were inaccessible due to the flames and danger of explosion. Some of the windows were either opened or broken and these were our means of exit.

"While Mary and I were waiting our turn to escape I saw a human form all aflame, running grotesquely past the streetcar in an easterly direction. Someone tackled him and smothered the flames. (I eventually learned that this victim of the accident had been in the RCAF and was the best friend of a chap with whom I had served in Gander, Newfoundland, earlier in the war.)

"I helped Mary out through a broken window and then got out myself. Mary discovered she had left her purse on the seat. I crawled back through the window and threw out several purses that lay scattered about. While looking for purses, I was somewhat startled to see what I first thought to be the wet end of some part of the human anatomy. It turned out to be a roast some panic stricken shopper had thrown on the floor. The total damage to myself was a cut suit and topcoat, singed hair and a minor cut on my back.

"Mary and I had to walk home due to the track blockage. At the time I lived with my parents on Pauline Avenue, two blocks west of Dufferin Street.

"Eventually the TTC paid (not willingly) to have my jacket and top coat mended. The shirt and undershirt were apparently my responsibility, I was somewhat chagrined. I had just blown most of my $100 discharge clothing allowance on these clothes and could ill-afford replacements.

"One other little anecdote, if I may. My girlfriend (now my wife) gave me hell for being late for our date that night. In all fairness, she was unaware of the reason for my tardiness. I also recall very well that the TTC inspectors, etc., on the scene wouldn't even take our

names. We weren't too upset about having to walk home because we were among the more fortunate passengers.

"Car #4076, which was built in 1938, was repaired and returned to service following the accident. It has only recently been scrapped due to "old age.""

These graphic newspaper photos from the Evening Telegram *show the inferno that erupted when PCC 4076 sliced into the Boyce Machinery Company truck's gas tank, May 3, 1946.*

Lighting Up the City's Past

April 24, 1988

Recently, Consumers' Gas Company published a particularly interesting little brochure entitled "The Lore of the Lamplighter" that documents the fascinating story about a man who, in the "olden" days, was as common a sight on the downtown streets of our city as the ubiquitous courier is today. As early as 1841 Toronto streets were lit by gas though in the beginning the company providing the service was privately owned. Torontonians' reliance on this private ownership eventually led to

Gas lamp in front of the restored St. Lawrence Hall, 1988.

Courtesy of City of Toronto Archives.

problems and seven years later, in 1848, a more responsible (and responsive) enterprise was born and given the name Consumers' Gas.

The company's first president was Charles Berczy, who for a time also held the position of city Postmaster. Charles was the son of William Von Moll Berczy, the gentleman responsible for the early settlement of much of the present Town of Markham. Toronto remembers this important family with Berczy Park on Front Street East, just west of the beautiful old Flatiron Building.

In its first year of operation Consumer's Gas was under contract to the 14-year-old city to maintain a grand total of 164 gas lamps positioned at strategic locations around town. In addition to producing gas for these street lamps, the company also distributed gas to homes and businesses for interior lighting, heating and industrial purposes. The customer paid the company direct.

In those days, the gas referred to was not the natural gas that we are all familiar with today, but rather manufactured gas obtained from the burning of coal in huge furnaces or retorts at plants situated around the city. Interestingly, portions of two former gas manufacturing complexes can be found on the south side of Eastern Avenue at Booth Avenue (Station B) and at the north-east corner of Parliament and Front streets and the south-west corner of Front and Berkeley streets (both part of the sprawling Station A). The coke by-product was eagerly sought by the common folk for use in their stoves and furnaces for warmth in the winter months.

In 1856, the company was able to reduce the price of gas to the city and in the following year, to save even more money, the city ordered the lamps extinguished on moonlit nights. This latter idea didn't last very long.

To maintain the gas streetlights,

which had increased to almost 2,000 by 1878, the company employed a number of lamplighters whose job it was to keep the lamps operational and in good repair. Included in their responsibilities, which occupied both days and evenings and for which each man received eight dollars a week, was the illumination and extinguishing of 90 lamps, the cleaning of burners, lamp housings, servicing the syphons, inspecting the frames, inspecting for gas leaks, and so forth.

The rules under which the city's lamplighters worked were extremely stringent and should the lamplighter violate any of them, he was "subject to a fine (not to exceed $1.00), suspension or dismissal at the option of the Inspector." In addition, "any property of the Company lost or injured by any Lamplighter must be paid for or made good by him." Then, in 1883, the city approved the trial use of a new invention, electric street-lights. Sensing serious problems ahead, senior officials of the gas company believed that they too should be allowed to get into the electric light business, but the city fathers said "no."

Within a few years, the more efficient and less costly electric lights were starting to take their toll on the traditional gas lights resulting in more than 30 lamplighters being dismissed. Then in 1901, Consumers' Gas lost their contract to light city streets and over the next few years the last of a once hearty breed of lamplighters disappeared from the streets along with the lamps they looked after.

Today, Consumers' Gas continues a 140-year tradition of supplying gas to Torontonians, though gas streetlamps are now the exception rather than rule.

Gas lamp at the north-west corner of Yonge and King streets, c. 1870. This view looks west along King Street.

Our Man Filey in the Slammer

March 24, 1991

The Don Jail sits on a hill to the right of this 1922 photo that was taken to show progress on the construction of the new Gerrard Street bridge over the Don River.

A couple of weeks ago, I went to jail. The operative word in that last sentence is "went." I wasn't sent.

As a matter of fact, I've always had an urge to visit (just visit, mind you) inside the old part of the Don Jail. Through the kindness of Joe DeFranco, senior assistant superintendent of the Toronto Jail (the present day name for the old Don), I was invited to come and take a look and see.

Joe introduced me to security manager Reg Smythe and after a brief chat in the relative comfort of the administration office in the newer red brick part of the facility, Joe returned to his paperwork leaving genial Reg to give me the $2 (plus GST) tour.

Prisoners have not resided (or whatever they call it when you're locked up) in the old part of the jail since the end of 1977. Therefore, though my trip to jail may have appeared to be the ultimate in bravery, it was really no sweat.

In fact, the only thing I saw in the old building (most of which is now devoted to the storage of old files and furniture) that looked halfway scary was one of those omnipresent copying machines over in a darkened corner with its lid up and lights flashing.

Reg showed me the cells where the notorious Boyd Gang members were incarcerated as they awaited trial for a series of bank robberies in the early 1950s.

These were the same cells, I was told, that Alonzo Boyd and a few of the boys had broken out of, not once but twice. Then cutting through the bars of the jail windows, the gang made their successful getaway.

Boyd's first escape lasted more than four months before he was captured and returned to the "hotel across the Don." Ten days after the September 8, 1952 breakout, Boyd and three of his pals were discovered in a barn near the present Leslie Street and Sheppard Avenue intersection.

Through a large steel door is the death chamber where 30 to 70 prisoners were dispatched at the end of a taut rope. The records are surprisingly vague on the exact number, though we know the first was in 1872 and the last, a literal double-header, was in 1962.

Looking inside the small, cold room

I could just make out where the gallows had been affixed to the stone walls and down there (the steel trap door has also been removed) was where the lifeless bodies were removed from the limp rope that had done its job.

Though it wasn't really necessary, Reg pointed out how quiet and ghost-like the room was. I couldn't hear a sound ... or could I?

In the jail's earliest days hangings were done in the jail yard, but as the area around the jail became more and more residential, the activity was moved indoors to avoid the leering eyes of those who had climbed rooftops (some having paid a fee) to witness the proceedings.

The quietness that pervades the old section of the Don Jail today is in stark contrast to the rousing ceremony that accompanied the cornerstone laying at the city's new Industrial Farm (as the place was originally called) more than 125 years ago.

The newspapers of the day reported that Monday, October 24, 1859, was cold and blustery. Late in the morning a clutch of dignitaries, accompanied by hundreds of curious members of the public, gathered on the old Scadding farm on the other side of the Don River to cheer lustily as the cornerstone of the young city's newest jail was "well and truly laid."

I emphasize newest because even though Toronto was just 25 years old it had already had three jails – the first near the site of the present King Edward Hotel, the second at the north-west corner of Church and King streets and the third, which was still in use while the Don was being built, near the foot of Berkeley Street.

Following the obligatory speeches and religious invocation, civic officials and their invited guests repaired to a downtown hotel for a celebratory lunch where many proceeded to get "bombed." And get this, Toronto City Council had even authorized either the free lunch or the booze.

The Don was off to a troubled start and worse was yet to come. Construction of the new structure was well underway when late one afternoon a serious fire broke out. The lack of proper fire fighting so far outside the city proper led to much of the building being gutted.

Work had to start all over and it wasn't until 1865 that the jail, the cost of which eventually exceeded $250,00 well over budget, was finally ready to accept "guests."

One of the least-known features of the Don is the tiny cemetery directly north of the centre block of the old section. It was here that at least eight poor unfortunates, who had met their end at the end of a rope and the bodies left unclaimed, were laid to rest.

Perhaps the most notorious of the group was George Bennett who was hanged July 23, 1880, following the death of George Brown, founder of the Globe newspaper and a Father of Confederation who Bennett, while in a drunken stupor, had shot less than four months before.

Today, the site of the little cemetery is a parking lot.

The Don Jail, 1991.

Parting is Such Sweet Sorrow

November 22, 1987

Recently I've had a number of readers ask me if I was aware that one of downtown Toronto's oldest restaurants had closed up shop and did I know whether good old Diana Sweets had really gone out of business.

Well, the first thing I did was to wander over to Yonge Street to see if the rumours were true and sure enough, the old Diana Sweets at number 187 Yonge was closed up tight. But, a quick phone call to the Diana Sweets number listed in the phone book put me straight as to the future of this long-time Toronto eating institution. But, first a little company history.

Diana Sweets founder
Constantine Boukydis (1885-1969).

Courtesy of Diana Sweets.

it Diana Sweets in honour of the statue of Diana, the mistress of the hunt that stood in the town square in Boukydis's hometown.

About 1928, the restaurant moved further north on Yonge where it would be closer to the busy Eaton's and Simpson's department stores, and over the next half-century staff of these two establishments became the business mainstay of the restaurant. In fact, it was the move of the Eaton store to the north end of the new Eaton Centre in the mid-'70s that ultimately led to the closing of Diana Sweets on Yonge Street.

The first Diana Sweets restaurant opened on Yonge Street in 1912, though at a location several blocks south of the 187 address. The young owner was Constantine Boukydis who had recently emigrated from Greece, first to the States where he became a pushcart vendor, then to London, Ontario, before a final move saw Constantine, his two brothers and a brother-in-law, new residents of the big and promising City of Toronto.

Pooling their financial resources, the boys opened a candy and ice-cream store at Yonge and Richmond streets, naming

In the early 1960s, a second Diana Sweets restaurant, which had opened in 1931 next door to the still-unfinished Queen's Park Plaza Hotel (to give hotel it's real name) at Bloor and Avenue Road, was closed when construction of the Bloor–Danforth subway led to the demolition of their building.

A replacement for this restaurant location opened in the Don Mills Plaza in 1962.

Now, though no longer in downtown Toronto, Diana Sweets is alive and well and living with Joe Bird in Yorkdale, Scarborough Town Centre, Square One and Don Mills Plazas.

The first Diana Sweets was located south of the busy Yonge and Queen intersection. In this c. 1930 view, the restaurant's new 187 Yonge Street location is visible between the Hair Goods and Try Our Upstairs Cafe signs to the right of the centre of the photograph.

A Victim of the 1904 Inferno

August 15, 1990

How's that old saying go? "There'll be a hot time in the old town tonight." Well it was especially hot in this old town 86 years ago this coming Thursday.

On April 19, 1904, about 8 pm, a conflagration erupted in the heart of Toronto, an inferno that remains to this day as the worst fire in our city's history.

It had been a cool day in southern Ontario, and as the sun set the wind picked up and flurries filled the air. The temperature began to fall and by 8 pm it was down to 24 degrees Fahrenheit.

John Croft (1866–1904), victim of the great Toronto fire.

Courtesy of Bruce Croft.

On Wellington Street, just west of Bay, a Toronto police constable, hunched over against the biting cold, patrolled his beat. Suddenly, sharp fingers of fire ripped through the roof of the Currie Building at No. 58 Wellington and seconds later, the building immediately to the east exploded in flames.

The constable raced to fire alarm box No. 12 at the corner of Bay and King, removed the gloves from his numbed fingers and turned the alarm key.

It was exactly 8:04 pm. Toronto's heart was on fire.

Plagued by high winds, low water pressure and dozens of unprotected old buildings, nearly 250 firemen spent the next nine hours trying to control an inferno that would eventually gut 123 buildings, destroy 139 businesses and throw almost 5,000 men and women out of work.

Concentrated at the Bay-Front intersection, the fire reached out south past Front down to the water's edge, east almost to Yonge, west to the site of today's Royal York Hotel and north to little Melinda Street, just a short block south of King. Mercifully, with searing flames dancing from building to building and block to block, no one was killed in the raging inferno, or at least, so I thought.

A couple of years ago, someone somewhere mentioned to me that indeed the Great Fire of 1904 had left a fatality in it's wake, though that poor victim didn't succumb on the night of the fire, but some days later. The details were sketchy and I was unable to substantiate the story – that is until a few weeks ago.

For the past few weeks, I've been in the offices of Toronto Trust Cemeteries going through registry books, compiling a list of some of the many interesting people buried in Mount Pleasant Cemetery for a book I've been commissioned to write. While searching for a burial plot for someone who died in 1904, the great Toronto fire suddenly flashed into my mind. I wondered if the person that was supposed to have died as a result of that fire might be in the Mt. Pleasant Cemetery registry?

All I really knew was the person's death occurred some days after the fire and he was killed in an explosion. Fortunately, the burial registry includes a column in which the cause of death is

*Bay Street looking north from Wellington before and after the worst fire
in the city's history.*

listed. I then spied the words "accidentally killed in a dynamite explosion." In
another column was the date May 5,
1904, and in another, the victim's name.
Could John Croft be the poor soul I was
looking for?

Next day, I visited the *Toronto Sun*
library where old editions of the
Telegram newspaper are on microfilm.
The nice ladies there got me started and
soon, on the screen, was the story I'd
been trying to track down for years.

"Croft dies of shock. First victim of
fire," screamed the headlines. And in a
subheading: "So terrible was the pain
that he was kept in an unconscious
condition by means of morphia."

The story went on to report that
John Croft was a part-time dynamiter,
hired by the city to demolish some of the
ruined buildings on Front Street West so
the immense task of rebuilding the
downtown core could start. Croft had
been working on the ruins of the W.J.
Gage building at 54–58 Front Street West
where, having set three charges of dynamite, he lit the fuse and sought cover.
Only two charges detonated. So, after a
short wait and with prodding from
labourers and teamsters who wanted to
return to work, Croft approached the
unexploded charge intending to disable
it by pulling out the fuse.

It detonated in his face.

Croft was rushed to hospital but his
injuries were so severe that he died the
following morning, never having
regained consciousness.

The registry book told me that the
38-year-old father of three was buried in
plot P-2242 in Mount Pleasant Cemetery
days later.

Aided by the people at the Toronto
Trust Office, I was soon able to track
down John Croft's grandson, Bruce,
who told me that his grandfather had
been born in Lincolnshire, England, in
1866, emigrating to Port Hope when he
was just 16 years old.

Eight years later, John moved to
Toronto where he worked for Canada
Printing Ink Company and lived at 144
Ontario Street. A few years later John
married and the young couple moved to
274 1/2 Parliament Street, where he was
residing when the accident occurred.

Croft's experience with dynamite
was obtained in the coal mines in
England where he worked as a youngster. When the call went out after the big
fire for help in clearing the area, Croft
eagerly volunteered.

Bruce confided that the unfortunate
John Croft left his adopted city a legacy
– Croft Street in the Bathurst-College
area was named in his honour.

A Voice from the Past

August 28, 1988

Lord Stanley (1841–1908).

Since that very first Exhibition held way back in 1879, the "grand old lady by the lake" has been the place where Canadians have witnessed the newest in household inventions or the latest in transit vehicles or the most modern appliances available to the public anywhere in the civilized world.

Take, for example, the electric streetcar experiments of the mid-1880s, the Rogers AC radio demonstration of the late 1920s, early TV experiments in the 1930s, the annual introduction of next year's automobiles and trucks (often before our friends south of the border had seen them), new food products in the Food Building, business machines in the Business Machine Building, washing machines and ovens in the Electrical Building, farm machines in the Coliseum, the latest in plant hybrids in the Horticultural Building, and so on.

The list of firsts is virtually endless.

In fact, the EX was the first fair in the world where people could see these things at night following the introduction of outdoor lighting in 1882. While we're on the subject of firsts, an event that occurred exactly a century ago at the fair is being featured in a special display in the Town Hall in Centennial Square. As the opening day for the 1888 edition of the Toronto Industrial Exhibition (as the CNE was then called and would be until 1912) approached, all was in readiness down by the lake.

The dignitary officiating at that year's opening was Lord Stanley of Preston, the young country's 6th Governor-General who had been in office for just a few months and would at the end of his term in office donate a cup for amateur hockey supremacy appropriately enough called the Stanley Cup.

As he toured the grounds that fall day in 1888 in the company of Alderman J.J. Withrow, the guiding force behind the formation of the EX and first president of the Exhibition Association, Lord Stanley came upon a display of newly developed cylinder phonographs, the creation of a young American inventor by the name of Thomas Edison.

Displaying one of the inherent traits of a true politician, the Queen's representative stepped forward and recorded for posterity this short, but sincere, welcoming message to all American citizens visiting the 1888 edition of the Exhibition:

Mr. President and Gentlemen:
The best use that I can make of this wonder of the age, the phonograph, is to bid you, on behalf of the citizens of the

Dominion of Canada, the most hearty welcome and to assure you that we are at all times most happy to meet our friends of the United States in the pursuit of song, of art and all that may embellish the human life. We bid you a hearty welcome.

That historic recording, done originally on a wax cylinder and now preserved forever using modern electronic techniques, has become the oldest example of recorded sound in the world.

Seeing the advantages in presenting new sound-reproducing products to the public at the EX, it wasn't long before most major phonograph manufacturers were presenting their inventions at the annual fair.

In fact, Emile Berliner, the inventor of the gramophone that used circular disks similar in shape to the well-known LPs rather than cylinders as pioneered by Edison, produced a special record for the 1904 fair on which he advised "the good people of Ontario" that his gramophone was "the most up-to-date talking machine in the world."

His recording went on to say that "every family should have a Berliner Gramophone, for it will brighten the home, amuse and entertain the children and instruct them too and [will] furnish music for dances or parties or it will play a hymn or read a prayer on Sunday."

Not only were phonographs introduced to visitors to the fair, but so too were virtually all the newly developed consumer products, stoves, furnaces, washing machines, ice boxes, refrigerators, freezers, tube-type radios, transistor radios, televisions, colour televisions, microwave ovens, cars, trucks, and so on.

In the teens, even aircraft were offered for sale to wide-eyed consumers visiting the Exhibition.

It wasn't long after Lord Stanley had recorded his voice for posterity at the 1888 edition of the Exhibition that various forms of recorded sound, spoken and musical, became popular attractions at the fair.

The Bugle Boy of Company "K"

March 1, 1992

Sixteen-year-old Charlie Bolton (right) with two unidentified comrades in New York City, January 1862.

Courtesy of Vera Wylie.

Meet Paul Culliton, a young man who calls himself a "student of the Civil War." Culliton is a member of a Civil War re-enactment organization in which he assumes the roll of Charles Augustus Robert Bolton (1845–1930), a Toronto boy who, at the outbreak of the American Civil War, crossed the border and became a "Billy Yank."

Canadians in the American Civil War? You bet!

Besides being one of approximately 270 Torontonians who served with either the "Blue" or "Grey" (historians estimate between 40,000 and 60,000 Canadians served south of the border during the 1861–1865 conflict), Charles

Bolton has yet another distinction. Following his return to this city after the war, he became an undertaker and introduced both embalming, a skill he learned while serving with the Union Army, and the first wooden coffins to Toronto.

Let's ask Paul Culliton to fill in the details.

The modern era of funeral practices in Canada may have been ushered in by a $25 bet between two young Torontonians.

It was April 1861, and the first angry shots of the American Civil War had been fired at Fort Sumter, South Carolina.

Several hundred miles to the north, two young Torontonians, Charles Bolton, 16, and pal Thomas Hughes, 21, made a $25 bet. The first to get a job would win the wager.

Word quickly reached the city that the Union Army was looking for recruits so off they both went to New York to enlist.

Who won the bet? Apparently Hughes did. Enlistment papers show he joined the 4th New York Volunteers on May 4, 1861, but for some unknown reason, Bolton's early military records are missing. We do know that he was a bugler with Company "K," 11th Ohio Regiment Volunteer Cavalry, for his name appears on a roster dated February 1864.

Where was the young Torontonian from 1861–64? No one knows for sure but a pension affidavit sworn on May 30, 1892,

152

lists Bolton as a carpenter at the time of enlistment. As the public turned to carpenters and cabinet makers to build coffins, conjecture is that when those in command learned that Bolton was a carpenter, his military fate was sealed.

In being detailed for burial service, Bolton may have come in contact with the concept of arterial embalming, a practice introduced to keep the corpse "lifelike" until returned to the family.

Following his return to Toronto after the war, Bolton worked for several local undertaking establishments and is said to have introduced not only embalming, but to have constructed the first wooden caskets, built the first horse-drawn hearse and conducted many of the first burials to take place in Mount Pleasant and Prospect Cemeteries.

He was buried in the latter on February 24, 1930, one of the last Canadian survivors of the Civil War.

Charles Bolton (1845–1930), carpenter and American Civil War veteran.

Toronto's Own Casino on Queen

January 14, 1990

Today, when we talk about old Toronto theatres, the recently restored Pantages and Elgin (originally Loew's) and Winter Garden immediately come to mind. But, the city was also home to almost a hundred less grand movie houses.

One of the best-known was the little Casino theatre that was located on the south side of Queen Street West, opposite today's Nathan Phillips Square and "New" City Hall.

Opening in 1936, the Casino was just another building in a long row of non-descript structures that filled the space between Bay and York streets along the south side of Queen.

Other structures in the block housed pawn shops, hotels and a slightly older theatre, the Roxy (later renamed Broadway), where manager A.A. Appleby was murdered in 1935.

The Casino was built as a combination vaudeville and burlesque house and in its early days featured such greats as strippers Sally Rand, Gypsy Rose Lee and Ann Corio as well as song and dance (and usually off-colour) funnymen like Red Buttons, Phil Silvers and Rags Raglund.

Entertainment was in the eye of the beholder in those days so that even

The biggest crowds to ever witness a performer turned out by the thousands in February 1952 to see and hear the Prince of Wails, Johnny Ray.

Toronto Telegram *photo.*

boxing legend Joe Louis appeared on the Casino's stage one week performing rather pathetic song and dance routines. Many thought he should have stuck to boxing.

Then came Basil Rathbone who recited Shakespeare. Some in the audience even listened.

At one point in 1944, the city's police chief thought some of the female entertainers had gone too far and recommended that the Casino's license be revoked as the theatre had become a "notorious centre of suggestive, objectionable entertainment and was a bad influence on the city." A large deputation of clergy agreed with the chief, but the board of police commissioners (who just happened to be frequent opening-night guests) didn't. The Casino remained in business.

In 1950, the era of the so-called "girlie shows" in Toronto ended (the Victory on Spadina Avenue at College Street revived that art form some years later) when the burlesque part of the Casino's program was deleted and "big name" vaudeville and family entertainment packages substituted.

In retrospect, the list of stars that appeared on the theatre's stage during this era of the theatre's life is like a

who's who of the entertainment world. Victor Borge was there as was Van Johnson, Billy Daniels, Eartha Kitt and the Mills Brothers. The house attendance record was broken in 1952 when the Prince of Wails, pop singer Johnny Ray, who's double-sided record hits "Cry" and "Little White Cloud that Cried" (thus the "Prince of Wails") topped the American music charts for 11 weeks in 1952, bringing in more than $20,000 in box-office admissions.

Interestingly, on "Cry," Ray was accompanied by four young fellows from Toronto who eventually got their own listing on the Casino marquee as The Four Lads.

As these performers became more and more popular, thanks in no small measure to frequent appearances at the smaller theatres like the Casino, showplaces in Miami and Las Vegas began to beckon. Before long fees were so high that venues like Toronto's Casino could no longer afford them. And then there was television.

So for the Casino it was back to an evening of "bump and grind" followed by something less than a first-run movie. Occasionally a big name act would liven up the place.

In 1961, the old theatre tried something different. The 1,100-seat Casino was remodeled, redecorated and reopened as the Civic Square theatre where it was hoped live theatre would flourish. In an effort to encourage the younger citizens to attend this alternate form of entertainment, tickets priced as low as $2.50 were made available.

A couple of years later, live theatre

was replaced by a string of "art films" in what is now called the Festival Cinema.

Unfortunately, both attempts to keep the old theatre going were for nought. In fact, for months plans were being formulated to redevelop the south side of Queen Street altogether. After all, Toronto couldn't have a sparkling new City Hall and Civic Square on one side of the street and a collection of dilapidated, collapsing old buildings on the other.

So it was that in mid-1965, the Casino/Civic Square/Festival theatre came crashing down. For a time a small park sat opposite Toronto's New City Hall and Nathan Phillips Square. But soon the park, too, vanished and today, the Sheraton Centre towers over the site of what was for years one of Toronto's most popular theatres.

"Toronto's New Amusement Palace," the Casino, on the south side of Queen Street just west of Bay, opened to theatre-goers on April 13, 1936. Admission prices – 16, 27, or 35 cents, depending on the time of day you wanted to go.

The Evening Telegram.

155

New Generation of Glitter

October 4, 1981

Cawthra Mulock (1884–1918), creator of the Royal Alexandra Theatre.

Nearly three-quarters of a century ago, Toronto boasted four legitimate playhouses in the downtown core. The Grand on Adelaide Street, steps west of Yonge, was the oldest. Next door was the Majestic and down on King, where modern day University Avenue cuts through, was the Princess.

And the 4th? It's the only one of the four that still stands recalling a time when wooden streetcars clattered all over town, the new City Hall was today's "old" City Hall, and Ambrose Small wasn't a statistic on the missing persons' ledger.

The Royal Alexandra on King Street West opened on August 26, 1907, with all the pomp and ceremony that the city of 272,000 souls could muster. Lieutenant-Governor Mortimer Clark was there, as was a beaming mayor Emerson Coatsworth. They were surrounded by a crowd made up of the élite of the city.

The Royal Alex, as the playhouse be-

came affectionately known, was built by a consortium of some of Toronto's wealthiest gentlemen led by Cawthra Mulock, Canada's youngest millionaire and representative of one of the city's most influential families. In this business venture he was joined by stock broker R.A. Smith, manufacturer Stephen Haas and entrepreneur Lawrence Solman.

"Lol," as he was known to most people, was a remarkable gentleman. Not only did he manage the Royal Alexandra but he also ran the Toronto Maple Leaf baseball team, the Toronto Island ferryboat service, the Arena on Mutual Street, Hanlan's Point Amusement Park and later, in the '20s, Sunnyside Amusement Park.

The architect of the theatre was John Lyle, who in later years participated in designing the city's new Union Station on Front Street, west of Bay.

The Royal Alex was erected on the former playing grounds of Upper Canada College that stood on the northwest corner of Simcoe and King and had some pretty impressive neighbours in those early days; the lieutenant-governor's residence across the street and a little further east, the old Parliament Buildings, due south of the theatre between Wellington and Front streets, the well-patronized Arlington Hotel along King Street to the west, and stately St. Andrew's Presbyterian Church at the south-east corner of Simcoe and King.

The work chosen to open Toronto's new $750,000 playhouse was entitled *Top of the World*. It was a musical extravaganza written by Mark Swain and had a cast of over a hundred. The play was an instant hit and was held over for two

The Cowboy and the Lady, *seen on the advertising boards in front of the theatre, premiered October 21, 1907 (just two months after the theatre opened), a fact that makes this one of the earliest photographs of the Royal Alexandra.*

The Evening Telegram *photo.*

weeks with the top seats selling for $2 each.

In the 70 years that the Royal Alex has operated just about anyone who is anyone in the field of legitimate theatre has stood in front of her footlights, including such luminaries as Sir Johnston Forbes-Robertson, Fred and Adele Astaire, Al Jolson, Eddie Cantor, Ed Wynn, Marie Dressler, Harry Lauder, Alfred Lunt and Lynn Fontaine, Lillian Gish, George M. Cohan, Maurice Chevalier, and the list goes on and on.

In all, more than 1,500 musicals, dramatic plays and even motion pictures have been seen at the Royal Alex.

Then, in 1963, the end of the theatre's remarkable career seemed to be waiting in the wings.

But, like a gallant knight right out of medieval days, Toronto businessman Edwin Mirvish came to the rescue. "Honest Ed" purchased the slightly wilted theatre for $200,000 and today the grand old lady of King Street continues to glitter and welcome a new generation of Torontonians and visitors.

Anne and Ed Mirvish. "Honest Ed" purchased the Royal Alexandra Theatre in 1962 saving it from certain demolition.

Canada Zoomed Ahead with Ambitious *Jetliner*

August 6, 1989

Forty years ago this August 10, we were number one in the aviation world, again! By "we" I really mean "Canada" for on August 10, 1949, exactly 40 years ago this coming Thursday, this country put North America's first jet passenger aircraft into the air. Named the *Jetliner*, a word that has now come to be a generic description of all jet passenger planes, the revolutionary craft was built by the talented people at the A.V. Roe aircraft plant adjacent to the Toronto airport when that airfield was still called Malton.

Work on designing a new passenger aircraft with the latest form of propulsion equipment, the jet engine, started in mid-1947 with the input of Trans-Canada Air Lines (renamed Air Canada in 1965) who were seeking an airplane that could transport 30 passengers 1,200 miles at a cruising speed of 400 mph.

Further, the new craft had to be able to operate from existing 4,000-foot runways and be as cost efficient as existing piston engine "transports."

Today, those parameters don't sound too stringent, but remember they were put forward in the spring of 1946 when the now seemingly "old fashioned" DC-3s and North Stars represented the "state-of-the-art" flying in Canadian skies.

Avro Canada responded positively to TCA's list of requirements stating that each of the proposed new aircraft would cost $350,000 (remember, that's per plane) with delivery starting on October 9, 1948, an incredibly short 2 1/2 months following the program's startup. Under the expert guidance and direction of Jim Floyd, a recent arrival from the A.V. Roe plant in Manchester, England, the project quickly got underway. Then they hit their first snag. Initially, the revolutionary new passenger plane was to be powered by two Rolls-Royce AJ.65 jet engines, but it quickly became apparent that British authorities would not release these powerful new engines for civil aircraft use. Avro then decided to substitute four smaller, less powerful Rolls-Royce Derwent jet engines. TCA was unhappy with this alternative and withdrew from their agreement with Avro Canada.

Nothing daunted, Avro continued on with the project alone and by August 8, 1949, a little more than two years after the project finally got under full steam, the new *Jetliner* had gone from a few lines on a drafting board inside the Avro plant to a complete aircraft undergoing, taxiing tests on the runway in front of the aircraft plant.

Two days later, with an air temperature of 103 degrees, our *Jetliner* rose gracefully from the hot tarmac.

What make's the *Jetliner* project even more incredible is that all of this took place five full years before the American-designed and -built Boeing 707 got off the ground. Even more remarkable is the fact that the 707 had taken four years, almost twice as long as the Canadian-designed and -built *Jetliner*, to get from the drawing board into the sky. Seems we had beaten the most technologically advanced nation in the world.

To be sure, Canada's *Jetliner* was actually the world's second passenger jet, the first being the de Havilland *Comet*. We missed being the world's first by a scant 14 days. However, those first *Comets* were plagued by problems, problems serious enough to result in several fatal crashes. The English craft was finally withdrawn from service leaving the *Jetliner* on its own, now unique in all the world.

Following its maiden flight, the *Jetliner* entered upon a seemingly endless test program. Many of these test flights actually became promotional marketing endeavours like the April 18,

dozen hours. It was all for naught, however. The worsening Korean War saw the *Jetliner* program scrubbed and Avro's emphasis placed on the continued development and production of the CF-100 jet fighter, another Canadian first. There were serious concerns that the Russians would attack the United States

The Avro Canada Jetliner: *first flight August 10, 1949, scrapped 1956.*

1950 effort that saw the *Jetliner* make a special trip into Idelwild (now Kennedy International) Airport in New York City making the usual 1 hour and 45-minute trip in a mere 59 minutes.

The American aviation industry was stunned. On board the craft were 15,000 specially canceled letters thus making the Toronto–New York City trip the first official "jetmail" flight in postal history. While several American airline companies were intrigued with the craft, as were the Canadian and American air forces, nothing definite happened even though a fellow by the name of Howard Hughes indicated he'd like a few *Jetliners* for his two airlines, National and TWA.

The Jetliner was flown to Hughes' plant in Culver City, California, where Hughes test flew the airplane for a

by way of the Canadian Arctic, therefore the RCAF must have more CF-100s!

And what was to be the ultimate fate of our *Jetliner*? While the prototype kept flying (it was in both the 1953 and 1954 CNE air shows) the *Jetliner* project, unlike the aircraft, was going nowhere fast. Following the end of the Korean War, there was a brief attempt to get the program back into the air, but that too failed. Then, in November of 1956, in a scene to be duplicated several years later with the *Arrow*, blow torches and axes carved the craft into little pieces. Seems the one thing we did better than create world class aircraft was to cut them into ever smaller pieces.

Today, all that remains of the one and only *Jetliner* is its nose section, now part of the Canadian Aeronautical Collection in Ottawa.

It's Time to Visit the Dock

September 13, 1987

Eglinton Park fitted out for battle. Note the guns mounted on either side of the bridge.

One of the nice things to do this time of year is to go for long walks in the brisk autumn air. Many people venture out into the countryside to do their walking, but may I suggest a trip right here in town where you can combine a healthful promenade with a heaping helping of good old Toronto history.

We've all heard about the things that are happening at Harbourfront, both good and bad. Right? Well this column, and those for the next couple of Sundays, dodge those issues and look, instead, at what it used to be like in the "good old days" down on the waterfront.

Ships of all shapes and sizes have always been a major component of activities on Toronto Bay, from the earliest days when Governor Simcoe arrived in the pristine pure water of Toronto Bay to establish what has become Toronto on board his sailing ship *Missisaga* [sic], right up to the present time as dozens and dozens of pleasure craft and sightseeing vessels crisscross the now less than sparkling waters of the bay.

It was a particularly hectic time on Toronto Bay during the wars years, those of both the First and Second, as numerous Toronto companies turned out ships by the hundreds for the war effort.

At the foot of Sherbourne Street (now, as a result of extensive landfilling, at a site that approximates the corner of Sherbourne and The Esplanade), the people at the Polson Iron Works (who had built the recently restored Island ferry *Trillium* in 1910) turned out dozens of freighters during the First War.

A couple of decades later and over at the other end of the bay, west of the foot of Spadina Avenue and close to where the spectacular King's Landing condominium now stands, a succession of companies built much needed minesweepers for convoy duty in the North Atlantic. The total number of Toronto-built minesweepers of the Bangor and Algerine class constructed during the Second War exceeded 50.

Today, only the shipyard's administration building remains as a reminder of those terrible years. It's now the Toronto Francophone Centre and stands on the west side of Spadina, just south of Lake Shore Blvd.

Assuming the more peaceful role as schoolhouse, and with a new name, Fuel Marketer, *the vessel was moored at Harbourfront until removed and cut up for scrap in 1989.*

There is, however, another reminder of the last war berthed at the foot of Peter Street. The Canadian Underwater Training Centre's floating "school-house," *Fuel Marketer,* was built by Marine Industries at its Sorel, Quebec, shipyard in 1944 as one of the Park-class flat-bottomed oil tankers designed specifically to permit this type of craft to get as close to shore as possible to off-load its precious cargo.

Originally named *Eglinton Park* (I've as yet been unable to find out if she was named for Toronto's Eglinton Park where I got my first job as a skating rink guard back in the '60s), the sturdy craft was reported to have taken a torpedo in the bow while leaving Halifax Harbour bound for the Normandy beaches. Quickly repaired, *Eglinton Park* made it overseas to complete her assigned duties in the days that followed the invasion of Europe.

Following the war, *Eglinton Park* remained overseas, transporting peanut and other vegetable oils off the coast of Africa. Eventually, she returned to Canada, was sold to the Canadian Oil Company, renamed *White Rose* (remember White Rose gasoline?) and began transporting fuel oil to depots up and down the St. Lawrence River. A few years later, the rugged vessel was renamed yet again, this time to *Fuel Marketer* following the sale of the Canadian Oil Company to Shell Oil in 1962.

Destined for the scrap yard in 1978, the *Fuel Marketer* was rescued by the operators of the Canadian Underwater Training Centre and now students are taught to be Category 1 commercial divers on board this much-travelled old vessel.

[In July, 1989, almost two years after this article appeared in the Sunday Sun, *Fuel Marketer* was towed from her Harbourfront berth, through the Welland Canal to Port Colborne, Ontario, where she unceremoniously was cut into pieces at a local ship scrapyard. The ship's bell, engraved with the original name, *Eglinton Park,* has been preserved and can be seen in the lobby of the Toronto Harbour Commission Building.]

A Towering Proposal

February 5, 1989

Events don't always have to have occurred dozens and dozens of years ago to make them historic. In fact, when you think about it, anything that has happened is now part of history. And while it's true that the majority of the items prepared for this column describe events that happened many, many years ago, this time the selection of a topic, timewise at least, is a bit different.

The year was 1973. The event? An announcement that Canadian National Railways intended to build the world's tallest communications and observation tower on Toronto's waterfront.

Actually, the idea of such a tower for Toronto was not totally new. A little more than four years before, in December of 1968 (to be a little more precise), a consortium made up of senior officials of Canadian National and Canadian Pacific Railways announced a billion-dollar plan (the cost estimate was to eventually top $1.5 billion) to redevelop the 187 acres of mostly undeveloped land situated between Front Street and the Gardiner Expressway, and from Yonge Street westerly to Bathurst.

Described as the biggest redevelopment scheme proposed anywhere on the continent, it was to be called Metro Centre and would include a new $25 million transportation terminal that would be built at the foot of an extended University Avenue (the old, "inefficient" Union Station on Front Street would be demolished, they said, a decision that would haunt the project and help eventually kill it), a mammoth convention and trade show centre, a 30-storey hotel and more than a dozen low and high-rise residential and office towers all tied together by pedestrian walkways leading to and from shops, department stores, theatres, boutiques and restaurants.

At each end of the hotel/convention centre there would be twin 26-storey office towers, one for CN and the other for CP. It was perceived that when the entire project was complete some 15 years in the future, more than 20,000 would live in Metro Centre with approximately 50,000 working there. City Alderman Joe Piccinini even suggested that a domed stadium might be built as part of the new Metro Centre. His idea didn't get much of a hearing. Imagine, a domed stadium on the waterfront! Back to reality.

The focal point of the proposed

Actual construction of the CN Tower began on February 6, 1973 and 1,263 days later, June 26, 1976, Toronto's newest landmark was opened to the public.

development was to be a 1,575-foot, three-legged communications tower complete with revolving restaurant up top and a new CBC broadcasting complex surrounding the base. Officials announced the new tower would be called the CBC Tower and work on it and the rest of the transportation terminal, to which it would be physically connected, would commence in 1969 with completion of this phase of the project scheduled for 1973.

The Tower was topped off when Olga, *a huge Sikorsky helicopter, put the final piece of antenna in place on April 2, 1975.*

However, just before work was to start, the federal government announced a spending freeze on all CBC projects, except those in Montreal and Vancouver. This, combined with the public's reluctance to see their magnificent Union Station pulled down (the developers finally agreed to save the Great Hall in an effort to get the preservationists off their backs), seemingly endless meetings with city staff plus the arrival on the scene of a new, and less enthusiastic City Council eventually brought the entire project to a standstill.

Then, on February 5, 1973, Canadian National rekindled the fire by announcing that they would proceed with the construction of the communications tower component of the project, albeit now redesigned and renamed the Canadian National Tower, or more simply the CN Tower.

It would be 230 feet and 5 inches higher than the CBC proposal and would go ahead with or without the stalled Metro Centre.

A little more than three years later, Toronto's CN Tower was officially opened June 26, 1976. The rest of the Metro Centre scheme lay dead on the drawing boards. And as for that domed stadium idea ...

Home Sweet Streetcar

September 9, 1990

A large number of antiquated Toronto streetcars are loaded onto railway flatcars prior to being shipped north to help those left homeless after a forest fire ravaged Haileybury, October 10, 1992.

Courtesy of TTC.

During my six-year stint as a director of the Ontario Heritage Foundation, I had occasion to visit the pretty little community of Haileybury where a meeting with local heritage groups had been scheduled.

Haileybury was established in the late 1880s by Charles Farr who had come to Canada from England to work for the Hudson's Bay Company. Farr was also involved in the surveying of the Ontario-Quebec border. In 1887, he acquired title land on the west shore of Lake Timiskiming with a view to creating a settlement there. He named his new community Haileybury after the public school near Hoddesdon, Hertfordshire, that he had attended as a child.

I had never visited what's called the "near north" before and when I was advised that Haileybury was on the itinerary, it suddenly dawned on me that there was indeed a Toronto–Haileybury connection. Perhaps while carrying out my Heritage Foundation responsibilities there, I could see if any vestiges of that connection were still in evidence. What was that connection, you ask? Here's the story.

The month of September 1922, and the early days of October had been unusually void of rainfall. As a result the forests and bush lands surrounding the communities of New Liskeard, Charlton, Cobalt, Heaslip and the district town of Haileybury were tinder dry. Small bush fires broke out all over the countryside, but for now they were manageable. As the morning of October four dawned, a brisk wind of 30 to 40 mph sprang up. Those little fires were about to cause a lot of trouble.

Raging out of control, a seething wall of flame roared out of the western forests towards the town of Haileybury. Within hours, virtually ever street of the once proud community of 5,000 was littered with the smoldering remains of office buildings, schools, churches and residences.

On that terrible day in early October, 1922, almost one-quarter-million acres of forest and woodland were obliterated and thousands left homeless. Forty-four others had been killed. A few days later, those same winds turned cold and snow began to fall. The winter of 1922 had come early to Haileybury.

Surveying the damage, it was obvious to government officials that the first priority, after arranging for supplies of food and water, was to provide shelter against the unusual cold for the hundreds of homeless families. An urgent call for help went out.

Three hundred miles or so to the south, the City of Toronto quickly

Number 124, a former Toronto horse-drawn streetcar that had seen use as a residence in Haileybury, sits in the community works yard awaiting restoration, July 19, 1990.

Partially restored car Number 124 on the occasion of the 70th Anniversary of the Great Fire that occurred on October 4, 1922.

Courtesy of Haileybury Fire Museum.

responded with food, clothing and building materials. And there was something else the city sent north to Haileybury. With the creation of the Toronto Transportation Commission in 1921, many modern new steel streetcars had been ordered, received and placed in service. As a result, dozens and dozens of older streetcars, those that had been operated by the TTC's predecessor, the Toronto Railway Company, had been taken out of service and stored at the Commission's Danforth carhouse along with large numbers of former horse-drawn streetcars and trailers.

While no longer fit for transit use, these cars could easily be turned into small houses for the shivering victims of the Haileybury holocaust. Within a week, 87 former Toronto streetcars had been loaded on flatcars and were on their way north where they would provide accommodation for the dozens of families that had lost everything in the great fire.

As I checked into the Leisure Inn in Haileybury, the young fellow behind the desk asked if I was the one interested in the old Toronto streetcars that had been sent north those many years ago. "Sure am," I think I blurted, somewhat surprised that anyone knew of my interest.

"Come with me," he replied, and a few moments later I was standing face to face with old number 124.

Built in 1904 (ironically, the same year Toronto suffered its big fire), car 124 was one of 35 trailers that saw years of service on the King, Dundas, Bloor and Carlton streetcar routes until they were retired from service in March of 1922. Twenty-nine cars in this group, including number 124, would get an unexpected reprieve from the wrecker's torch when they were shipped north six months later.

Serving as a temporary residence in Haileybury until a new home could be built, car 124 then reverted to use as a storage shed. Years later, it was enclosed in a garage-like structure where it remained until just a few weeks before my visit when, following the town council's agreement to replace the garage, number 124 was removed from its cocoon, hopefully to be restored and given a place of honour in town as a reminder of the day when Haileybury was nearly wiped off the face of the earth.

"Lady Lindy" in Toronto

July 8, 1990

It was 53 years ago this month, July 1937, that American aviatrix Amelia Earhart disappeared while attempting to complete an around-the-world flight. Speculation abounds, but to this day no one is sure what fate befell the 38-year-old pioneering American flyer who was the first woman to fly solo across the Atlantic Ocean.

One thing is sure, though, "Lady Lindy," as she was dubbed in friendly comparison with "Lucky" Charles Lindbergh, was first bitten by the aviation bug right here in Toronto. In a speech she delivered to guests at the Canadian Club meeting in December of 1932, Amelia referred to her days as a nurse's aid with the Canadian Red Cross during the latter months of the First World War. Assigned to the old military hospital located in the circle on Spadina Avenue just north of College Street, Amelia had come to Toronto to visit her sister who was attending St. Margaret's College. But when Amelia witnessed the pathetic condition of many of the returning airmen, without the brass bands and colourful parades

Amelia Earhart in Toronto, 1917.

Courtesy of The Seaver Centre.

to disguise the wounds and amputations, the young American quickly decided to stay in Toronto and help as best she could as a nurse's aid.

Amelia continued to render aid until an armistice was declared on November 11, 1918, then stayed on to help out in the wards during the devastating Spanish flu outbreak that followed. It was while working in Toronto that the young lady took an interest in flying, having been taken out to the small Armour Heights airfield out in the countryside north of the city (near today's Avenue Road/ Highway 401 interchange) on several occasions by some of the wounded airmen.

Overwhelmed with the urge to "soar with the birds," Amelia eventually returned to the States where she quickly mastered the art of flying. In 1928 she became the first woman to fly the Atlantic crossing from Newfoundland to Burry Point, Wales. On July 2, 1937, Amelia Earhart and her co-pilot, Fred Noonan, vanished without trace over the Pacific while attempting a round-

The Spadina Military Hospital, 1916.

the-world flight in a Lockheed 10-E Electra.

[This article appeared in the July 8, 1990 edition of the *Sunday Sun*. In March, 1992, Associated Press reported that wreckage of what was thought to be her plane had been found on the remote South Pacific atoll of Nikumaroro. Since unequivocal confirmation of the wreck's identity has still to be made, the Earhart mystery still exists.]

Past Easters on Parade

April 3, 1988 (Easter Sunday)

Courtesy of Toronto Harbour Commission.

Torontonians were forced to put up with cool and windy weather during their traditional Easter stroll along the old Sunnyside boardwalk in 1943.

"On Easter Day, all the young people come out in something new and bright like butterflies. It is almost part of their religion to wear something new on this day. It was an old saying that if you don't wear something new on Easter Day, the crows will spoil everything you have on." (Francis Kilvert, 1840–79, English cleric and diarist.)

The origin of the term Easter Parade, an event during which both sexes display items from their new spring wardrobe, seems to be lost in antiquity, or to put it another way, I can't find out when the first one was held. I do know that as early as the turn of this century, Torontonians were parading on Easter Sunday down at

Sunnyside, that part of the city near the foot of Roncesvalles Avenue bordering the old Humber Bay.

Contemporary photos show Toronto belles and beaus all decked out in their finest wardrobe, covered from head to toe, strolling along the wooden sidewalk on the south side of the old Lake Shore Road. For them the perfect ending to a perfect day would have included a 25-cent fish or chicken dinner at Pauline Meyer's Banquet and Refreshment Parlour overlooking Lake Ontario near the mouth of the Humber River.

A slight digression. To most people the term Sunnyside conjures up visions of a busy amusement park complete with dance halls, swimming pool (oops, it was always called the Sunnyside tank), rides and hot dog stands. Historically, the community known far and wide as Sunnyside originated much earlier than the popular amusement park which didn't arrive on the scene until 1922.

Named after the residence of George Cheney, an American stove manufacturing mogul living in Toronto who revered works by Washington Irving whose residence on the Hudson River was also called Sunnyside, our Sunnyside was located approximately where the parking garage serving St. Joseph's Health Centre on The Queensway now stands. The community of Sunnyside, all 115 acres, was annexed by Toronto on January 2, 1888, 14 months before the adjacent and much larger Town of Parkdale entered the fold.

With the opening of Sunnyside Amusement Park in June of 1922, an Easter Sunday stroll along the lake's edge became an annual tradition in all kinds of weather. What helped ensure the tradition would remain at Sunnyside was the presence of a wooden boardwalk built by the Toronto Harbour Commission between 1919 and 1921 as part of their massive 1912 waterfront redevelopment plan.

Constructed of 2-foot wide planks of white pine laid on pine stringers (which in turn were laid on a new beach reclaimed from the old Humber Bay), the new boardwalk stretched along the south side of the new "trafficway" (now Lake Shore Boulevard, West) commencing near the foot of Dowling Avenue and running west for a total of almost 10,000 feet.

For more than three decades Toronto's Easter Parade along the Sunnyside boardwalk signalled the return of spring for thousands of citizens. Then in 1954, due in part to the deterioration of the wood but more, perhaps, to the gradual demise of Sunnyside Amusement Park as a place to visit, the boardwalk slowly began to disappear.

First it was just a few planks here and there, but within a year all 13,092 planks had been ripped up and replaced with unattractive asphalt. But, the boardwalk and the old park just weren't the same. Shortly after the end of the 1955 season, the park, too, was just a memory.

Sensing the end of the Sunnyside Easter Parade was close at hand, in 1954 the business community along Bloor Street, west of Yonge, decided to hold their own annual Easter Parade. A few years later, another version of the parade was held on lower Yonge Street between Gerrard and King. In fact, the 1961 edition of Easter Parade was held on a stretch of Yonge that had actually been painted pink.

Sure, Easter Parades are still with us (the Queen Street East community hosts a dandy each spring in the Beaches area), but we certainly lost something special when the parades were discontinued at Sunnyside.

Ontario's Taj Mahal

March 4, 1990

Perched on a hill just a short drive north of the pretty little Town of Uxbridge is Ontario's own Taj Mahal, at least so it would appear. In reality, it's the Tommy Foster Memorial, but it sure looks like a miniature Taj Mahal. And there's a good reason for that, but to understand why, we first have to understand the man who built it.

Tommy Foster was born in 1852 on what was then called the Yorkville and Vaughan Plank Road, a short distance south of the Third Concession, Township of York. In

Mayor Thomas Foster, 1852–1945.
Courtesy of City of Toronto Archives.

today's terminology, his birthplace would have been on Vaughan road a little south of Dufferin street.

While still a young boy, Tommy's mother died and the youngster was sent to live with an uncle in the small community of Leaskdale, a few miles north of Uxbridge. The years past and in 1867, at the age of 15, Tommy Foster moved to the big City of Toronto where he took on a position of apprentice butcher in the shop of the Richardson Brothers at 206 Queen Street East.

After three years of learning the trade, Tommy opened his own butcher shop in a building a little further east along Queen. One day several years later, the son of the building's owner let slip the fact that his father was soon going to give the building to his children and they would probably put Foster out into the street. The possibility scared Foster and right then and there he decid-

ed to buy his very own building, thereby securing his future and, coincidently, introducing the young man to the often lucrative world of real estate.

As the years went by Foster lived frugally, investing much of his hard-earned money in property. Then, after 18 years in the butcher business, he decided to retire to try his hand at municipal politics. He was elected alderman in 1891 serving in that capacity until 1909 when he was returned to City Hall as controller, a position he filled from 1910 until 1917.

Foster then decided to try his talents at the federal level and was elected to represent East York in the House of Commons from 1917 to 1921. Then it was back to the municipal arena where he served as controller for a further three years. In 1925, he contested the mayor's position, won and held onto the office until 1927 when he was succeeded by the often cantankerous Sam McBride. An interesting event that occurred during Foster's term as mayor that confirms his overwhelming anxiety about municipal financial matters is the fact that it was Foster who demanded that the words "City of Toronto" be emblazoned on city vehicles to prevent their use for anything other than official city business.

Though regarded by all as a highly successful businessman and politician, there was still a void in "Honest Tom"

Foster's life. Elizabeth Foster, Tom's wife of many years, had died in 1920 and this, combined with the loss of his beloved daughter, Ruby, who had passed away in 1904 at the tender age of 10, weighed heavily on him. They were both given magnificent funerals and buried in expensive plots in St. James' Cemetery on Parliament Street. But, for Tommy that just wasn't good enough.

The grieving father and husband sought solace in travel and in 1931, while visiting Agra in India, saw the beautiful Taj Mahal. Erected over a span of 17 years (1629–49) by more than 20,000 labourers, this "most beautifully perfect building in all the world" was Shah Jahan's memorial to his recently deceased wife.

The instant Foster saw the structure, he knew that nothing less than his own version of the Taj Mahal would do as his memorial to the two people who were taken from him much too early.

Returning to Toronto, Foster contacted local architect H.H. Madill who, like Foster, had spent much of his childhood in the Uxbridge area and commissioned him to create another "Taj Mahal."

Erected over a period of three years, the $200,000 Thomas Foster Memorial Temple (to give it its proper name) was

Grieving Torontonians pay their respects at the Foster Memorial and Mausoleum near Uxbridge, Ontario, following the former mayor's death on December 10, 1945.

Toronto Telegram *photo.*

dedicated by Foster himself in 1936. He died nine years later.

The awesome memorial in Scott Township was by no means the only thing that we have to remind us of Tommy Foster. In his will (which contained bequests totalling $1,168,555) Foster decreed that for 4 successive 10-year periods (1945–55, 1948–58, 1951–61 and 1954–64), the woman having the most children in each decade (she must be "in lawful wedlock") would receive $1,250 for her efforts. Second and third place mothers would receive $800 and $450 respectively.

Foster also left thousands of dollars to a variety of churches, a bequeath of $5,000 to feed wild birds and another $15,000 to help protect wildlife. Central Technical School got a 45-foot wooden flagpole worth $3,500 from the Foster will and every year hundreds of children continue to be entertained at the annual Tommy Foster picnic.

Oh, one other thing. Foster wanted to make sure that the highway entrances leading into his city were prettied up. See all those trees on Highways 400 and 401 on the city's outskirts? Many were planted thanks to a provision set out in the former mayor's will directing that his executors use the interest accrued on $100,000 for the planting and maintenance of trees along highways leading into his city. Quite a man, Tommy Foster.

Transferring TTC History

March 13, 1988

What's an inch and three-quarters wide, has a length that varies with the time of day and more than a half-million of them are given out free right here in Metro every day? Give up? The common, everyday TTC transfer, that's what.

Today, riders of the TTC take the lowly transfer, whether it be dispensed from a machine or handed out by a bus driver or streetcar operator, completely for granted. Actually, that little slip of paper which, when used properly, allows passengers to move between different transit vehicles on different transit routes without paying an extra fare, a relatively unique commodity in the modern-day public transit business.

Though the first paper transfers were issued in 1892, historically, the idea of free transfer privileges between streetcars started a year earlier when Toronto Railway Company, the predecessor of our modern TTC, introduced the "verbal" transfer. Using this method, if six people got off one car to board another, the operator of the first car or a transfer agent (if one were stationed at the intersection) would shout out the number of passengers wishing to transfer (in this case six) to the other operator, who would then permit the first six to approach to board free. There's no mention of what happened if a seventh showed up at the door of the second car.

In 1892, a slightly more practical method of transfering between vehicles was introduced when the paper transfer itself was introduced. At first it was necessary for the operator to punch a hole with a pencil through the name of the route the passenger wished to take, tear off the corner representing direction of travel, then sign his name along with badge number and time and date of issuance on the back of the transfer.

Obviously, all this fuss was holding up service and after various alterations were made a transfer, approximating the tear-off type we now get on buses and streetcars, was introduced in 1909. Next time you get a transfer (forget the subway transfer), take a close look at it. The V-notch and where it's cut off at the bottom will indicate the hour and closest minute that the vehicle left the terminal (with a top NIGHT stub if issued after 5 pm). Also recorded is the car's direction of travel (U means north or westbound, D, south or eastbound). The numbers beside the cross-streets in the box on the left side of the transfer indicate the approximate running time in minutes from the terminal to that intersection. Imagine, all that information on a small but historic piece of paper.

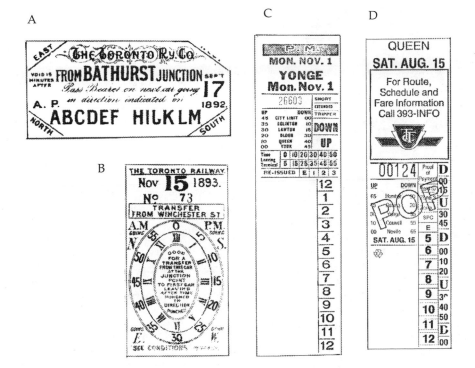

Types of transfers

A *The first free transfer required that the conductor punch a hole in it, write time, date and his badge number on it and tear a corner off of it. All in all, not very efficient especially at rush hour.*

B *Second style required four- punch holes and was in use 1893–95.*

C *In use Sept. 27, 1925–32. First "tear-off" transfer.*

D *Transfer presently in use.*

Rebirth of a Toronto Landmark

December 13, 1987

Greek-born American theatre mogul, Alexander Pantages, after whom Toronto's Pantages was named. Incidentally, there is no record of Pantages ever visiting Toronto.

You probably read in the paper or saw on TV recently stories about the proposed reopening of the partially restored Pantages Theatre on Victoria Street. Initially the new owner of part of the theatre, Cineplex Odeon, planned to hold a combined official opening and company Christmas party on the evening of December 10, 1987. However, due to legal games played by the owner of the other half of the theatre, both events were canceled at the last moment leaving four or five hundred invited guests out in the cold.

As part of the opening ceremonies, I had been asked by Cineplex Odeon president, Garth Drabinsky, a former graduate of North Toronto Collegiate Institute like myself, to say a few words at the opening about the history of the theatre. But for the reasons outlined above, I was unable to do so. However, the research is done so permit me to at least share the story of the Pantages Theatre with you, dear readers.

Toronto's magnificent new Pantages theatre opened on Saturday evening,

August 28th, 1920, and as *the Evening Telegram* newspaper published the following Monday (there were no Sunday papers in those days), "Never before has a Toronto theatre had such a gala opening."

Pantages, which could seat 3,700, was what was known as a combination house; that is, where both vaudeville acts and motion pictures were presented. On that summer's evening 67 years ago, six vaudeville acts were featured on the stage including monologue entertainer Fred P. Allen (I wonder, was he the Fred Allen, Jack Benny's nemesis?), The Marconi Brothers, Maude Earl and Company, McGrath and Deeds, followed by a play entitled "On The High Seas" (which was as one critic described "a dramatic wartime playlet with an explosive and patriotic finale") and two silent films – *Sick Abed*, with heart-throb Wallace Reid, and *High and Dizzy*, starring comic Harold Lloyd.

And the admission prices? Matinees, 25 cents, Evenings 45 cents, both including tax.

The opening night was a smashing success and Toronto's newest theatre was off to a great start.

The Pantages theatre was the creation of Nathan Louis Nathanson, an American citizen who moved to our city in 1907 from Minneapolis, Minnesota, to pursue a career in the outdoor advertising business. Before long he found himself in show business and eventually head of an organization that we know today as the Famous Players Canadian Corporation. It was this company that in 1919 decided to build a new theatre in Toronto, a theatre they'd call Pantages.

It would be a gigantic 3,700-seat house, the largest in the country and the third largest in the world.

The main entrance would be on Yonge street with a secondary entrance on Victoria. The name selected for the new theatre was borrowed from one of

Victoria Street entrance to Toronto's new Pantages Theatre soon after the official opening on August 28, 1920.

---

the most influential theatre owners and booking agents in the business, Alexander Pantages.

Pantages was born in Greece in 1872 and emigrated to the States while still a young man. It wasn't long before the lure of gold in the Klondike beckoned him north. Eventually, though, Pantages decided that using a pick and shovel to get rich wasn't for him. Instead he decided to get rich by opening a dance and music hall in an entertainment-starved Dawson City.

As the months went by, Pantages realized a small fortune, which he parlayed into an even larger fortune by opening vaudeville and moving picture houses in major cities all along the west coast of the United States. In addition, he created an extremely successful vaudeville booking agency and it was through this latter enterprise that he met "Nate" Nathanson who decided to name his new theatre after the influential Mr. Pantages.

The City of Toronto in which the sparkling new vaudeville house opened those many, many summers ago was a much, much different city than the one we enjoy today. The population stood at just over a half-million citizens. Their mayor and the man who officiated at the theatre's opening was popular Tommy Church who, it is said, possessed a photographic memory for names, welcoming home most of the troops returning

from the great war a couple of years earlier by name. Sadly, 10,000 young men from this city would never receive Tommy's warm welcome home.

In the Toronto of 1920, many families were still mourning their dead sons and daughters and the TTC was still a year in the future. Back then, transportation was provided by an extremely lucrative private enterprise known as the Toronto Railway Company that charged a nickel for a ride on their dilapidated old wooden streetcars up and down city streets including the busy Yonge line that ran right in front of the new Pantages.

To put those far off times and prices in perspective, an 11-room house at 54 Avenue Road near Bloor was being listed for $12,500 while over on Queen Street, just west of Bathurst, a six-room brick house was up for grabs at $3,300. Dining suites were on sale at Adams just down the street from the new theatre for $385 with brass beds selling for $33.95. A 9' x 9' Wilton rug was on special for $68.95.

Hungry? Fresh lean boneless beef was 30 cents a pound, and freshly caught, dressed salmon and trout sold for 25 cents a pound in the market at Robert Simpson's store down the street at Queen (phone direct, Adelaide 6100 for free delivery).

Within a decade following the Pantages opening, Pantages, the man, was involved in a sex scandal (of which he was later found to be guiltless), and times being what they were the theatre's name was quickly changed to the more pristine Imperial, a name that was changed again, slightly, to Imperial Six after the 3,700 seat hall was converted into six separate theatres in 1973.

Thirteen years later, 1986, the theatre was closed following a dispute between Famous Players and Cineplex Odeon, the latter company having purchased a portion of the theatre including the 900-seat balcony of the original Pantages. It is the Cineplex Odeon portion of the theatre that has been restored and will soon reopen with the theatre's original name back up on the mar quee.

[This column originally appeared on December 13, 1987. Almost two years later, on September 20, 1989, the fully restored Pantages reopened with the Canadian premiere of *The Phantom of the Opera*. A Toronto landmark was reborn!]

Fort York History Unearthed

June 26, 1988

Imagine this scenario. The boss is having some important people over for dinner. Better use the best dishes. In fact, better bring out the Spode ironstone serving plate. Soon the guests start arriving and all the preparations are going well when, just as the guests are getting ready for the meal to be served, CRASH!!, The Spode plate hits the floor and shatters into a thousand pieces. Quick! Clean up the mess before the boss comes in. Now, where to hide the pieces? I know. Bury them in the farthest corner down in the basement. They'll never find them down there.

Andrew Murray examines the excavated pieces of plate in the wine vault in the basement of the Officers' Quarters at Fort York

Courtesy of the Toronto Historical Board, Fort York..

Now imagine that the above took place at Toronto's historic Fort York almost 200 years ago. The pieces of that dropped plate were buried in the basement of the officers' quarters where they remained hidden for almost a century and a half. Then, during a recent excavation program, wouldn't you know it, someone went and found that broken plate. Boy, is that servant ever in trouble now!! All kidding aside, a broken Spode plate is but one of more than 70,000 items unearthed during last year's archaeological dig at the city's most historic site, Fort York. From late March through October 30, 1987, Dr. Donald Brown and his nine-member crew examined in minute detail two specific areas of the old fort which had been established nearly two centuries ago by our community's founder and the province's first lieutenant-governor, John Graves Simcoe.

The purpose of the fort, as Simcoe saw it, was to provide some sort of defence against American military invasion that Simcoe knew was coming, though where and when he wasn't sure. But, he reasoned, it was a good bet that the invaders would attack his new community which, in tribute to King George's son Frederick, the Duke of York, he had renamed York from the original Indian word, Toronto.

By establishing a fort on the mainland (small as that fort would be) and a blockhouse, complete with cannon, on the peninsula opposite to it, Simcoe felt that the harbour and townsite could be protected against invading warships.

(In 1858, the narrow isthmus at the east end of the peninsula was breached and the land mass became an island, today's Toronto Island.)

Unfortunately, Simcoe was unable

to convince his superiors that more substantial defenses should be constructed to protect York, and so for the early part of its existence little Fort York was an ill-equipped, poorly manned cluster of buildings located in a clearing in the forest west of the townsite. Eventually, tired of arguing the point with a defiant Governor-General who saw no need to secure York, an ailing Simcoe eventually set sail for England and other duties. Within a few years, Simcoe was dead.

Back on this side of the Atlantic, relations between the United States and Britain began to sour and, having the same fears as Simcoe, the province's new lieutenant-governor, Major General Isaac Brock, again sought to improve the fort's defences, this time with more success.

In June of 1812, the States declared war on Great Britain and a month later attacked Upper Canada near the site of today's Windsor, Ontario. Numerous skirmishes ensued, followed on April 27, 1813 by an attack on York, which had become the capital, by a force numbering in excess of 1,700 troops transported across Lake Ontario on board 14 warships.

The ensuing battle was short-lived with the 700 or so British and Canadian troops, militiamen and Mississauga Indian allies eventually surrendering to the much superior invading force. For the next six days, our community struggled on under the "Stars and Stripes" with the Americans eventually withdrawing from the province only to return in July of 1813 to continue their plundering and destruction.

Following the end of British-American hostilities in December 1814, and as a precaution against further invasions by anyone, the authorities ordered much of the fort rebuilt. These are the buildings that make up much of today's Fort York.

In 1870, the British Army left Fort York and Canada, to be replaced by locally recruited Canadians. Many of these Canadian troops were assigned to Fort York where they remained until the 1930s when the site was decommis-

sioned and work started on the fort's restoration, a major project that would see historic Fort York the centre-piece of Toronto's centennial celebrations in 1934. As part of an ongoing program to investigate various Toronto Historical Board sites around the city "in depth," an archaeological dig was commenced

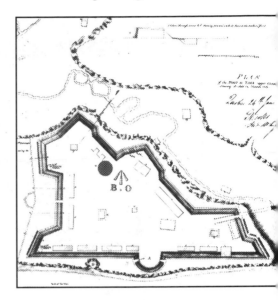

Map of Fort York, 1816. The dot indicates where the pieces of plate were unearthed.

Courtesy of Toronto Historical Board, Fort York.

early last year. This is the project that resulted in the discovery of the "hidden," c. 1810–25 Spode dinner plate, no doubt used for a time in the Officers' Quarters, a structure that was built following the American invasion and one of many restored in 1934.

In addition to the handsome plate, the 1987 dig uncovered many, many other items that give us a much better idea of the day-to-day lifestyles of the earliest Torontonians and why, as Mrs. Simcoe pointed out in her famous diary, it was necessary on May 2, 1794, for her friend, Mr. Pilkington, to go fishing with his gun and not a normal fishing rod. One of the excavated items was a sturgeon bone 5 3/4 feet in length from a fish that it is estimated would weigh in at 80 to 100 pounds!!

Putting Toronto on the Map

November 6, 1988

One day while perusing some documents in the City of Toronto Archives, which is located in the basement of New City Hall, I came across a development proposal for an immense area of downtown Toronto put forward by an American company, United Engineering and Construction Company. The organization's head office was located in Los Angeles, California, with a Canadian branch, run by Andrew J. Little, on the second floor of the Confederation Life Building at Yonge and Richmond Streets.

In September of 1911, United Engineering approached the city's Board of Control with a proposal to build a huge structure that would occupy the entire area bounded by Yonge, King, York and Queen streets, a total of almost 60 acres. The mammoth building would burrow three storeys below ground and tower 20 storeys above street level. In total, the Toronto Union Terminal and Commercial Building, as it was to known, would provide 40 million square feet. (For reference purposes, the recently approved $500 million Bay-Adelaide Court that will sit right in the middle of the Yonge, King, York, Queen site contains only 2 million square feet of space or only 5% of that specified in the 1911 plan.)

This massive terminal would serve the country's three transcontinental railways (Grand Trunk, Canadian Northern and Canadian Pacific, the first two eventually becoming part of Canadian National), an enormous hotel, rows and rows of retail stores, several hundred business offices, numerous theatres and several banks. And, to quote from the prospectus, there would be provision made in the building for "all lines known to the commercial world." The prospectus goes on, "Even at $1 a square foot, the project will bring in a substantial revenue."

A solution to the city's railway problem was also included in the development company's proposal. "Have all trains enter the heart of the city in long tunnels, thereby removing all tracks from the city streets." Simple. Railway tracks, over which pedestrians and vehicular traffic had to cross to get to and from the harbour had been an ongoing headache for the city fathers ever since the first steam train chugged out of town in 1853.

By the turn of the century, steam tracks in downtown Toronto were one enormous problem. The federal government finally ordered the construction of a cross-waterfront viaduct, that opened in the late 1920s. Therefore, in retrospect, one can see how welcomed United Engineering's proposal must have been to both city politicians and a public concerned about deteriorating safety conditions down at the water's edge.

Another selling feature of the proposal was the plan to use the earth excavated from the below-ground phase to fill and improve the city's waterfront. This improvement was in anticipation of the huge ocean-going freighters and passenger liners that would arrive at the city's docks upon completion of a deep water canal through the St. Lawrence Valley. (In reality, the St. Lawrence Seaway didn't open until 1959, almost 50 years after this proposal was tabled at City Hall.)

In the drawing accompanying United Engineering's proposal, multi-funnelled passenger vessels similar to

WATCH TORONTO GROW TO THE MILLION MARK

Courtesy of City of Toronto Archives.

The massive scope of the 1911 proposal to erect the Toronto Union Terminal and Commercial Building is evident in this artist's drawing.

the White Star Line's new *Olympic* are depicted moored alongside four massive wharves constructed just south of Front Street. And, who knows, they may even have been thinking about the day that *Olympic's* sister, still under construction in the Belfast shipyard of Harland and Wolff and known only as SS400, would arrive in Toronto. SS400 would never even make it to this side of the Atlantic, let alone to the Port of Toronto. In April of the following year, RMS *Titanic* would hit an iceberg and sink on its maiden voyage.

The method of financing United Engineering's project is interesting in itself. The proposal suggested that the numerous land and building owners occupying the site of the company's proposed skyscraper offer their property on a stock ownership basis. United also suggested various local building material companies take stock in the project instead of cash payments in a manner similar to the way Maple Leaf Gardens was financed during the Great Depression.

To quote directly from the proposal: "It is not too colossal an enterprise for Canada's Queen City to undertake to place herself on record before the world centres of doing things. In the advanced events of today, ranking among the survival of the fittest, to whom the better part of the world belongs Toronto will surely show them; then keep your eye on Toronto."

Nevertheless, in spite of all the hoopla, the plan never got past the Board of Control.

So You Think Our Winters Are Cold?

February 21, 1987

Was it Mark Twain who once said, "Everybody talks about the weather, but nobody does anything about it ... " or words to that effect. Well, in this week's column I thought it might be interesting to take a look at Toronto's winter weather in years gone by.

Let me start with a rather chilling thought for you to ponder while you're turning up the thermostat another degree. Almost two centuries ago, when Lieutenant-Governor John Simcoe decided to establish the new, but temporary, capital of Upper Canada on the north shore of Lake Ontario at a place the Indians called Toronto, the newcomers were forced to live in tents until proper wooden structures could be readied.

It may have been colder back at the turn-of-the-century, nevertheless these hearty sportsmen seem to be enjoying themselves as they ice-boat across a frozen Toronto Bay.

Simcoe's wife, Elizabeth, a prodigious and colourful writer, describes in her diary that for the first little while at Toronto she, the Governor and their three children (one, a child who was to die in less than a year in April of 1794, just fifteen months old) resided in what she called "the canvas house," a tent that had belonged to James Cook, the famous explorer with whom Simcoe's father had traveled. A comment in the diary dated December 27th, 1793, reveals that the day was so cold that "some water [that] spilt near the stove froze immediately."

While official records obviously don't go back that far, we do have temperature records for the latter part of the 1800s. In fact, the coldest day in Toronto's history occurred on January 10, 1859, when the thermometer fell to -33 degrees Celsius (-27 degrees Fahrenheit). In 1875, the average or mean (in more ways than one) temperature for the entire year was only 4.7 degrees Celsius (40.5 degrees Fahrenheit). The normal mean is about 10 degrees Celsius (50 degrees Fahrenheit).

Snow has been sparse in the earlier part of this winter, though February has tried to make up for it. Hopefully, we won't be setting any records before spring arrives, but if we do we'll have to beat the record set in December of 1944.

Early in the evening of December 11, it began to snow lightly and as the hours

Curlers and a clutch of warmly attired onlookers brave the cold on a frozen Grenadier Pond in High Park, c. 1900.

went by, the intensity of the storm got worse. By 4 in the morning, several of the TTC's streetcar lines were blocked by heavy drifts. Then as the rush hour approached, what few vehicles were still able to operate got caught in the traffic tie-ups caused by stalled trucks, cars and buses. Streetcars on North Yonge Street between Willowdale and Richmond Hill were stranded from 9:40 am until 10 that night. The Carlton cars out near High Park stopped running at 8 in the morning and didn't start moving again until 8 that evening. In total, 16 routes were paralyzed for various periods of time.

Things could have been worse, though. With fuel rationing in place because of the war, fewer than the normal numbers of cars could even get gas, let alone get out of the garage. In total, almost 22 inches of snow fell in less than 12 hours; a record they can keep!!

Doubling Up in Downtown Toronto

May 21, 1989

You may have noticed while traveling the streets of downtown Toronto that a new, longer type of streetcar has become prominent on the Queen, Bathurst and King routes. It's called an Articulated Light Rail Vehicle, or ALRV for short, and no, its not because it's particularly eloquent or expressive that it gets that fancy name, but rather because it is able to articulate or bend in the middle thereby allowing longer streetcars that are able to move more people. You may also hear them called "two rooms and a bath" or, as some TTC operators refer to them, "Slinkys."

This vehicle, the latest in a long line of Toronto streetcars, is a creation of UTDC Inc., a division of The Lavalin Group, one of Canada's leading engineering procurement, construction, project management and consulting firms.

The articulated, or bendable streetcar evolved from the Canadian Light Rail Vehicle (or CLRV) that first began operating in Toronto in the fall of 1979. It in turn was designed and built as a response to the TTC's request for a replacement vehicle for the aging Presidents' Conference Committee (PCC) streetcar that in one version or another had been in operation on Toronto city streets since 1938.

The ALRV, of which there will ultimately be 52, is 75 feet in length, stands 11 feet high (not counting the trolley pole, of course) and weighs in (when empty) at just over 4 tons. Each vehicle has a seating capacity of 61 passengers with a design load of 159 and "crush" load of 257. The cars operate on 600 volts DC, have three "trucks" or "bogeys" with two electric motors per "powered truck" (the centre truck is unpowered) and can move at a maximum design speed of 50 mph.

The idea of extending streetcars to increase carrying capacity is really nothing new, trailers being the first such

Complete with trailer coupled on behind, the TTC's Peter Witt streetcars were the "state-of-the-art" back in 1950 when Yonge was the city's busiest route. In this view the Yonge trains are being diverted via Dundas, Church and Adelaide during Yonge subway construction. Note the black police car exiting the lane left of centre and the soon-to-open Brown Derby Tavern at the north-east corner of Yonge and Dundas.

example. In the very early days of electric streetcar operation, it was not unusual to see an old horsedrawn vehicle (without the horse, of course) hooked on as a trailer behind the "motor" or lead car. These old horsecars couldn't stand up to the beating they'd get in the faster traffic of the 1890s and the idea (and the horsecars) didn't last very long.

Soon after the turn of the century, the Toronto Railway Company, which had a 30-year monopoly to provide the public transportation service within the city's boundaries, built a number of specially designed "convertible" trailers, convertible in that the sides could be removed in the summer months, turning the closed trailer into a nice, cool open vehicle. However, in 1915 the government banned all "open" cars, both motors and trailers. Then, following a serious fire in late 1916 in which a large part of the company's streetcar fleet was destroyed, a number of these old, retired "motors" were converted into trailers and so used for many years.

Interestingly, many of these vehicles had yet another job to fulfill when in October of 1922 they were withdrawn and sent to Haileybury, Ontario, following a devastating forest fire that virtually wiped out the northern town. Here, the former Toronto streetcars finished out their lives as much-needed offices and residences.

In 1903, the TRC took 30 of their smallest electric streetcars and by ingenious carpentry work were able to turn them into 15 "twin body" cars with large seating and standing capacities, but because the door arrangements were unsatisfactory, the loading and unloading of the "twins" was very slow. The cars also sagged badly under the increased weight. All eventually burned or were retired from service.

With the establishment of the TTC in 1921, a new type of streetcar was soon in regular service. Called the Peter Witt, after its Cleveland, Ohio, designer, these cars were the state-of-the-art. Complementing the 350 new cars that were put in service between 1921 and 1923 were 225 Witt-type trailers, some of which were

The TTC's new Articulated Light Rail Vehicles entered service in 1988. Its design was based on the Canadian Light Rail Vehicle that had entered service seven years earlier. ALRVs accommodate almost 160 passengers and are especially suited for the busiest present-day streetcar routes, Queen and Bathurst.

Courtesy of TTC.

retrofitted with a third door and a movable barrier inside the car which resulted in faster loading of the car downtown and, with the barrier removed, faster unloading uptown. These cars were called Harvey trailers after the designer, D.W.Harvey, the TTC's assistant general manager who came up with the idea of the moveable barrier.

The motor-trailer combination, called Witt trains, hauled hundreds of thousands of passengers up and down Yonge Street and on several other busy routes. The use of this combination of vehicles ended with the opening of the Yonge subway on March 30, 1954.

There was a time when 225 Witt motor-trailer combinations and another 33 Witt motor-TRC trailer combinations were in daily service throughout the city. Even the new PCC cars saw a kind of trailer service, though in this case a coupled pair of PCCs was referred to as multiple unit or a "M-U," to use streetcar jargon.

Torontonians may recall these multiple-units on the Bloor-Danforth route from 1950 until the cross-town subway opened in 1966 and then on Queen for a period of 10 years, 1967–77.

Killer of the Seas
Took Toronto by Storm

April 2, 1989

*The captured First World War German submarine UC-97 was on its way to a museum
in Chicago when the United States Navy brought it into Toronto Harbour
June 10, 1919, and put it on exhibit for a few days.*

There's been much in the news these past few months about whether or not Canada should invest some $8 billion to acquire a dozen or so nuclear submarines and, if we do in fact buy them, from whom. The French or the British?

Whether the deal is good or bad morally or financially, I really don't know. What I do know is that even by working out the best deal possible, each of the 12 craft will cost the country (read taxpayers) $666,666,666.70 each. That figure is almost equal to the entire assessed value of the entire City of Toronto when many of its 499,278 citizens saw their very first submarine away back in June of 1919.

The "war to end all wars" had been over for one day short of seven months when the captured German submarine UC-97 steamed under its own power into Toronto Harbour on June 10, 1919.

Tremendous crowds lined the railing in front of the Harbour Commission Building which, in 1919, was still brand new and stood right at the water's edge. Out in the harbour, hundreds of others gazed at the craft from the decks of the steamers *Lakeside* and *Chippewa* that were just leaving for their destinations across the lake, and from the decks of the Island ferries *Mayflower*, *Primrose*, *Blue Bell* and *Trillium*. And all along the harbour's edge people stared in awe at this craft of destruction.

Submarine UC-97, 191 feet in length with a draught of 12 feet had been commissioned just prior to the armistice signing and was outfitted for mine-laying detail. Then, at the conclusion of the war, the almost new craft was handed over to the British by her German crew at the port of Harwich. In turn, the British gave the UC-97 and four other

captured submarines to the American government and now UC-97 was on her way to the Great Lakes Training Station in Chicago where she would be dissected "to see what made her tick." But before that, the vessel was taken on a goodwill tour of various ports along the Great Lakes. Towed by the U.S. Navy's Revenue Clipper *Iroquois* from port to port, the American crew of the German craft unhooked the hawser outside the East Gap and UC-97 was allowed to steam into Toronto Harbour propelled by her own three-diesel engines each rated at 300 HP.

Contemporary newspaper accounts of the sub's arrival here in Toronto described the heavy saw-toothed device rising from the bow of the "dreaded U-Boat" that was used to cut cables and nets. The papers also commented on the cannon jutting up "at a jaunty angle" in front of the conning tower.

Mention was also made of the brass plaque with the words "TELEGRAPH IMMEDIATELY U-BOAT BASE AT KIEL. UNDERSEA BOAT HERE SUNKEN." Attached to a buoy aft of the conning tower, it was to be released when the vessel went down. Then, as almost an expression of relief, the reporters went on to praise the engaging young American officer (Lieutenant-Commander Charles Lockwood) who brought the craft into the harbour as well as his crew of "friendly American Jackies."

Only a year earlier, this "dreaded U-Boat" would have typified all the cunning and treachery of the German navy but here, in the Toronto Harbour of 1919, manned by its friendly American crew and proudly flying the American flag, the UC-97 looked more like a "large toy."

Seven decades later, and with all due respect to those in charge of our country's military preparedness, submarines certainly have become very expensive toys!

An Unsinkable Legend

April 26, 1992

During a recent visit to Boston, Massachusetts, I attended a convention held by the Titanic Historical Society to honour the memory of those who died that cold April night 80 years ago when, on the fourth day into her maiden voyage, the world's largest ocean liner sideswiped a gigantic iceberg and plunged beneath the icy waters of the North Atlantic.

This occurred in spite of the fact that many said even God himself couldn't sink the mighty *Titanic*.

Of the 711 passengers that survived the calamity, four were special guests at the gathering along with one who boarded the ill-fated

Charles Melville Hays (1856–1912)
President, Grand Trunk Railway.

craft at Southampton, England, making the short hop across the English Channel disembarking at Cherbourg, France, *Titanic's* second port-of-call (the third and final was at Queenstown, now Cobh, Ireland) to commence a tour of the continent.

I was able to chat briefly with spirited Eva Hart who was seven at the time of the sinking. With her parents, Eva was bound for a new life in Canada, a dream interrupted by the iceberg. Eva and her mother survived. Her father did not.

Miss Hart confided to me that she did eventually make it to the family's original destination, Winnipeg, many, many years later though she wasn't sure which was colder, Winnipeg in winter or the North Atlantic the night *Titanic* went down. Interestingly, the day after I met Eva, she flew to Toronto to be interviewed for the forthcoming IMAX film, a unique Canadian/American/Russian co-production about *Titanic* that features footage of the vessel 2 1/2 miles below the surface on the ocean floor.

An interesting sidelight to the convention was a trip to the Maritime Museum in Fall River, a small community an hour's drive south of Boston. Here, members of the society were able to view the *Titanic* model made for the 1953 film on the disaster and to see and touch a beautifully carved oak panel that formed part of the decor over the first-class passenger stairway.

This artifact had been recovered from the ocean by the steamer *Minia* that had been dispatched from Halifax several days after the scope of the tragedy was apparent. *Minia's* job was to recover bodies that had drifted with the current. During the search period, *Minia* retrieved 17 cadavers plus four large oak panels found floating amongst the flotsam. The bodies were interred in various Halifax cemeteries. The panels were eventually turned over to the Public Archives of Nova Scotia who then loaned them to the Fall River museum for its *Titanic* display.

RMS Titanic, *Launched May 31, 1911, sank April 15, 1912, with the loss of 1,517 souls.*

One of the bodies recovered by *Minia* was that of Charles M. Hays, American-born president of Canada's Grand Trunk Railway (GTR) who was a resident of Montreal. (The GTR became part of CNR in 1923.) He was but 1 of 20 Canadians who were to lose their lives (out of a total of approximately 37 Canadian passengers on board) in a tragedy that is usually described as either American or British, depending on who's telling the story.

Other prominent Montreal citizens to die in the sinking were well-known stock broker Thornton Davidson, who six years earlier had married Hays's daughter and was traveling with his father-in-law, and 56-year-old Henry Markland Molson, grandson of John Molson, founder of the Molson brewing empire.

Winnipeg, Manitoba, lost Mark Fortune and his son, Charles, while Mrs. Fortune and her three young daughters were rescued. Hugo Ross, who was born in Toronto and educated at Upper Canada College, and George Graham, head chinaware buyer for the T. Eaton Company in Winnipeg, who had recently lived and worked in Toronto, were other Winnipeg victims. Out of respect for the popular Graham, the Eaton's Toronto store closed at 1 pm on Saturday, April 20, the same day that the Toronto church Graham had attended held a service in his memory.

J.J. Borebank, who was born in Toronto in 1877 and had moved to Winnipeg at the age of 26 to set up his own real estate concern, also died in the sinking. Borebank, his wife and young daughter had gone to England to enrol the child in a private school. While Mrs. Borebank had decided to remain in England for a time until the daughter had settled in, business pressures back home forced her husband to book passage on *Titanic*. In so doing, his fate, along with that of 1,502 others who had also selected the White Star Line's "unsinkable" *Titanic* in which to cross the Atlantic, was sealed.

AFTERWORD

Visitors to Toronto, aboard Imperial Coach's solid-rubber-tired sightseeing vehicle, King, *pause on their journey in front of the Parliament Buildings.*

What you have just read are but a few of the many hundreds of columns that I have submitted to the *Sunday Sun,* each having been selected because of the reader feedback that they prompted.

Many of these stories have come from my readers, and I always welcome their input. As I continue to submit these vignettes of our city's past, who knows? Perhaps Volume 2 will appear somewhere in the not-to-distant future, especially when one realizes that next year, 1993, marks the 200th anniversary of the founding of the town of York, which in 1834 became our city of Toronto.

Happy Anniversary, Toronto.

Mike Filey